# J.R.R. Tolkien's Utopianism and the Classics

Classical Receptions in Twentieth-Century Writing

**Series Editor: Laura Jansen**

Each book in this groundbreaking new series considers the influence of antiquity on a single writer from the twentieth century. From Woolf to Walcott and Fellini to Foucault, the modalities and texture of this modern encounter with antiquity are explored in the works of authors recognized for their global impact on modern fiction, poetry, art, philosophy and socio-politics.

A distinctive feature of twentieth-century writing is the tendency to break with tradition and embrace the new sensibilities of the time. Yet the period continues to maintain a fluid dialogue with the Graeco-Roman past, drawing on its rich cultural legacy and thought, even within the most radical movements that ostentatiously questioned and rejected that past. *Classical Receptions in Twentieth-Century Writing* approaches this dialogue from two interrelated perspectives: it asks how modern authors' appeal to the classical past opens up new readings of their oeuvres and contexts, and it considers how this process in turn renders new insights into the classical world. This two-way perspective offers dynamic and interdisciplinary discussions for readers of Classics and modern literary tradition.

Also new in this series:
*Fellini's Eternal Rome*, Alessandro Carrera
*Foucault's Seminars on Antiquity: Learning to Speak the Truth*, Paul Allen Miller
*James Joyce and Classical Modernism*, Leah Culligan Flack
*Tony Harrison: Poet of Radical Classicism*, Edith Hall
*Virginia Woolf's Greek Tragedy*, Nancy Worman

**Editorial Board**
Prof. Richard Armstrong (University of Houston)
Prof. Francisco Barrenechea (University of Maryland)
Prof. Shane Butler (Johns Hopkins University)
Prof. Paul A. Cartledge (Cambridge University)
Prof. Moira Fradinger (Yale University)
Prof. Francisco García Jurado (Universidad Complutense de Madrid)
Prof. Barbara Goff (University of Reading)
Prof. Simon Goldhill (University of Cambridge)
Prof. Sean Gurd (The University of Texas at Austin)
Prof. Constanze Güthenke (University of Oxford)
Dr Ella Haselswerdt (University of California, Los Angeles)
Dr Rebecca Kosick (University of Bristol)
Prof. Vassilis Lambropoulos (University of Michigan)
Dr. Pantelis Michelakis (University of Bristol)
Prof. James Porter (University of California, Berkeley)
Prof. Patrice Rankine (University of Chicago)
Prof. Phiroze Vasunia (University College London)

# J.R.R. Tolkien's Utopianism and the Classics

Hamish Williams

BLOOMSBURY ACADEMIC
LONDON • NEW YORK • OXFORD • NEW DELHI • SYDNEY

BLOOMSBURY ACADEMIC
Bloomsbury Publishing Plc
50 Bedford Square, London, WC1B 3DP, UK
1385 Broadway, New York, NY 10018, USA
29 Earlsfort Terrace, Dublin 2, Ireland

BLOOMSBURY, BLOOMSBURY ACADEMIC and the Diana logo are trademarks of Bloomsbury Publishing Plc

First published in Great Britain 2023
Paperback edition published 2025

Copyright © Hamish Williams, 2023

Hamish Williams has asserted his right under the Copyright, Designs and Patents Act, 1988, to be identified as Author of this work.

For legal purposes the Acknowledgements on p. vi constitute an extension of this copyright page.

Cover image: 2nd December 1955: John Ronald Reuel Tolkien (1892–1973) at Merton College Oxford. Photo by Haywood Magee/Picture Post/Hulton Archive/Getty Images

All rights reserved. No part of this publication may be reproduced or transmitted in any form or by any means, electronic or mechanical, including photocopying, recording, or any information storage or retrieval system, without prior permission in writing from the publishers.

Bloomsbury Publishing Plc does not have any control over, or responsibility for, any third-party websites referred to or in this book. All internet addresses given in this book were correct at the time of going to press. The author and publisher regret any inconvenience caused if addresses have changed or sites have ceased to exist, but can accept no responsibility for any such changes.

A catalogue record for this book is available from the British Library.

Library of Congress Cataloging-in-Publication Data
Names: Williams, Hamish, author.
Title: J.R.R. Tolkien's utopianism and the classics / Hamish Williams.
Description: London ; New York : Bloomsbury Academic, 2023. | Series: Classical receptions in twentieth-century writing | Includes bibliographical references.
Identifiers: LCCN 2022046406 | ISBN 9781350241459 (hardback) | ISBN 9781350241466 (paperback) | ISBN 9781350241473 (ebook) | ISBN 9781350241480 (epub)
Subjects: LCSH: Tolkien, J. R. R. (John Ronald Reuel), 1892-1973–Criticism and interpretation. | Utopias in literature. | English literature–Classical influences. | LCGFT: Literary criticism.
Classification: LCC PR6039.O32 Z898 2023 | DDC 823/.912—dc23/eng/20220926
LC record available at https://lccn.loc.gov/2022046406

ISBN: HB: 978-1-3502-4145-9
PB: 978-1-3502-4146-6
ePDF: 978-1-3502-4147-3
eBook: 978-1-3502-4148-0

Series: Classical Receptions in Twentieth-Century Writing

Typeset by RefineCatch Limited, Bungay, Suffolk

To find out more about our authors and books visit www.bloomsbury.com and sign up for our newsletters.

# Contents

| | |
|---|---:|
| Acknowledgements | vi |
| List of Abbreviations | viii |
| Series' Editor Preface | x |
| | |
| Introduction: Utopianism and Classicism: Tolkien's New–Old Continent | 1 |
| 1   Lapsarian Narratives: The Decline and Fall of Utopian Communities in Middle-earth | 17 |
| 2   Hospitality Narratives: The Ideal of the Home in an Odyssean *Hobbit* | 59 |
| 3   Sublime Narratives: Classical Transcendence in Nature and beyond in *The Fellowship of the Ring* | 97 |
| | |
| Epilogue: Ancient Trees in Tolkien's Forest | 137 |
| | |
| Notes | 143 |
| References | 181 |
| Index | 199 |

# Acknowledgements

I cannot possibly list all the individuals who contributed to the germination of ideas that eventually found their way into this book, and I apologize to those who are not mentioned here by name. First and foremost, this research would not have been possible without the support and encouragement of Prof. Thomas Honegger, of the Institute of English and American Studies at Friedrich Schiller University Jena. A special thanks to the 'Fellowship of Friends' who contributed to my edited volume *Tolkien and the Classical World* (Walking Tree Publishers, 2021), and who produced many great essays which challenged me to revise my own interpretations, including Ross Clare, Giuseppe Pezzini, Austin Freeman, Peter Sundt, Michael Kleu, Łukasz Neubauer, Philip Burton, Juliette Harrisson and, not least, Graham Shipley. I am most indebted to Prof. Katarzyna Marciniak, of the University of Warsaw, who provided me with numerous platforms to discuss my work with students and colleagues in Poland. Also thanks to the interest and encouragement of my research fellows at the Polish Institute of Advanced Studies, including Prof. Geoff Roberts and Prof. Sergei Erofeev, and of course to the head of the Institute, Prof. Przemysław Urbańczyk. I am grateful for the editorial support of the staff at Bloomsbury publishing, including Lily Mac Mahon, Georgina Leighton and Alice Wright, as well as the series editor, Dr Laura Jansen, for helping me hone my proposal. Grote dank voor de steun van de leden van Unquendor, het Nederlands Tolkiengenootschap (the Dutch Tolkien Society), met name Jan van Breda en Renée Vink. в конце концов, большое спасибо моей жене Ксении и двум мальчикам, Константину и Саше.

    This book project was funded through the support of The Alexander von Humboldt Foundation and the Polish Institute of Advanced Studies, realised during research stays in Jena and Warsaw, respectively, from 2019 to 2022. Certain parts of this monograph are based on, and developed substantially from, book chapters and journal articles which I have written over the past five years. My thanks to the editors, peer reviewers and other publication staff of the following books and journals, in which my work was first published, for helping to advance the quality of my papers (in chronological order): *Rewriting the Ancient World: Greeks, Romans, Jews and Christians in Modern Popular Fiction* (Leiden: Brill, 2017), edited by Lisa Maurice, for the chapter '"Home is Behind, the World Ahead": Reading Tolkien's *The Hobbit* as a Story of *Xenia* or Homeric Hospitality' (174–97); *Lembas Extra 2019: The World Tolkien Built* (Beverwijk: Tolkien Genootschap Unquendor, 2019), edited by Renée Vink, for the chapter 'Tolkien's Trolls: Intertextuality in "Roast Mutton" and Monstrous Incarnations After *The Hobbit*' (111–27); *Sub-Creating Arda: World-Building in J.R.R. Tolkien's Work, Its Precursors, and Its Legacies* (Zurich, Jena: Walking Tree Publishers, 2019), edited by Thomas Honegger and Dimitra Fimi, for the chapter 'Mountain People in Middle-Earth: Ecology and the Primitive' (285–311); *The Journal of the Fantastic in the Arts* (2020), for the article 'Westwards, Utopia; Eastwards, Decline: The Reception of Classical Occidentalism and Orientalism in Tolkien's Atlantic Paradise' (31(3): 404–23); *Tolkien Studies* (2020), for the article 'Tolkien's Thalassocracy and Ancient Greek Seafaring People: Minoans, Phaeacians, Atlantans, and Númenóreans' (17: 137–62); *Tolkien and the Classical World* (Zurich, Jena: Walking Tree Publishers, 2021), for the chapters 'Classical Tradition, Modern Fantasy, and the Generic Contracts of Readers' (xi–xxvi) and 'Tolkien the Classicist: Scholar and Thinker' (3–36); *Lembas Extra: Númenor* (Beverwijk: Tolkien Genootschap Unquendor, 2022), edited by Renée Vink and Jan van Breda, for the chapter 'The Five Ages of Tolkien's Greek Thalassocracy: A Comparative Study of Númenórean Narrative History'.

# Abbreviations

Abbreviations are followed by the full title of the work and a short citation referring to reference list.

| | |
|---|---|
| BLT2 | *The Book of Lost Tales Part II* (Tolkien 1984) |
| BT | *The Birth of Tragedy out of the Spirit of Music* (Nietzsche [1872] 2003) |
| CM | *The Colossus of Maroussi* (Miller [1941] 2016) |
| FR | *The Lord of the Rings: The Fellowship of the Ring* (Tolkien [1954] 2001a) |
| GI | *The Greek Islands* (Durrell [1978] 2002) |
| Hobbit | *The Hobbit* (Tolkien [1937] 2006a) |
| KMD | *The King Must Die* (Renault [1958] 1961) |
| Knossos | *The Palace of Minos at Knossos* (Evans 1921) |
| Letters | *The Letters of J.R.R. Tolkien* (Tolkien [1981] 2006b) |
| LfgrE | *Lexikon des frühgriechischen Epos* (2004) |
| MC | *The Monsters and the Critics and Other Essays* (Tolkien [1983] 2006c) |
| OFS | *Tolkien On Fairy Stories* (Tolkien [1947] 2014a) |
| OH | *Of Hospitality: Anne Dufourmantelle invites Jacques Derrida to Respond* (Derrida [1998] 2000) |
| PESB | *A Philosophical Enquiry into the Sublime and Beautiful* (Burke [1757] 2015) |
| PK | *At the Palaces of Knossos* (Kazantzakis [1981] 1988) |
| PME | *The Peoples of Middle-Earth* (Tolkien [1996] 1997) |
| RK | *The Lord of the Rings: The Return of the King* (Tolkien [1955] 2001c) |
| S | *The Silmarillion* (Tolkien [1977] 2002b) |
| SD | *Sauron Defeated: The History of The Lord of the Rings Part 4* (Tolkien [1992] 2002a) |
| SL | 'Sigelwara Land' (Tolkien 1932) |

| | |
|---|---|
| *TT* | *The Lord of the Rings: The Two Towers* (Tolkien [1954] 2001b) |
| *UT* | *Unfinished Tales of Númenor and Middle-Earth* (Tolkien [1980] 2014b) |
| *WR* | *The War of the Ring* (Tolkien [1990] 2000) |
| *ZG* | *Zorba the Greek* (Kazantzakis [1946] 2008) |

# Series' Editor Preface

The present volume marks the sixth innovative contribution to the series *Classical Receptions in Twentieth-Century Writing* (*CRTW*), a project that seeks to explore the modalities and textures of modern classicisms in the works of writers recognized for their global impact on modern philosophy, poetics, politics and the arts. *CRTW* approaches this aim from two distinct yet interrelated perspectives: it asks how modern authors' dialogue with the classical past paves the way to new understandings of their oeuvres and contexts, and it considers how this process in turn renders new insights into the classical world and its sense of impact on our modernity. In plotting twentieth-century receptions of Graeco-Roman antiquity from this two-way perspective, the series aims to promote dynamic, highly interdisciplinary discussions for readers of Classics and Literary and Classical Studies. Indeed, a key feature of the series is its extensive range and scope. It looks at both Anglophone and non-Anglophone writers from modernities around the globe, as well as writers still or until recently active in their field, such as Tony Harrison in the fourth volume of the series, or our forthcoming studies in Wole Soyinka and Simon Armitage. Each of these authors is considered primarily as a writer whose interest in antiquity has contributed to a significant revision of philosophical and political thought, aesthetics, identity studies, gender studies, translation studies, visual culture, performance studies, urban studies, and cultural criticism, amongst other areas of knowledge. In this sense, *CRTW* aspires to promote a new intellectual space and critical direction for those producing research on Twentieth-Century Studies with a focus on Classics and vice versa.

The series furthermore aims to re-energize aspects of reception premises and practice. Over the last two decades, Classical Reception has developed broadly into four main fruitful areas of investigation: periods and/or movements (e.g. Humanism; the Enlightenment; the Victorians), media (e.g. film; sculpture; painting; the stage; musicology; comics), theory and criticism (e.g. psychoanalysis; gender studies; deconstruction; postcolonialism); and geopolitical regions (e.g. Africa; the Caribbean; Latin America; Eastern Europe; Australasia). These lines of enquiry have been instrumental in shaping methodological agenda and directions, as well as offering tremendous insights into discourses of Graeco-Roman antiquity in space and time. Yet, within the histories of classical receptions focusing on periods and regions, the twentieth century has been underexamined as a thematic unit. On the one hand, there has been a preponderance of focus in studies in English on Anglophone, Francophone and Germanophone receptions. This has been in part corrected by postcolonial reception studies with a focus on geopolitical regions outside of Western Europe. What has been missing is a perspective that combines not only an appreciation of Western and non-Western receptions, but also an understanding of these reception phenomena within a global, and not merely regional, framework. *CRTW* seeks to address this tangible gap, moving beyond isolated treatments and into full-scale investigations of authors recognized both for radical re-readings of the classical past and for challenging received ideas about the identity and cultural mobility of antiquity in the Western tradition. Interdisciplinarity is at the heart of such a reconsideration of reception in the series. Instead of treating reception as a sub-discipline of Classics, or as an expansion of the disciplinary boundaries of Classics, *CRTW* conceives it as a hub for knowledge exchange amongst multiple subjects, disciplinary practices and scholarly expertise. It addresses some of the most profound shifts in practices of reading, writing and thinking in recent years within the arts and humanities, as well as in the strategies of reading the classics that one finds in twentieth-century writing itself.

Beyond matters of reception, each individual study in the series draws attention to the specific quality of a modern author's classicism, as well as the ways in which that author negotiates classical ideals and values. Such is the case with English writer, poet and scholar J.R.R. Tolkien (Bloemfontein, Orange Free State 1892–Bournemouth, Hampshire 1973), best known for his novels *The Hobbit* (1937) and *The Lord of the Rings* (1954–5). During his lifetime, Tolkien maintained an ongoing dialogue with the classics. At a young age, while home-schooled by his mother, he acquired Latin, then to perfect on his knowledge of classical languages at King Edward's School in Birmingham and Exeter College, Oxford. In his academic career, classical antiquity continued to inform his main interests in Anglo-Saxon literature, amongst other subjects, while in his fictional writings, he actively drew on ancient Graeco-Roman themes to recreate his high fantasy narratives, principally, those informing the utopia of Middle-earth. How, and to what effects, Tolkien's classicism interacts with his utopian thought is the focus of the present volume. In *J.R.R. Tolkien's Utopianism and the Classics*, Hamish Williams offers a distinctive reading of how Homeric/Odyssean, Platonic, and Ovidian ideals and motifs substantiate Tolkien's utopian world. At the heart of Tolkien's regard for antiquity is what Williams terms 'retrotopianism', a process by which the author looks back into the classics to familiarise his readers with the hidden, unknown fictional aspects of his utopian environments – most prominently, those of cities, homes and forests. These three themes form the backbone of Williams' analysis, which charts the allusive and/or symbolic role that narratives of Platonic moderation, Augustan restoration, Homeric hospitality and the Ovidian material sublime play in Tolkien's utopian poetics and design. Each chapter explores retrotopianism as a strategy that allows Tolkien to insert a series of broader classical concepts into three accounts of Middle-earth: 'lapsarian' narratives of decline and fall of the kind that mark ancient Rome, which temporally frame the ancient paradisical island or the city (Chapter 1); the hospitality narratives of Homer's *Odyssey* which occur in the home-settings of *The Hobbit* (Chapter 2); and the sublime narratives of voyages into the old, dense forest, the *silva vetus*, in *The Lord of the Rings* (Chapter 3). Williams' discussion also stresses the ethical, political and spiritual implications of Tolkien's retrotopian classicism. Thus Chapter 1 examines how utopian narratives of the decline and fall of distinctly 'classical' communities provide Tolkien with a blueprint for future political restorations. Chapter 2 considers the Homeric narrative of home as a model where an ethical reciprocity between host and guest can be sought in Middle-earth, while the focus of Chapter 3 is on Tolkien's transformation of Ovid's ancient forests into ambiguous, unsettling sites where his utopian characters can experience forms of awakening. A look back into the classical-as-blueprint is but one facet of Tolkien's engagement with antiquity. Williams further shows how Tolkien's classical knowledge opens his utopian experiments to stimulating intellectual enquiry about how past and present interact, and how older, well-known narratives, once strategically reworked, can speak powerfully to the modern *imaginaire* about ideal urban, domestic and natural environments. In the closing pages of his study, Williams sheds more intimate light on the significance of Tolkien's classicism for his branch of utopianism. Tolkien does not simply rethink antiquity to invest his utopian world with a steady paragon of 'Platonic' virtue. Instead, he makes certain epistemic demands on the classical tradition itself, recasting classical cities, home and forest in all their perfect and imperfect aspects. It is at this intersection that both Classical and Utopian Studies align productively to draw attention to this author's awareness of the (ins)stabilities that equally mark the classical and the Western modern world, as well as demystifying his utopian poetics and thought. Tolkien's utopianism, often regarded as unfashionably conservative and hermetically sealed from the real world (Epilogue), here seems refreshingly permeable to a fuller spectrum of classical and modern realities – utopian and otherwise – than one might at first suspect.

*Laura Jansen, University of Bristol*

# Introduction

## Utopianism and Classicism: Tolkien's New–Old Continent

### Between strangeness and familiarity

A literary genre is essentially a pragmatic, ever-evolving category that is assigned to a large group of literary works within which readers expect the fulfilment (or occasionally, within reason, some deviation from) a number of codes, the recurring signposts that are stock characteristics of the genre.[1] For the codes of the horror genre, for example, one might expect claustrophobic spaces, supernatural intrusions, a concentration on the vulnerability of the body in all its corporeality, inverted hospitality rites, villains who personify the primitive, irrational side of the human psyche and so on.[2] For science fiction, one could anticipate voyages through outer space, a fascination with technology and its potentials, interactions with the non-human and temporal disorientation. For the fantasy genre, one expects J.R.R. Tolkien's Middle-earth:[3]

> [The fantasy genre] existed before Tolkien [...] and it is possible to say that it would have existed, and would have developed into the genre it has become, without the lead of *The Lord of the Rings*. This seems, however, rather doubtful. [...] One of the things that Tolkien did was to open up a new continent of imaginative space for many millions of readers, and hundreds of writers – though he himself would have said [...] that it was an old continent which he was merely rediscovering.[4]

Shippey astutely points to a key principle in the aesthetic appeal of Tolkien's works for modern readers: a delightful tension between the strange and the familiar, between the unknown and the known. The spatial, continental metaphor which Shippey uses to help us visualize the aesthetic reasons for Tolkien's hugely successful reception, from roughly the mid-twentieth century to the present era, aptly introduces the two intersecting schools of thought which inform the present study, and which revolve around this aesthetic tension between strangeness and familiarity in Tolkien's writings: *utopianism* (opening up a 'new continent of imaginative space') and *classicism* (an 'old continent which he was merely rediscovering').

## Utopianism

Utopianism, if one breaks down the three etymological components of the term – two of them hidden in a verbal pun ($u = ou$ (no); $u = eu$ (good))[5] – might be defined as a form of thinking which generally triangulates around: (i) space, thinking in terms of place (*topos* (place) in Greek), thus distinguishing it from the more general, but related, 'a-topical' notion of idealism; (ii) alterity, imagining a strangeness, newness or foreignness to place, which gives it its distinct quality of 'nowhere-ness' (*ou-topos* (no place)); and (iii) idealism, speculating on the perfection (or imperfection) of place (*eu-topos* (a good place)).[6] To paraphrase with a working definition, *utopianism is a form of thinking which defamiliarizes physical space for the sake of exploring and evaluating an ideal.*

This is both similar to and quite different from the prevailing vernacular definition of 'utopianism' in the *Oxford English Dictionary* (OED): 'The belief in or pursuit of a state in which everything is perfect, typically regarded as unrealistic or idealistic'.[7] The reasons for definitional disputes regarding 'utopianism' and its concrete (positive) realization of 'utopia' in the burgeoning, interdisciplinary academic field of utopian studies are primarily discipline-related:[8] literary studies, political studies, philosophy, psychology, sociology and history all adopt discipline-specific discourse and norms to understand this important concept. In particular, the OED definition above is coloured by a pervasive analysis of twentieth-century social and state history on the part of many liberal-minded, realist critics in political or historical studies, who have regarded this period as marked by ambitious, failed utopian projects[9] – hence, the definitional reference to pejorative terms such as 'belief', which denotes an irrational, religious form of thought, and 'unrealistic', as well as the focus on the pragmatic idea of a 'pursuit' and on the 'state' as a unit of analysis. This is truly a discourse of political studies which has invaded the popular vernacular, such that the average person defines the 'utopian', in vernacular terms, as 'referring in almost all cases to an idea or scheme far beyond the range of possibility, though perhaps intriguing in theory [... often] used without precision to denigrate any idea the user finds implausible if not ridiculous'.[10] Alternatively, for instance, scholars from psychological and philosophical-cognitive perspectives may be more interested in defining 'utopianism' in terms of drives such as 'desires' and 'hopes'.[11] For scholars from sociological and socio-historical perspectives, the focus is far more on the possible realization or actualization of utopias in society than on the speculative wanderings of literature.[12]

Now with all due respect given to different academic disciplines and their objects of study (and to the popular usurpation and denigration of the term), literature has long been recognized in academic scholarship as an important avenue of utopian thinking and expression, at least since the time of Thomas More's *Utopia* (1516),[13] although the roots of modern explorations of these imagined realms go back to ancient thought.[14] At any rate, it is worth starting with More since he has become central to modern critical understandings and discourses of what utopian literature is,[15] which often entails the formal question of genre in structuralist analyses, as well as what *utopianism is in literature*, which is a more exploratory, ambiguous, conceptual question on literary thought, and which is the focus of this book. More's early-sixteenth-century literary treatise is spatially rich in its topographic descriptions of different regions of the world, of the cities and the rural countryside, and of course in the detailed description of his eponymous island community called Utopia,[16] which is a wholly imagined, constructed place, seemingly nowhere on our maps (*Ou-topia*), and which is, apparently, far better (*Eu-topia*) than the real world of More's represented European societies of England, Holland, Portugal and so on. More's utopian text has important implications for how utopianism in literature is defined in terms of spatial richness, defamiliarization ('nowhereness') and perfection. But it also raises certain ambiguities in defining utopianism in literature, which can help us appreciate the nuances of utopianism in Tolkien's writings.[17]

The first ambiguity lies in the *eu* of utopianism. One significant distinction between utopianism in a literary text such as More's and, for example, in a political pamphlet lies in the ambiguity of representations of the utopian in the former and the positivism in the latter (absolute eu-topias) – a tendentious positivism to which modern political and historical realism reacts unfavourably, and which it often unfairly attributes to literature as well.[18] To be clear, More's Platonic dialogue called *Utopia* includes *both* imperfect societies in the form of early sixteenth-century European feudal communities, beset by social inequalities, princely abuses, warring armies and religious intolerance, among other ills, *and* the apparently ideal society of Utopia, which provides a critique of, and perhaps a solution to, contemporary ills.[19] However, even within the generally perfective description, many critics have noticed apparent scepticism or satire on the part of More.[20] Furthermore, as a sidenote, if one wanted to explore the history and reception of the idea of the utopian rather than More's own literary interrogations, one would have to concede that many modern, particularly female readers have found More's island to be especially dystopic.[21] In short, in most literary texts which are concerned with 'utopianism' (again, a term which is not understood in this book in the political or vernacular senses),[22] there is an explicit or implied comparison in the representations of perfect and imperfect societies, whether this contrasting is spatial (utopia to be found across the ocean away from an imperfect society) or temporal (utopia, or *uchronias*, to be found in the distant past or future, away from a corrupted present).[23] And, furthermore, however perfect the spatially or temporally removed utopias seem to be, 'contradictions are betrayed in the utopia in the form of ruptures underlying its apparently smooth and seamless surface'.[24] Likewise, in Tolkien's creative fiction, which is teeming with both eu-topian constructs (the Shire, Rivendell, Lothlórien) and dystopian constructs (Moria, Isengard, Mordor), the oscillation both in space and in time between positive, negative and ambiguous places renders his literary eu-topianism as a form of critique, an exploration of ideas, rather than an attempt to promote an actual vision of absolute utopia, which for Tolkien – as a Christian – lay outside of time, history and human space.

The second ambiguity lies in the *topos* of utopianism. One notable bias which More's *Utopia* introduced in scholarly studies on literary utopias is a topographic bias towards understanding the place of 'utopia' in macro-social, even civilizational, terms, in particular as a condensed sociopolitical 'community' or 'state'[25] that often resides on a faraway island or some other remote terrain such as a mountain valley or in the middle of a jungle.[26] This is indeed a common trope in utopian literature in the early modern period, but it is not necessary to restrict the analysis of utopianism as a general form of literary thought to such a *topos*. For instance, the environmental turn of the 1960s and the more recent post-humanist turn of the past decade have been reflected in many creative works of literature and film which provide us with distinctly non-human ecotopias. In Richard Adams' *Watership Down* (1972), the freedom-seeking rabbits manage to find a peaceful, animals-only paradise atop a country hill in rural England, not completely isolated but sufficiently removed from the cruel machinations of men as well as humanized rabbits, who display forms of social utopianism in the form of fascism (General Woundwort's Efrafans) and communism (Cowslip's warren).[27] Certainly, in recent films such as *The Happening* (2008), the existence of human agents is problematized as the very dystopian element which needs to be destroyed within beautiful natural idylls. Aside from de-emphasizing the anthropological structure of the *topos*, literature concerned with utopianism can also focus less on the discovery of a perfectly running community than on an individual's quest to find some kind of personal utopia: for example, the cognitive peace or ontological bliss within the ideal mountainous interior of Crete which the Truman couple discover in Lawrence Durrell's *The Dark Labyrinth* (1947);[28] or the personal *plutotopia* which Daniel (Sean Connery) and Peachy (Michael Cane) mistakenly try to find in John Huston's *The Man Who Would Be King* (1975). Lastly, in contemporary works, the colonial desire to find or found utopia in distant, isolated places (islands and mountain vales) can be inverted,[29] and an idealization of the mundane, of the everyday is an image which can be endorsed.[30] One recent example is Alexander Payne's film *Downsizing* (2017), with its humorous emphasis on the desirability of the small, the local and the mundane for modern human or consumer happiness (utopia is to live in a kind of doll's house).

There is, in short, no need to be too essentialist when deciding what the *topos* of utopianist thought can be in fiction; likewise, when this study examines forms of 'utopias' in Tolkien's writing, the focus is on a diverse range of idealized *topoi*: sociopolitical communities, the individual, mundane home and vistas of the natural world. To be very clear to literary critics coming from a tradition of reading certain literary texts in generic harmony, however, it must be emphasized that this book does not understand Tolkien's *utopianism or utopian literary thought* as lying within the very specific, post-Morean genre of so-called 'utopian fiction' or as only being concerned with the intratextual *topos* of utopia itself.[31] Strictly speaking, his narratives in Middle-earth generally do not meet the formal requirements of the 'utopian novel' or the 'utopian narrative', with the focus on, for example, a traveller from our real world who comes across the utopian society (among other generic characteristics).[32] It is, therefore, not the purpose of this book to compare and contrast Tolkien's imagined world with those in the writings of More, Bacon, Butler, Bellamy, Morris, Wells, Orwell, and other writers.

Yet J.R.R. Tolkien's creative fiction, particularly his works which focus on Middle-earth such as *The Hobbit* (1937), *The Lord of the Rings* (1954–5), and *The Silmarillion* (1977), still deserve an important place within the *canon of literature which explores utopianism* because, like More's seminal text and its ancient predecessors, his writing triangulates over the defining components of spatial richness in narrative, of imaginative defamiliarization (nowhereness) and of (im)perfectionism or idealism; in other words, to return to my earlier working definition, as a literary thinker Tolkien 'defamiliarizes physical space for the sake of exploring and evaluating an ideal'. This is his 'utopianism'. The proof is in the pudding, of course. Nevertheless, Tom Shippey's astute observation – 'one of the things that Tolkien did was to open up a new continent of imaginative space for many millions of readers' – provides a tantalizing opener to this project since it implicitly presents the appeal of Middle-earth for modern readers as an extension of utopian representations in literary history, stemming from that of More's *Utopia*. More's utopian text was immensely exciting for his own readers in the so-called Age of Exploration precisely because just some twenty years prior the *new* continent of America had been opened up for imaginative adventurers (colonial ambitions aside). Such early modern utopian literature, like that of More and Bacon, offered the reading public the food they desired – an exploration of newness, of an otherness beyond the known European world, of a *genus* of land hitherto unknown (No-place, *Ou-topia*).[33] Conceived around the start of the twentieth century, when there were no more physical frontiers to be found in the western or the southern hemisphere,[34] Tolkien's Middle-earth was one of a number of important 'genre-fiction' places in the twentieth century which allowed readers to explore *new*, alternative, constructed spatial-temporal worlds in science fiction and fantasy, from H.G. Wells to Isaac Asimov, from C.S. Lewis to J.K. Rowling and George R.R. Martin.[35] 'If travellers' tales brought audiences to imaginary worlds and utopias gave them some sense of how their inhabitants lived, the genres of science fiction and fantasy invited audiences to live in them vicariously.'[36]

Tolkien's constructed world is an exciting *topos* of desire for many modern readers, who will stick a map of Middle-earth onto their walls[37] and traverse this new continent with the help of the third-person narrator. This imaginative adventure is a genuine ou-topian exploration of the strange, of the unknown, of the other, which is aptly aided by the author's near-unrivalled expertise in spatial worldbuilding, in constructing a secondary world seemingly divorced from our own known world, and which has its own hermetic system or internal logic of 'maps, timelines, genealogies, nature, culture, language, mythology, and philosophy'.[38] In his discussions of Tolkien's exemplary worldbuilding as a modern speculative fiction writer,[39] Wolf mentions the degrees of otherness or strangeness which are possible in a new (subcreated, secondary) literary world such as that of Middle-earth[40] – and thus, implicitly, the disorientation or defamiliarization which a reader experiences when entering such a realm. Wolf argues for hierarchical levels of invention in terms of 'the nominal, cultural, natural, and ontological':[41] for instance, strange place names, strange social customs, strange plants and strange physics. One might add that the breadth and depth of Middle-earth seemingly have no bounds and are currently still under construction, given that the continued fan fiction as well as filmic and gaming receptions only add to this sense of an ever-expanding universe, which goes beyond the limits of Tolkien's narratives.[42]

Such a reader-reception-based approach to the world of Middle-earth might make Tolkien's utopianism appear almost colonial or colonizing; alternatively, it might also remind us of Dutch historian Rutger Bregman's claim that utopias are at best always horizontal imaginaries, landscapes (literal or metaphorical) to be continually discovered at the edge of sight, and that utopianism is at best always an investigation into the perfect, a search for alternate worlds.[43] The search for new horizons is undoubtedly part of the persisting appeal of *The Lord of the Rings* for new readers. However, the appeal of newness in Middle-earth should not blind the reader to the processes of re-familiarization which coexist with those of defamiliarization in Tolkien's complex worldbuilding.[44] As the next section identifies, his utopianism is, in large part, a kind of retrotopianism, a rediscovery and rewriting of an older continent. Such a retrotopianism intersects, furthermore, with another defining feature of Tolkien's utopianism: his eu-topianism, the exploration of space on the level of ideals and ethics.

## Classicism

The second part of Shippey's dualistic statement – 'it was an old continent which he was merely rediscovering' – leads onto this book's second category of analysis for the aesthetic appeal of Tolkien's works: *classicism*. In a straightforward geographic sense, the 'old continent' is what ancient and early modern cartographers have called 'the old world', in other words, Eurasia and northern Africa. What was Tolkien 'rediscovering' while hovering over this old continent? A sizeable part of the scholarship in Tolkien studies has been devoted to studying the different ways in which the writer's inherited cultural, literary, mythic and (not least) philological histories shaped his thought and were manifested in his literary creations.[45] Depending on the methods employed by the individual scholar and their disciplinary background, such scholarship may variously be called source studies, reception studies, comparative literature studies, comparative mythology, folklore, religious studies, comparative philology or historical linguistics.

By sheer weight of critical studies, it would appear that the greatest influence on the fantasy writer can be ascribed to two domains: (i) medieval language, with a particular focus on Germanic languages (Old English, Middle English, Old Norse), and medieval literature (heroic epics such as *Beowulf* and romances such as *Sir Gawain and the Green Knight*),[46] and (ii) Christian or Catholic writings, particularly the Old and New Testaments and the works of theologians from the times of St Paul and Augustine to the present.[47] Both of these fields of influence make perfect biographic sense, given that Tolkien was, firstly, a medievalist by academic profession and an expert researcher of Old English literature and so-called Anglo-Saxon society⁴⁸ and, secondly, a staunch, conservative Roman Catholic by personal faith.⁴⁹ Yet Tolkien's inherited 'old continent' was a diverse melting pot, a compost heap. It was composed of different types of cultural texts: literary, theological, mythic, oral, philosophical and historiographic. It was built up from different regional contexts: certainly, the north-west of the 'old continent', but also the Mediterranean, the east, and even the far south, since Tolkien's personal knowledge of (and vague affiliation with) southern Africa extended beyond pre-modern cartographic limits. And it was assembled from different periods: pre-classical ('primitive' or 'prehistoric'), classical (Greece and Rome), late antique, medieval, early modern, romantic, Victorian, and Edwardian.

Of these many different sources, this book hones in on the importance of Graeco-Roman or 'classical' literary, mythic and other cultural texts to Tolkien's literary works and thought. As was the case for many young boys who grew up in late Victorian, Edwardian England at the turn of the century, much of Tolkien's early education bears testament to an undeniably strong education in 'the Classics'.⁵⁰ First tutored in Latin by his mother at the age of four (1896),⁵¹ young 'Ronald' (J.R.R.) Tolkien entered King Edward's School in Birmingham in 1900, a school with a strong Classics-focused education,⁵² and he soon added Ancient Greek to his growing repertoire of languages.⁵³ As Tolkien reflected succinctly in his later years, 'I went to King Edward's School and spent most of my time learning Latin and Greek'.⁵⁴ More concretely, this classical education included standard classroom fare such as prose composition (translating from English back into the ancient languages);⁵⁵ the study of classical grammar or linguistics;⁵⁶ the requisite schoolboy business of translating Latin and Greek literature into English;⁵⁷ and the study of Graeco-Roman history, society, and culture.⁵⁸ But the discipline of Classics was also broached in extracurricular activities, such as school debates held entirely in Latin (or in Ancient Greek, for the ambitious polyglot Tolkien)⁵⁹ as well as the performance of a Greek play during the year-end festivities.⁶⁰

From the evidence of biographic accounts, reflective letters and old school examination reports, Ronald Tolkien seems to have been a conscientious, hard-working Classics pupil at King Edward's: thus, he obtained a book prize in 1905, *Roman History* (1879) by W.W. Capes, for tying for first place in the Sixth Class;⁶¹ he was competitive about his knowledge of ancient literature;⁶²

and in passing his school leaving examinations, the Oxford and Cambridge Higher Certificate Examination,[63] the examiners singled him out for praise for his papers in 'Greek prose' and 'ancient history'.[64] Having graduated from school and having obtained an acceptable scholarship for admission to the University of Oxford,[65] Tolkien's academic career seemed geared towards becoming a classical philologist like his tutor, the eminent Classics scholar Lewis Richard Farnell.[66] Yet around this time of his undergraduate career Tolkien seems to have suffered something of a 'burnout' in Classics, to have become 'bored'[67] with the discipline, to hanker after other literatures and languages; this movement away from Classics is clearly reflected by a drop in his grades, which included the threat of losing his scholarship, by less than brilliant examination results for his Honour Moderations, and by his own later admissions.[68] The biographer Humphrey Carpenter establishes the canonical biographic narrative when he writes that in the summer of 1913: 'he [Tolkien] abandoned Classics and began to read English'.[69]

The reasons for Tolkien's change in academic career were probably various.[70] In all likelihood, he attained an overfamiliarity with classical texts from the time of his early school days – after all, Classics consumed roughly fifty per cent of the school timetable in the average English public school at that time;[71] his naturally creative imagination longed for something new.[72] Perhaps his philological imagination did as well: although Latin and Greek afforded Tolkien the positive platform for some of his earliest linguistic experimentations in designing his own languages,[73] he did not, in all likelihood, want to be restricted to a meagre two languages.[74] From the perspective of subject matter rather than form or language, on the other hand, Tolkien's love was more narrow than his linguistic tastes and clearly always directed to great epics, sagas and romances – hence his continued love of Homer and Virgil throughout his life (alongside Beowulf, Norse sagas and medieval romances) – rather than to the full gamut of classical literature, including genres such as oratory (Tolkien professed a marked dislike for Cicero and Demosthenes), love poetry and lyric poetry.[75] At this point in his professional career, biographers have typically pointed to a 'northern turn' in Tolkien's creative sensibilities, a turn away from the Classics – an idea which is backed up by Tolkien's own, often quite romantic, patriotic sentiments on his desire to establish a legend for England, for 'the clime and soil of the North West, meaning Britain and the hither parts of Europe; not Italy or the Aegean, still less the East'.[76] Some scholars, such as Tom Shippey, have also taken this biographic consensus (reinforced by, for example, John Garth) as a cue to downplay the classical influences on Tolkien's works, which they regard as substantially less important than 'Northern' sources.[77]

However, to paraphrase the hugely popular Internet meme which is based on the speech of the Gondorian hero Boromir in Peter Jackson's adapted film version of *The Fellowship of the Ring* (2001), 'one does not simply ... *abandon seventeen years of classical education*'! And Tolkien never really abandoned the classical world, in any case, because, apart from 'educational indoctrination', he never abandoned the pervasive cultural-historical sense that he, as a creative writer, was working in a Western literary tradition, in a long line of literary texts leading back to ancient Greece and Rome: thus, in Tolkien's own estimation, *The Lord of the Rings* had its clear precedents in Homer, Greek tragedy, Virgil, Beowulf and Shakespeare.[78] There was a time when the study of classical influences on an important, 'classic' writer such as J.R.R. Tolkien would require little scholarly justification. The advent of classicism and our cultural sense of residing in a post-classical tradition since at least the Renaissance[79] had imbued the Graeco-Roman world with cultural notions of being complete,[80] paradigmatic, essential, even approaching perfection.[81] These connotations are captured in the definitions of the related noun and adjective 'classic' in the *Oxford English Dictionary* (2nd edition):[82] 'A writer, or a literary work, of the first rank and of acknowledged excellence; esp. (as originally used) in Greek or Latin'; 'Of the first class, of the highest rank or importance; approved as a model; standard, leading'.[83]

In cultural studies, theoretical approaches such as postcolonialism, which has questioned the primacy of Western or classical thought in academic fields and which has shown the implicit power structures which lie behind the construction of knowledge,[84] have heightened our sense of ethical unease when we capitalize and emphasize, for example, 'Classical history' or the 'Western tradition' and, thus, when we construct more broadly the classical world as the temporal past-perfect foundation for orienting ourselves in modernity. This deconstruction of the seminal place of the classical tradition, for various reasons, has meant that many modern readers who have been educated in (post-)postmodernity, roughly since the 1980s, are not necessarily equipped with the necessary training to detect classical figures and tropes in certain allusive texts they read, and they, therefore, find different kinds of meanings in such texts. This is also true of Tolkien's texts, which have become canonized in a modern fantasy genre that is, in many respects, defined by its anti-classical, medieval, even gothic genre-codes.[85] This book is one of several classical-reception studies of Tolkien's works which attempt to recodify the 'lost' or hidden classical elements into his literature for readers. Tolkien was generally not a post-colonial, postmodern thinker – ways of thinking in the twentieth century which have ousted the primacy of the classical tradition in the humanities. He was essentially a traditionalist, a historicist, a comparativist in his philological or literary proclivities; more specifically, he was a medievalist by trade – a specialist in the Middle Ages (a category not always distinguishable from Late Antiquity), with a strong sense of what had come before, in the classical world and, indeed, the pre- and extra-classical world of Indo-European studies.[86]

In fact, in his reflections on his own writings, Tolkien is not shy to compare his own constructed peoples and characters to classical paradigms in Homer or Sophocles, for example;[87] nor was Tolkien averse to using a classical motif or myth to inspire himself in the very generative act of creation (as evidenced by his manuscripts), such as the device of the Homeric catalogue or the Atlantis myth.[88] While there were doubtless parts of a prescribed classical education that Tolkien was very happy to leave behind, there were also, as this book illustrates, classical writers (Homer, Plato, Virgil, Ovid, various Greek and Roman historiographers), classical characters or personages (Odysseus, Aeneas, Orpheus, Augustus) and, importantly, classical narratives (of decline and restoration from a former golden age, of hospitality encounters, of sublime experiences) that lived on and endured in the creative mind-compost of the English writer for the rest of his days. On a related note, it is fascinating to observe the retired Oxford don being absorbed in his seventies by *The King Must Die* (1958) and *The Bull from the Sea* (1962) by English-South African writer Mary Renault,[89] which are modern retellings of classical Greek (especially, Plutarch's) myths on Theseus – just as he was absorbed in his twenties by the classical receptions of William Morris, whose rewritten version of Apollonius' story about Jason's quest for the golden fleece, *The Life and*

*Death of Jason* (1867), inspired the young Tolkien at the very point at which he had apparently 'abandoned the classics'.[90]

In short, for the rest of his professional and intellectual life, Tolkien continued to read classical and classical-inspired fictional works; he gave lectures on Latin influences on English at Oxford;[91] he used classical historiography to come to terms with modern political situations during Second World War Europe;[92] he helped his sons with their Latin homework;[93] he opposed the modernization of the Catholic Church, which saw the use of Latin in the liturgy fall away;[94] he used classical exempla to orchestrate or reflect on his own writings; and he moderated Latin and Greek exams at Oxford.[95] Classics continued to be an important part of his life, and while it cannot be claimed that classical influences in his works are on the same level as the medieval, Germanic, or Victorian, they can still be felt in subtle ways in the canvas of his stories. To return to Shippey's metaphor, Tolkien provides a telling analogy between his constructed 'old continent' of Middle-earth and our own real world by including southern, Mediterranean or classical locales – thus familiarizing this strange new world, this *ou-topia*, for modern readers:

> Minas Tirith [...] is at about the latitude of Florence. The Mouths of Anduin and the ancient city of Pelargir are at about the latitude of ancient Troy. [...] The progress of the tale ends in what is far more like the re-establishment of an effective Holy Roman Empire with its seat in Rome than anything that would be devised by a 'Nordic'.[96]

Tolkien's formative education, personal remarks, reminiscences, uses of the classical, and his general integration in an English society and academic community which still placed a prestigious value on Classics[97] all provide the justification, the bedrock, for this study of classical reception – a field, to be clear, in which sufficient proof of authorial sources *does matter* (unlike comparative literature studies). After a few scholarly outliers in the 1970s and 1980s,[98] academics started to show a more concerted interest in the possible classical sources for Tolkien's writings during the 1990s. These first articles and chapters (as well as some more recent ones) were generally in the tradition of comparative mythology and folklore studies: they were concerned principally with exacting parallels in characters, places, events, and motifs. They showed, for instance, that Bilbo's story in *The Hobbit* seems informed by that of

Odysseus, or that *The Fall of Gondolin* is closely modelled on the fall of ancient Troy.[99] These studies have provided further proof that Tolkien was using classical models to construct his fabricated world. Yet it has become important in classical reception studies not simply to ask *what?* but *for what purpose?* From a reader's perspective: how do these classical receptions shape our understanding of key concepts or ideas in Tolkien's works?[100]

To date, there have been some innovative studies which have used the clear transmission of classical data in Tolkien's work as an avenue for further discussion of essential concepts and themes in the Englishman's writings: for example, how his construct of the hero mediates between Germanic, Christian, Roman Catholic, modern and, importantly, classical models, whether they be Homeric, Roman or Virgilian;[101] how by reappropriating the classical *topos* of the underworld, Tolkien could rewrite typical classical 'katabatic' associations of despair, forgetfulness and death in his elegiacs, but also write the essentially joyful Christian epic of *The Lord of the Rings*;[102] and how notions of divine intervention from classical epics have been rewritten in ways which are more commensurate with Tolkien's own compassionate Christian worldview.[103] The list could go on. The past few years have seen the publication of the first edited volume devoted wholly to Tolkien and the classical world,[104] a special issue on Tolkien and the Classics by classical-reception journal *Thersites* is expected in 2022, and further workshops and conferences related to Tolkien's classical reception and ideas of fantastical worldbuilding in the classics are arising.

The above examples give some idea of how classical-reception approaches can facilitate our comprehensive understanding of central concepts in Tolkien's writings: heroism, death, elegy, memory, creativity, the divine, and so on. For this book, the focus is very much on how Tolkien's reusage of classical knowledge intersects with and informs his literary utopianism. Certain hidden, unexplored parts of the new continent of Middle-earth, this Ou-topia, become familiarized to us through classical readings as part of the old continent.[105] Such a *retrotopianism* on the part of Tolkien involves his receiving and rewriting not only the analogous, cartographic bearings, which would, for example, equate a renewed Gondor with a restored Rome, but also – and more importantly for a literary writer whose medium is narrative (as opposed to a map-maker) – *broader classical narratives* which develop around and explore certain common *topoi*: 'lapsarian' narratives of decline and fall which temporally frame the ancient paradisical island or the city (Chapter 1); hospitality narratives which occur in and around the home or *oikos* (Chapter 2); and sublime narratives during voyages into nature, for example, the old, dense forest, the *silva vetus* (Chapter 3).

The narratives which develop around these *topoi* are, as this book illustrates, essentially ancient eu-topian thought exercises: What precise ideals constituted the ancient paradise or city, and can these ideals actually be restored in our fallen present (Chapter 1)? What is a good home and what is a bad home (Chapter 2)? What awakenings beyond our ordinary life can be stimulated by ventures into the realms of the natural world (Chapter 3)? The core of this monograph relates to Tolkien's reception of such narrative constructs of space and the exploration of ideals and ethics that they imply – the 'Platonic' ideas which one can find lying in the misty valleys and secret woods of Middle-earth. It should not come as a surprising claim to most readers of his works that Tolkien's writing exhibits eu-topianism, that his world is littered with eu-topian (Shire, Rivendell, Lothlórien) and indeed dys-topian (Moria, Isengard, Mordor) constructs, and that he invests his imagined places with meaning and with ideals which he explores; however, the particular relevance of his retrotopianism, of his looking back at the classical world, to his eu-topianism has not yet been broached.

Finally, on a more methodological note, while the Epilogue pays more attention to Tolkien's forms of classical reception, two features should be noted from the outset, since they are so readily apparent in the subsequent analysis: firstly, there is the admixture of the classical with the non-classical, particularly the Germanic and Christian sources, which cannot be discounted.[106] Throughout this book, reference is made to the mingling of the classical with the non-classical, to illustrate the compound nature of Tolkien's utopianism, which is in large degrees reflected by his Christian beliefs, not to mention his personal political and social opinions as a man often unwillingly stuck in the modern world. Secondly, there is the propensity for Tolkien not simply to transmit classical data in straightforward ways ('direct borrowings' or 'influences') but to subtly reimplement and fundamentally *rewrite* classical stories and ideas in ways which reflect his own personal worldview.[107]

# 1

# Lapsarian Narratives: The Decline and Fall of Utopian Communities in Middle-earth

## Introduction: Lapsarian narratives in Tolkien and the classics

There is general agreement that 'the fall' is a pervasive element in Tolkien's literary narratives.[1] Tolkien stresses the importance of such *lapsarian narratives*:[2] 'There cannot be any "story" without a fall – all stories are ultimately about the fall.'[3] In Tolkien's instructive summary of his legendarium to Milton Waldman, the word 'fall' and its variants ('fallen', 'falling', 'unfallen', 'downfall') can be tallied to twenty-three occurrences.[4] The importance which Tolkien gives to lapsarian narratives in his stories can be variously interpreted: they reflect a Christian worldview; they frame the internal chronology of his constructed histories; they accentuate the tragic and elegiac qualities of his writing; and, not least, they facilitate Tolkien's exploration of utopian communities.

Tolkien's lapsarian expressions in his private thoughts owe a great deal to his knowledge of the Old Testament, particularly Genesis. Writing to his youngest son Christopher, he laments the fallen state of modern, 'postlapsarian' man after our expulsion from an original 'Eden' (the 'sad exiled generations from the Fall', 'this very unhappy earth') and the moral, ontological decline from 'the nobler part of the human mind' which that exile has engendered ('[w]e shall never recover it').[5] In a letter to his middle son Michael, in identifying possible real-world signs of decline ('this is a fallen world'),[6] Tolkien grounds these societal failings in terms of an original Adamic Fall, and his description of our postlapsarian state draws on characteristically Christian notions of sexual guilt, the debased body, and asceticism in the face of temptation.[7]

Turning from Tolkien's personal reflections to his creative writings, we may note that Chapters 6 to 9 in *The Silmarillion*, which describe the fall of the elves, seem broadly constructed from various biblical and later Christian narratives of the Fall. A group of elves called the Noldor, spurred by the temptations of the 'Satanic' or 'serpentine' Melkor, decide to leave their Edenic paradise of Valinor, which is watched over by the angelic Valar; these elves are subsequently banished from Valinor and are forced to suffer in the wider, corrupt, 'postlapsarian' world of Middle-earth.[8] There are, moreover, recurring motifs throughout Tolkien's legendarium which pick up the Adamic fall. For instance, the temptation of the forbidden fruit, which grants increased knowledge at the cost of a fall from Edenic bliss, seems to be reflected through the numerous tainted 'jewels and precious objects'[9] (the Silmarils, the many rings, the palantíri) which pervade the long history of Middle-earth:[10] these objects are often associated with increased perception; however, despite such epistemic promise, the best approach for morally benign characters such as Frodo, Sam and Pippin towards these tempting objects is a Christian strategy of 'denial' and 'suffering'.[11] In contrast, those characters who are tempted by these objects, for example Boromir or Denethor (the One Ring; a palantir), inevitably suffer tragic falls.[12]

Tolkien's religious beliefs affected his views on the directionality of human history. Rather like St Augustine,[13] Tolkien understands history in our world (the City of Man) as a process of general decline and fall: 'Actually I am a Christian, and indeed a Roman Catholic, so that I do not expect "history" to be anything but a "long defeat" – though it contains (and in a legend may contain more clearly and movingly) some samples or glimpses of final victory.'[14] The term 'final victory' alludes to Christian eschatology (the Second Coming), where the return to the City of God (an ahistorical heaven) effectively terminates our stay in the City of Man (history). Tolkien's invitation to consider representations of historical decline and Christian renewal (or victory) in legends is informative. In his own legendarium, the canvas of historical decline is ruptured by brief glimpses of 'Christian' victory and renewal at important moments in the stories.[15] The *Silmarillion* narrates the decline and fall of various elven communities in Beleriand because of the growing evil of Morgoth, but this downward process is stopped by the Valar during the War of Wrath at the end of the First Age; the Last Alliance towards the end of the

Second Age halts the geopolitical dominion of Sauron, which had caused the downfall of the great human settlement of that historical aeon, Númenor; and in the Third Age the final defeat of Sauron, a villain who 'devours all',[16] again halts a period of civilizational waning in Middle-earth. These moments are all noteworthy pauses to narratives of terminal historical decline, where the world seemed destined to end in catastrophe, ruin and destruction, and where there would be no further events for historiography to narrate.

Such hopeful moments apparently distinguish Tolkien's Christian chronologies from the 'pagan' chronologies of classical writers such as Hesiod and Ovid, where the degeneration from a Golden Age to a Silver Age to a Bronze Age to the hopelessly corrupted Iron Age is terminal, a sort of *transsaecular decline* (literally, a trans-Age decline).[17] Given that these ruptures seem to occur roughly at the end of historical epochs or 'Ages' in Tolkien's legendarium and that they trigger restored golden ages, such as in Númenor at the start of the Second Age or in Gondor at the start of the Fourth, one might regard history in Tolkien's legendarium as somewhat cyclical rather than linear.[18] Societies decline, fall and are renewed in different guises – *intrasaecular decline* with *intersaecular renewal*. Then again, proponents for a more linear view of unremitting *transsaecular decline* in Tolkien's chronologies might well point to macro-narratives of consistent falling across the epochs:[19] for example, the steady dwindling of the elves or ents, from an ethnic, populational perspective, which only seems to worsen as the ages progress.[20] Perhaps a term such as *extrasaecular decline* might be even more appropriate: the fall of Melkor, just like the Fall of Satan, stands outside the recorded,[21] chronological history of Arda (the Four Ages); this suggests that 'historical' decline is rather an absolute principle in Tolkien's moral universe, revolving around Christian conflicts between good and evil (as the instigator of decline), irrespective of the aeon.[22] Decline is always present: for the elves, the seeds of their downfall are sown as soon as they enter paradise, at the very start of their story.[23]

Changing tack from the historical to the personal, we may note that Tolkien's claim that every story is about the fall implies tragedy as a literary genre or mode. Many characters in his declining legendarium suffer their own individual falls and catastrophes. Summarizing the decline of Arda in one letter, Tolkien cites perhaps his most tragic tale, that of Túrin,[24] whose 'blindness' at the point of his death recalls the Sophoclean Oedipus and the

Finnish Kullervo,[25] and whose fall conforms to Aristotle's theoretical discussion on the typical tragic man.[26] Tolkien links the tragedy of Túrin to the historical tragedy of greater Middle-earth: 'There are other stories almost equally full in treatment, and equally independent and yet linked to the general history.'[27] Tolkien had a particular fondness for Greek and Shakespearean drama (on stage, not in textual form),[28] which is reflected in many of his tragic characters: Boromir as Ajax,[29] Denethor as Priam or Lear,[30] Saruman as Macbeth.[31] Yet Tolkien's Christian worldview often requires a rewriting of the fatalistic, 'classical', Aristotelian concept of a terminal downward trajectory, the *katastrophē*, which a tragic character suffers;[32] instead, characters such as Bilbo Baggins and Peregrin Took experience the *eu-katastrophē*, a turn for the better when all hope seems lost, at the very moment of their imminent destruction, at the Battle of the Five Armies and the Battle of the Black Gate, respectively.[33] Here, again, Tolkien's Christian view of historical ruptures transforms the apparently tragic arc of his stories into joyful, hopeful fairy tales, even 'divine comedy'.[34]

Apart from an oscillation between a tragic (catastrophic) and a fairy-story (eu-catastrophic) literary mode, scholars have also pointed to an elegiac mode;[35] Middle-earth spatially marks historical decline and cultural collapse through sorrowful monuments, ruins, battlefields and graveyards.[36] The appropriate response by Tolkien's characters to this pervasive *feeling* of decline, felt in space and time, is the elegiac mode.[37] Tolkien's writing is emotionally charged with narratives of characters coming to grips (often through poetry or song) with fading memories of past glories, with forgetfulness, a losing fight against oblivion.[38] This gives Tolkien's characters their elegiac view of history and *The Lord of the Rings*, in particular, its elegiac tone. Such a gloomy threat of forgetfulness is pervasive. The ents have long lost track of the whereabouts of the entwives, who 'are only a memory' to them, a circumstance which breeds 'sorrow';[39] Númenor is a faint memory to be recalled by its descendants in the obscure realm of dreams;[40] only the elves seem to possess perfect memories, and yet such accurate recollection does little to abate elven gloominess and elegy as they fade away from (Middle-)earthly memories.[41] Indeed, *The Lord of the Rings* as a whole self-consciously defines itself as an epic text which has been entirely lost by our modern world.[42]

The pervasiveness of the fall in Tolkien's writings reveals his Christian framing of history and is reflected on a literary level by an oscillation between tragic, elegiac and fairy-story modes; but for Tolkien lapsarian narratives also operate as a means of reflection on utopian communities. Tolkien's world spatially brims with isolated communities, whether urban or more rustic settlements, 'a wilderness dotted with centres of civilization, pinpoints of light in the darkness'.[43] These communities are regarded as better in distinct ways with respect to the surrounding (postlapsarian) world at large, and decline and usually fall (or simply fade away from the known human world), thus losing their special, perfective, utopian status over time. Doriath, Nargothrond, Gondolin, Númenor, the Shire, Rivendell, Moria, Lothlórien and Minas Tirith (Gondor) are all isolated communities that approach perfection in their own distinct fashions, depending on whether the character travelling into the utopia is a gardener like Sam (the Shire), a poet like Bilbo (Rivendell), a 'business-dwarf' like Gimli (Moria) or a soldier like Boromir (Minas Tirith); importantly, almost all these settlements decline, ultimately collapse, or otherwise fade away from human memory, with the exception of a few which experience (ephemeral) restorations, where decline is arrested and renewals occur.

In creating such constructs of utopian communities or cities (*poleis*) that decline and fall, Tolkien was, probably consciously, placing his own (re)created *topoi* in a long post-classical tradition of literary, historiographical, and other cultural texts that have received this narrative from important works of classical literature and philosophy. In an early manuscript of 'The Fall of Gondolin', Tolkien's narrator compares the sacking of this elven city thus: 'Nor Bablon, nor Ninwi, nor the towers of Trui, nor all the many takings of Rûm that is greatest among Men, saw such terror as fell that day upon Amon Gwareth [the hill on which Gondolin is built] in the kindred of the Gnomes [i.e. the elves]'.[44] In a proto-version of this sentence, Tolkien had probably written 'Babylon, Nineveh, Troy, and (probably) Rome'.[45] Given Tolkien's self-conscious, playful inclusion of his own fallen city within such an ancient-inspired tradition, it is unsurprising that two important, interconnected human communities in Tolkien's world – Númenor and Gondor – closely receive and rewrite ancient lapsarian narratives. As this chapter illustrates, such a classical reception entails not only some of the more superficial details and events that occur during the corresponding sequences of decline and fall (the sinking of 'Atlantis'-Númenor; 'Carthaginian' elephants marching on 'Roman' Minas Tirith) but also an exposition on what cherished *ideals fall* as a community declines. In other words, Tolkien employs ancient lapsarian narratives as a basis for meditating on the loss of the ideals (political, social, moral, religious etc.) which a community represented – what made it utopian.

This is not to say that Tolkien's utopian speculations are always going to be classical in their ideological desires. Lapsarian narratives from the ancient world have been received in literary, historiographic and political traditions and discourses in the post-classical period: thus, the story of Troy, both its fall and restoration, was prominently represented in medieval traditions;[46] the downfall of Atlantis has been consistently rewritten since the Renaissance;[47] and the decline, fall and restoration of an ideal Rome has been represented by Christian theologians of Late Antiquity,[48] medieval mythmakers,[49] Enlightenment thinkers such as Montesquieu and Gibbons,[50] and twentieth-century historians such as Spengler or political figures such as Mussolini.[51] The ancient narrative of 'civilizational' fall has a long history of being rewritten in terms which respond to various post-classical contexts and ideals. This chapter concludes by putting Tolkien's lapsarian narratives in dialogue with other twentieth-century reimaginings of ancient fallen cities, where diverging modern ideologies are shown to be behind the appropriated ancient narratives.

To give some further background to these lapsarian narratives: it was a common technique in Graeco-Roman literary and social thought to employ narratives of decline and fall in order to articulate certain visions of utopia or paradise, communities in the past which were somehow more perfect and more desirable, and *which represented superior values*. Discussions of such ancient lapsarian narratives usually start with the so-called golden-age myths. Texts such as Hesiod's *Works and Days* and Ovid's *Metamorphoses* have provided the classical blueprint for these golden-age paradises.[52] These places are temporally removed from the present time and set in the mythic or heroic past;[53] they can also be described in terms which reflect spatial isolation or removal.[54] Importantly, they have a superior, perfective status: the blessed inhabitants are free from normal human sufferings and toils; their lands boast a natural profusion and perenniality; and there is direct contact with the divinities and the supernatural.[55] Not all classical paradises are such *ab origine* constructs as those in creation myths, but places such as the Isles of the Blessed[56] or even Homer's Scheria, a natural fertile paradise[57] where live the toil-free,[58] divinely blessed[59] Phaeacians, nevertheless replicate many typical golden-age characteristics.⁶⁰ One common feature of many (but not all) of these golden-age paradises is that they undergo decline, fall, and/or (imminent) collapse. Such a 'steady moral and physical deterioration from the beginning of human history to the present'⁶¹ is manifest in the creation myths of Hesiod, Ovid and other Graeco-Roman writers,⁶² where there is (variations and exceptions notwithstanding), a transsaecular decline in the relative perfection of humanity: a perfect Golden Age descends into a somewhat less ideal Silver Age (with various flaws revealing themselves in the inhabitants), then into a more violent, war-like Bronze Age, and finally into the most corrupt, evil Iron Age of contemporary society, which will ultimately also collapse and be destroyed like the others.⁶³ Other classical communities which bear paradisical, golden-age characteristics such as Plato's Atlantis and Homer's Scheria also tend to suffer collapse (physical catastrophe): the former undergoes a dramatic physical disaster,⁶⁴ while the latter is more discreetly removed from the Hellenic world of men by the promised imposition of a mountain.⁶⁵

Tolkien picks up on the classical motif of the golden-age paradise in the rural, 'Hesiodic' character of his remote, isolated paradises: depictions of natural, even 'golden' perenniality (thus, the mallorn trees of Númenor, golden- and silver-leafed, and resisting seasonal decay),⁶⁶ labourless bliss (the characteristic otium of hobbits, shirking work in favour of gossip, beer and good cheer),⁶⁷ and divine interaction (the elves living with the Valar in Valinor).⁶⁸ And, as discussed from an historical perspective, Tolkien also adopts the golden-age motif in the sense of pervasive temporal and mythic decline: 'in his fictional world the ideal social-political state is located in the distant past [...] rather than in the eschatological future.'⁶⁹

But can one talk about 'utopian thought' – eu-topian reflections on 'the ideal social-political state' or community – in these narratives of decline from golden-age-like paradises, both in classical texts and in Tolkien's writings? Two broader, antagonistic scholarly assessments are likely to present themselves here: either these backward-looking narratives are part of nostalgic, conservative, even primitive ways of thinking, or they are useful constructs for explorations of the perfect, of lost ideals in the past, which could even shape our contestations with the present. The former assessment is likely from scholars in utopian studies and other tangential fields, which give preference to the novelty of the early modern period. Such scholars have tended to regard such fallen or lost 'paradises' as ontologically distinct topologies from 'true utopias', which commenced (with some leeway usually given towards Plato, depending on the critic)[70] in the early modern period.[71] In such a structural division, 'paradises' are characteristic of ancient and classical literature, of post-classical narratives which draw on the classical or biblical *topos*, such as the works of Milton, Spenser and Tennyson,[72] as well as of the mythic mode in modern retrospective genres such as fantasy and historical fiction.[73] 'True utopias', on the other hand, are to be found, for example, in utopian fiction from the early modern period, in twentieth-century dystopian fiction or satire[74] and in science fiction writings.[75] This scholarly dialectic identifies different topical characteristics. 'Paradise' invokes pastoral landscapes[76] and (anti-modern) religious ethics; modern 'utopias' are pictured as urban, institutional and social, with a secular, humanistic, Enlightenment code of ethics.[77] Most important are the temporal engagements and the ways of thinking which are believed to define these temporal desires: paradises enact restorative nostalgia, a conservative (unreflective, primitive, simple, unquestioning) longing to return to an idealized, static past, 'a transhistorical reconstruction of the lost home';[78] modern utopias are, instead, regarded as progressing towards different potentialities of the present or even of the future,[79] providing an 'alternative historical hypothesis'.[80]

Some classical scholars have, however, rebutted this generalization and reduction of the lost paradisical *topos* to nostalgic, primitive, retrogressive or unreflective thought patterns, 'that the good old days were just better'.[81] In his analysis of Hesiod's 'lapsarian' myth of the five races, for instance, Glenn Most essentially argues for a persuasive text that is aimed at the moral inclinations of Hesiod's present context and listeners (such as his brother Perseus).[82] For Most, the construction of a golden-age past (along with a silver-age and other pasts) in the poem is not designed to be regarded mournfully, nostalgically, as a hopelessly lost or irretrievable past, but, rather, as a comparative thought exercise which shows forms of behaviour which are just not possible for biological human beings (the un-human labourless bliss of the golden age)[83] in order to reinforce definite moral and social virtues – namely, 'to act righteously and to work hard rather than to try to make [one's] fortune by crooked means'[84] – something which is required for a generic human community to thrive or 'flourish',[85] a positive, future-oriented, even utopian vision.[86] Rhiannon Evans, in *Utopia Antiqua*, strongly argues for the relevance of such declining golden-age structures, such as Ovid's myths of the ages,[87] to contemporary sociopolitical contexts and thought in late Republican Rome – in other words, that these golden-age paradises that have fallen in the distant past are literary creations that engage with ideals (political, moral etc.) in present 'dystopian' contexts in a way characteristic of utopian literature:

> [The] function [of Golden Age narratives] is historically determined, and the evocation of Golden Age mythology is particularly important in harnessing the political and cultural potential of the utopian. The Golden Age in Roman texts transforms Hesiodic and Hellenistic models in ways which are telling in their particular context, and texts which deal with the return of the age or its decline to the present are especially revealing.[88]
> 
> [...]
> 
> The Roman Golden Age [...] partakes of a central utopian trope, or at least of the positive utopia ('*eu*topia') which can be defined as a device for critiquing contemporary *mores*.[89]

Furthermore, classical narratives depict decline and fall not only from absolute, original, golden-age paradises of the Ovidian or Hesiodic vintage but also from relatively better sociopolitical structures in the historic past, such as actual urban communities[90] in the form of Athens (for instance, in the histories of Thucydides) or Rome. In his illuminating monograph *The Eternal Decline and Fall of Rome: The History of a Dangerous Idea* (2021), Watts discusses the pervasiveness of the particular lapsarian myth of ancient Rome, which he regards as 'the state in history that is most strongly identified with the idea of decline'.[91] It is a narrative thread which was well established even in the early second century BCE (after the first two Punic Wars), articulated by the skilled orator and austere censor Cato the Elder;[92] it gained added force and the semblance of political, societal reality in the turbulent, violent years of the late Roman Republic, as reflected in the historiographical writings of Sallust;[93] and after Augustan, Trajanic and Antonine renewals or revivals in the early Principate,[94] the decline 'definitely happened' to the Western Empire (in the contemporary popular imagination at least) during the fifth century CE as Rome succumbed to raiding barbarian hordes and religious change.[95] Watts conclusively shows that the adoption of lapsarian narratives (the myth of decline) serves definite ideological purposes, functioning to consolidate certain past ideals or virtues (for example, Roman austerity, discipline, aversion to luxury and so on) which have been lost and should, therefore, be reclaimed and renewed in a corrupted present.

Furthermore, Watts's discussion shows that narratives of decline and narratives of restoration (or renewal, revival, recovery etc.) are closely linked because our interaction with the past always entails a reflection on and contestation with the contexts of the present, which can entail 'utopian' reconstructions in a renewed present, even projected into the future.[96] It is not only in Roman historiography that the relationship between decline and restoration is evident; in fact, it seems a general trope of ancient-world writings.[97] Narratives of decline, then, exist as utopian thought exercises: not only to identify specific ideals or virtues which were lost in the past but also to suggest the possibility of restoring former periods of pre-lapsarian bliss, renewed golden ages. Moreover, it is important to note, as both Evans and Watts do in their excellent monographs, that narratives of restoration are persuasive, rhetorical exercises which are often making play of returning to an ideal, pre-lapsarian past (*re*-storation, *re*-vival, *re*-covery), while in fact engaging with the changing contexts of their times to suggest new, different, hybrid visions of utopia.

Equally, when Tolkien receives and rewrites specific classical lapsarian narratives – paradigms of ancient communities that have fallen, such as Platonic Númenor and Roman Gondor – within his own world of Middle-earth, his interest is not simply in mourning for a lost golden age or absolute paradise, a form of nostalgic, primitive, dogmatic, mythic-religious thinking. Rather, in a more philosophical, 'Platonic' bent, Tolkien is interested in establishing precisely which ideals or values were evident in better, relatively more perfect, past communities;[98] these are precise 'utopian' configurations related to ideal moral behaviour, internal political government, international relations, economic conduct, religious observation and so on. Secondly, the universal applicability of these ideals – in other words, that they are not restricted to a lost past – is evident through narratives of restoration in Tolkien's worldbuilding, where narratives of decline and fall are halted, and a renewed golden age, or even a quite different utopian present, is attainable.

## Platonic ideals in the archetypal fall of Númenor-Atlantis

The great settlement of the Second Age of Tolkien's legendarium is the island of Númenor: established by the Valar and inhabited by a superior civilization of men, this Hesiodic paradise boasting perennial fertility, connections with the divine (elven) and vigorous longevity for humans,[99] is described in the chapter 'Akallabêth' in *The Silmarillion* and three chapters in *Unfinished Tales* (1980). Although casual readers of Tolkien's works may not be familiar with this legendary island, it was in fact one of the core archetypal myths of Tolkien's legendarium,[100] and, as later discussed, the utopian past which Númenor represents is a force that motivates several characters in Tolkien's *The Lord of the Rings*, including Aragorn and Faramir.

By enumerating multiple points of similarity, scholars have shown that Plato's mythic island of Atlantis, as presented briefly at the start of the *Timaeus* and in more detail in the incomplete dialogue *Critias*,[101] was a definite primary source for Tolkien in constructing his own mythic, paradisical island of Númenor.[102] This consensus is backed up by Tolkien's own reflections in his *Letters* (1981), where he juxtaposes the names of *Atlantis* and *Númenor* on at least eleven occasions;[103] by his philological wordplay, in translating *Númenor* as *Atalantë* in his constructed elven language;[104] by his comments on his own manuscripts;[105] and by his ludic assertion that Atlantis was itself derived from the original myth of Númenor.[106] The similarities between Plato's and Tolkien's island paradises are plentiful: the isolated location of the island west of Eurasia/Middle-earth, the attention given to natural fecundity, the centrality of a mountain with religious associations, the importance of harbours and so on.[107] There is no need to venture further into these already-well-trodden similarities.

The key event that united Tolkien's story with that of Plato's Atlantis was the *downfall* of the island paradise. In Tolkien's own reflections, it is difficult to disentangle the very name of Númenor from associations of decline and fall. He termed this story 'The *Downfall of Númenor*'[108] and framed its chronology annalistically in terms of three successive stages of decline – 'the first stage', 'the second stage' and 'the last [phase]'[109] – which culminates in a 'catastrophic end, not only of the Second Age, but of the Old World, the primeval world of legend'.[110] This last sentence, in particular, seems to draw closely on Plato's description of the end of the entire primeval world in his *Timaeus*, with the catastrophic destruction of both Atlantis and Athens leading to a temporal rupture which divorces the whole world of primitive legend from the then-present Greek world.[111] In examining the events surrounding the catastrophic collapse of Númenor (the tail end of a long narrative of decline), there are certainly some similarities with Plato's Atlantis, but equally there are also similarities with other ancient stories of fallen coastal or island paradises.[112] In his *Letters*, Tolkien repeatedly invoked the idea of an 'Atlantis tradition' or 'legend', out of which individual versions of the myth emerged, such as that of Plato and his own Númenórean version.[113] Tolkien understood[114] this mythic archetype as centred on seafaring communities that had attained some kind of higher utopian quality, which is prefigured by him calling them 'culture-bearing'[115] (in other words, 'utopian' as hyper-civilizational, a relic of nineteenth-century discourse occasionally found in Tolkien's writing), only to suffer the inevitable decline and collapse; the collapse of this archetypal community was often spatially visualized by Tolkien through the 'Jungian' image of a destructive wave which engulfs the archetypal island, an image which had haunted the unconscious space of his dreams since childhood.[116]

What were the other (ancient) versions of this mythic archetype of 'the culture-bearing men of the Sea'[117] who suddenly collapsed and disappeared? Unfortunately, Tolkien is never explicit, but at any rate he was not the only creative-minded academic in the first three decades of the twentieth century to have speculated about a connection between the various classical myths of seafaring peoples. Several classical philologists triangulated connections between Plato's men of Atlantis, the Homeric Phaeacians and various stories of the Bronze-Age Cretans (modernized as 'Minoans').[118] It is tempting to speculate whether Tolkien has perhaps combined elements from various classical and classical-inspired stories of perfective seafaring peoples who suffer some manner of catastrophic downfall in his narrative of Númenórean downfall. Thus, the aggressive Númenórean fleet, which forms an invading armada like that of Plato's imperial men of Atlantis,[119] is drowned in the sea rather like Minos' great Cretan fleet, which is, according to Herodotus, wrecked by a sea storm.[120] The last king of Númenor, Ar-Pharazôn, and his men suffer physical (and perhaps historiographic) petrification at the hands of Ilúvatar, being 'buried under falling hills'[121] in Valinor, while the Phaeacian ship which transported Odysseus home is actually turned into stone by Poseidon, who also threatens the paradisical seafaring community of Scheria with petrification, being blocked off from the Hellenic world by a mountain.[122] In Tolkien's narrative of his island's downfall, there are earthquakes, a volcanic eruption on Meneltarma, a tsunami and the sinking of the island, a sequence which would appear to combine the Platonic description of the sinking of Atlantis with modern speculations on the collapse of Minoan Crete caused by a compound natural disaster of earthquake, volcanic eruption (Santorini/Thera) and tsunami, as later espoused by the well-known hypothesis of Spyridon Marinatos.[123]

A more specific link between the falls of Tolkien's Númenor and Plato's Atlantis might lie in the narrative of mnemonic distancing and decline, which is used to separate the event of the fall from subsequent generations, relegating the world of legend to an almost-forgotten past. In the case of Atlantis, the Greek reader has to cross great temporal, generational (several intradiegetic narrators), geographic (to Egypt) and cultural distances – as well as a global apocalypse – in order to 'reach Atlantis';[124] yet despite such efforts, this story still lies on the edge between human memory and forgetfulness.[125] On several occasions Tolkien gives descriptions which represent how Númenor is remembered in later ages of Middle-earth, and the depiction of this memory is characteristically fragmentary – 'the story of Ar-Pharazôn and his impious armada was all that remained generally known in later ages'[126] – illustrating an island past which has been entirely or almost entirely lost and forgotten (apart from the collapse itself as an archetypal event).[127] Moreover, like Plato's Egypt,[128] Gondor (like Rivendell) represents a unique place where ancient history can be accessed, a dynastic land of many 'Kings'[129] and thus of many generations.[130] Nevertheless, even in Gondor, the information has been subject to the wear and tear of history, and much of the memory of the island has been lost through 'neglect'.[131]

In short, the downfall of Númenor is a powerful classical palimpsest in Tolkien's writing, invoking perhaps not only the fallen island paradises of myth, such as Plato's Atlantis, the Homeric Phaeacia and ancient (and modern Minoan) Crete but also the tragic historiographies of thalassocratic[132] Athens in the Classical period, as reflected by Herodotus and Thucydides,[133] whose collective writings depict a great sea empire which had attained a utopian, 'hyper-civilizational' status in the eyes of Western posterity, only to suffer inevitable decline and fall.[134] Having established Tolkien's reception of the narrative motif of the fall from various ancient versions of his Atlantis tradition, we must now turn to the applicability of lapsarian narrative to utopian thought. What ideals, values or virtues were lost when Númenor declined? In this regard, Tolkien is in close concord with the philosopher Plato, who meditated on the decline of his own native community of Athens through various thought exercises, which are captured in the fall of Atlantis in the *Timaeus* and *Critias* and in the decline of hypothetical city-states (*poleis*) in the *Laws* and *Republic*. More concretely, the archetypal fall of Númenor-Atlantis communicates Platonic (and, more broadly, Greek) utopian desires for a moderate, ascetic (Occidental), pious, economically self-sustainable and 'sophocratic' community.

Plato's ethnographic characterization of Atlantis, in tandem with his prehistoric Athens, provides us with some telling clues as to the reasons for the island's fall. Atlantean decline might, in part, relate to various forms of immoderation (political, religious, material, social) that are observable in this state, an ethnic denigration which Plato implicitly achieves through what the Greek imagination would regard as an unfavourably Orientalist discourse.[135] To be clear, Plato's Atlanteans, while cartographically a far western people, are actually characterized as an Oriental, particularly a Persian, power:[136] their story is recreated through the mnemonic voyage of the Platonic interlocutor (Critias) to the cultural East, in Egypt;[137] and Atlantis is physically described (topographically, architecturally) in terms which closely resemble Herodotus' Ecbatana (Iran)[138] and Babylon (Iraq).[139] According to Rowe, 'Atlantis is [...] Persia transformed, and transported from the east to the west, and way back from the fifth century to an earlier, dreamlike time'.[140] Such an Orientalized Atlantis naturally triggers Greek antipathy towards the immoderate 'East', which is geographically defined through immense stretches of land and imperial dominion: not only is the island of Atlantis itself strangely massive,[141] but its inhabitants control even more territories, including Plato's imagined 'western continent' and significant parts of Eurasia.[142] Plato even describes Atlantis through a hyperbolically Oriental analogy: 'an island larger than Libya and Asia combined'.[143] But even this is not enough land for Atlantis.

Because of the fragmented textual state of the *Critias* and the brevity of the *Timaeus*, one cannot claim that Plato directly attributed the ultimate fall of his mythic islanders to their immoderate behaviour as a quasi-Persian imperial power.[144] Nevertheless, a strong sense of *hybris* – a concept which Douglas Cairns paraphrases as 'to increase power and prestige beyond a vague limit of what is enough', 'thinking big'[145] – marks Plato's description of the magnitude and endeavours of the Atlantean Empire in the *Timaeus*, which is extrapolated in the *Critias*,[146] and such a hyperbolic grandeur in behaviour (and thought) beyond normal human boundaries typically leads to a Greek audience's implicit expectation of divine or divine-inspired ill-will (*phthonos*) and, consequently, punishment.[147] Importantly, then, the (fragmentary) sequence of divine punishment for Atlantean excesses is initiated by a god,[148] who incites the islanders to attack Athens;[149] thus, their huge but ill-starred naval attack might represent one excess too many, a divinely prompted excess which will quite naturally incur divine punishment.[150] Furthermore, apart from literary and social-religious conventions of punishable *hybris* as possible historical contexts behind the Atlantis myth, Plato certainly had the ill-fated examples of the Persian invasion of Greece under Xerxes in Herodotus[151] and the Athenian invasion of Sicily in Thucydides as paradigms for what disastrous results such naval armadas could bring to the 'hybristic' imperialists who reached too far.[152]

In Tolkien's lapsarian narrative, Númenor gradually transitions from an early moderate island realm, more akin to Plato's idealized prehistoric Athens, to a later immoderate, massive, Orientalized kingdom which resembles Atlantis' dominion. The early Númenóreans, then, might have 'surpassed'[153] the evil kings of Middle-earth in war-mongering and weapon-making, but they choose peace;[154] even though they do not fully understand the geographic boundaries imposed on them by the Valar, the islanders have no 'desire to overpass the limits to their bliss'.[155] Tolkien's selection of verbs, of not 'surpassing' and 'overpassing', describe a form of wisdom realized through moderation of geopolitical power.[156] But gradually the Númenóreans depart from moderation, regarding their island as a limited space: 'for their own land seemed to them shrunken'.[157] And like Plato's Atlanteans, they conquer the quasi-Eurasian mainland of Middle-earth, thus becoming a huge Oriental realm, located *east* of Númenor: '[T]he Númenóreans first made great settlements upon the west shores of the ancient lands; [...] and they desired now wealth and dominion in Middle-earth since the West was denied. Great harbours and strong towers they made, and there many of them took up their abode'.[158] Finally, like the Atlanteans, who might be a later Platonic mythologization of historical *hybristēs* in the form of Herodotean Persians and Thucydidean late-Athenians, the men of Númenor engage in a final demonstration of collective *hybris* in the form of a massive naval armada, an immoderate act of hyperbolic, global imperialism which garners divine punishment and results in the sinking of their island.[159]

The punishment which the Númenóreans as *hybristēs* incur at the end of their histories raises the matter of the religious-divine reasons behind their fall. In several of the Greek mythic versions of the 'culture-bearing men of the sea' which Tolkien might have inherited, there is a sense that declining piety and divine benediction lead to collapse or the possibility of catastrophe. Plato's early Atlanteans possess a kind of divine nature or essence, because of which they are rewarded by the divinities with golden-age blessedness and wealth.[160] Such benediction is complemented by Atlantean piety: Poseidonic laws are inscribed on a pillar;[161] they partake in ritual slaughter, libations and oath-swearing to their patron god;[162] they build temples for deities.[163] But the key moment of decline seems to occur, rather suddenly, when 'the portion of divinity within them was now becoming faint and weak',[164] the result of which is that they impiously disregard the laws and their former virtuous, harmonious ways of life and start the process of decline proper.[165] The Homeric Phaeacians are pious: they uphold the divine rights of suppliants and guests[166] and build temples;[167] and they are blessed by the gods through their golden-age bliss. Yet one might observe the importance of impiety in the looming fall of Homeric Scheria, where King Alcinous' earlier haughtiness towards the sea god Poseidon[168] is reconciled by his later pious behaviour as he hastily tries to atone for the Phaeacians' having ignored their founding god's prophecy and, thus, to prevent further punishment.[169]

Likewise, there is a remarkable piety in early Númenor: the sacred mountain Meneltarma is a place of reverence to Eru Ilúvatar,[170] analogous to the Poseidonic mountain on Atlantis;[171] at this site, there are seasonal rituals, prayers and pious observation of a collective silence.[172] The perennial state of golden-age perfection on Númenor is achievable because of a harmony between humans and 'gods', a sense of harmony and balance between 'top-down' blessedness and 'bottom-up' piety in the realm; indeed, rather like Evans's modern imagination of Minoan 'priest-kings'[173] and Platonic kings of Atlantis, Tolkien's early Númenórean kings function as quasi-priests during their rituals[174] – the most blessed are also the most pious. Unfortunately, this cannot last for ever: as with Plato's Atlantis, there is a simultaneous lessening in the 'divinity' of the Númenóreans' being, reflected through a shrinking lifespan,[175] and in their piety with respect to elves, customs and so on.[176] One architectural manifestation of this growing impiety is that the place of worship to Eru, which is a sort of early-Christian open glade, is replaced by the domed 'pagan' temple of the Satanic Sauron.[177] Ultimately, this religious decline culminates in collapse when the islanders try to flout the divine injunction which prohibits sea travel beyond a certain limit, namely too far westward beyond sight of their island.[178] The attempt to conquer divine Valinor is an act of extreme immoderation: the Númenórean desire to break the physical or spatial limitation imposed on them (imperial immoderation) is a symbol of a more significant attempt to break the ontological limitation imposed on man by god – their innate mortality, their limited lifespan.[179] In short, the blessed islanders want to become like gods (or Valar) themselves, but in reaching beyond their human ontological limits, they inevitably discard both their pious habits and the divine blessedness, which kept their early society in harmonious balance.

Moderation is a complex virtue, then, which is flouted by the 'Atlantean' Númenóreans on geopolitical, imperial, religious and ontological grounds. In his ethnographic description of Atlantis, Plato also introduces the problem of immoderation by drawing on the Graeco-Roman motif of excessive materialism, on the corrupting influence of extravagance, luxury and wealth on good morals; such materialism is often associated with an increased contact with the Orient.[180] Thus, the great temple in 'Oriental' Atlantis is decorated with silver, gold, ivory and the mysterious 'orichalcum'.[181] Plato also connotes Oriental extravagance through the construction of greatly adorned baths,[182] in which not only kings but also private individuals, and even horses and cattle, luxuriated.[183] '[T]he picture of Atlantis contains some echoes of the Persian empire's wealth and technology';[184] furthermore, the moral decline of Atlantis is implied, at least in one part of the *Critias*, by an excessive love of wealth,[185] which is analogous to the decline of Persia in Plato's *Laws*.[186] In contrast to such material immoderation which triggers moral decline, Plato idealizes (in the *Critias*) the ancient 'Occidental' community of Athens, the rival of Atlantis, as governed by austerity: Attica, in which province lies Athens, is 'austere',[187] especially in its lack of infrastructure such as complex temples, market places, harbours and mines[188] – all elements that Plato, in other dialogues, criticizes for 'making the Athenians worse by indulging and increasing their desires instead of disciplining and reducing them'.[189]

Rather like Plato's lapsarian constructions of Athens across his dialogues, from an originally utopian, prehistoric city-state (*Critias*) to a declining, 'fallen' community (*Gorgias*), which is becoming too Persianized, too Oriental (*Laws*), a little too much, indeed, like this 'imaginary' Atlantis (*Critias*),[190] Númenor is characterized by a decline from a frugal, idealized Occidental culture – a population kept to a moderate size through its reproductive values,[191] a people not given to excessive *aedificatio* (building), as signified by their lack of roads[192] – to a civilization increasingly attracted by material and architectural immoderation: 'they begin to seek wealth rather than bliss [...] and they lavished wealth and art on tombs and memorials'.[193] Tolkien assesses the growing luxury of Númenor: 'gifts of gold and silver and jewels [...] were rare and prized in earlier centuries, until the power of the Kings was spread to the coasts of the East'.[194] Interactions with the East are associated with excessive materialism and luxurious, inappropriate, pleasure-seeking forms of social behaviour, which trigger moral decline: '[t]hose that lived turned the more eagerly to pleasure and revelry, desiring ever more goods and more riches';[195] 'they drank and they feasted and they clad themselves in silver and gold'.[196]

That Tolkien cherished Platonic ideals of moderation (on different levels), piety and asceticism and, moreover, that he used a narrative of decline in 'Númenor-Atlantis' to mourn these lost virtues would not be ethically problematic to many modern readers; on the other hand, the association of immoderation with the cultural Orient and moderation with the Occident, as a trope inherited from classical narratives, is a less palatable taste in post-colonial times. Still, Plato's discussions of societies that are susceptible to decline need not have an entirely Orientalized aspect, even when directed at the problem of economic trade. In the fourth book of the *Laws*, an interlocutor called the 'Athenian Stranger' hypothesizes the suitability of both the seaside and the hilly inland as potential sites for a *polis* (city-state). Each location characterizes its native populace with respect to economic activities, military endeavours and, perhaps most importantly, moral disposition. Economically, coastal settlements partake in mercantile trade, acquiring goods from foreign lands, while inland regions are characterized as being more concerned with the actual production of commodities from natural resources.[197] Militarily, the marines, as the typical coastal soldiery, are naturally accustomed to retreat and flight rather than standing ground, fighting and dying like the landlocked soldiers of the interior.[198] From these discussions, it becomes logically evident that a *polis* built in a hilly interior is conducive to 'the acquisition of virtue'[199] among its citizens, while a seaside settlement is most likely to descend into 'luxurious and depraved habits'[200] and to lead its population to 'knavish and tricky ways'.[201] Such a decline occurs partly because of the business ethics of mercantile traders and the effect of foreign luxuries on a people, and partly because the citizens of such a *polis*, especially the soldiers, become craven and weak-willed. This is in contrast to people of the interior, who, one might say, are in touch with the soil, who stand their ground. As to why Plato has created such an ethno-topography: it is perhaps not coincidental that an origin myth of the city of Athens, as a coastal settlement, is referenced in this part of the *Laws*: that of King Minos and the periodic ransom of Athenian youths to the Cretan Minotaur.[202] Despite the heavy cost of Minos' ransom, the Stranger insists that Athens was in a better moral state in those foundational times *before* it started capitalizing on the military and economic potential of its coastal position.[203] This narrative of moral lapse in a coastal settlement, in tandem with 'international' economic growth and greater focus on maritime endeavours, is suggestive of the historic decline of Athens herself in Plato's lifetime, with the 'Sicilian adventure' marking a turning point.[204]

While the hydrophilic orientation and abilities of Tolkien's Númenóreans are clear from the start,[205] these early islanders are entirely restricted to their own hermetic environment: they feel no need to traverse the seas or to engage in communication – much worse, trade – with other peoples.[206] Tolkien's ethno-topographic account of early Númenor spends far more narrative time describing the interior – mountains, forests, rivers – than the coast.[207] The very advent of sea trade and navies, as per Plato's warning for Athens, gradually and inevitably corrupts.[208] The Númenóreans become imperial 'tax-gatherers'[209] rather like Thucydides' Minoans, and they return home from their colonial subjects in ships laden with gold and silver. Tolkien's story of the Númenórean prince Aldarion in *Unfinished Tales* exemplifies this decline caused by the growth of seafaring trade and an expanding empire:[210] 'Aldarion was a man long-sighted, and he looked forward to days when the people would need more room and greater wealth'²¹¹; '[h]is [Aldarion's] immaterial desire manifests itself materially, in collecting gold and jewels, in building ships and towns'.²¹² Importantly, the Platonic contrast between an insular community which lives in the interior and a coastal, 'international' community is picked up on a gendered level between Aldarion and his wife Erendis, who in contrast to her husband has no interest in ships and seafaring, who becomes estranged from him and who dwells right in the interior of Númenor.²¹³ The estrangement of Aldarion and Erendis is a personal, gendered tragedy which marks an important shifting point for the paradisical island as it transitions from a hermetic, isolated society, an inland, maternal, even 'omphalic' community to a seaside, trading, ultimately international community, which is patriarchal and aggressive. The decline of Númenor starts from the 'divorce' of this relationship.

Finally, perhaps Plato's most well-known utopian idea, at least in contemporary popular memory, pertains to the philosopher-state of the *Republic*, a kind of oligarchy or 'sophocracy' ruled by the wise rather than by the demagogues of democracy, beautifully described through his metaphor of the state as a ship, skilfully guided by a knowledgeable pilot rather than by the mob of the crew or a demagogic captain.²¹⁴ Tolkien was definitely familiar with Plato's political thought on rule by the wise. At the end of one letter to his youngest son, Tolkien meanders from a discussion of the weather to English politics; in particular, the Oxford professor is annoyed by a certain Anthony Eden, a speaker in the House of Commons,²¹⁵ who lamented the 'occurrences in Greece "the home of democracy"'.²¹⁶ Tolkien's response to the generic Western idealization of ancient Greece, 'the home of democracy', is to allude to Plato: 'δημοκρατία [*dēmokratia*] was not in Greek a word of approval but was nearly equivalent to "mob-rule"; and he neglected to note that Greek Philosophers – and far more is Greece the home of philosophy [than of democracy] – did not approve of it.'²¹⁷

In the most Platonic of Middle-earth communities, Tolkien praises the early 'sophocracy' which heralded the golden age of the island:

> [T]hough this people [the Númenóreans] used still their own speech, their kings and lords knew and spoke the Elven tongue, [...]. And the loremasters among them learned also the High Eldarin tongue of the Blessed Realm, in which much story and song was preserved from the beginning of the world; and they made letters and scrolls and books, and wrote in them many things

of wisdom and wonder in the high tide of their realm, of which all is now forgot.[218]

Firstly, this passage provides a wonderful exemplum of how Tolkien blends a narrative of decline – from an older 'high tide' to a present age of forgetfulness – with utopian thought. And the latter idea relates to the Platonic idea of rule by the wise. The common people, who presumably do not demand voting rights in Tolkien's island regency, use the vernacular tongue, which in Tolkien's myth means that they do not have access to special knowledge or wisdom, which is garnered through knowledge of the elven language; this wisdom is, in turn, the province of the few, the 'kings' and 'lords' who are simultaneously 'the loremasters'. There is, in other words, no division between political and epistemological (linguistic) superiority. Tolkien, incidentally, is not particularly forthcoming on what this knowledge entails, but part of it, at least, might have cosmological value since it is preserved from 'the beginning of the world'. The decline from this wisdom is repeatedly referenced by Tolkien throughout the remainder of the narrative of the 'Akallabêth', pertaining to the downfall of Númenor: in the early stages of decline, the wretchedness of the island community is not too severe because 'the kings and their people had not yet abandoned wisdom', although the formerly 'wise men' start to turn their intelligence to improper studies (gerontology in modern scientific terms);[219] and, continuing the earlier linking of wisdom to linguistic knowledge, the abrogation of elven tongues on the island – 'the twentieth king [...] ascended the throne [...], forsaking the Elven-tongues and forbidding their use in his hearing'[220] – is a further marker of decline from sophocracy.

In summary, like Plato's Atlantis and other ancient versions of island or coastal paradises, Númenor declines and eventually collapses. This decline is not a mere nostalgic device which hankers for the good old days, but it is a means of establishing what ideals or virtues defined the once-utopian community of Númenor – a moderate, pious, ascetic, economically insular, sophocratic and, to an extent, ideally Occidental community. This kind of 'utopological' thought exercise by Tolkien draws on similar constructs from Plato's philosophical dialogues, as well as other myths on the 'culture-bearing men of the sea'. Finally, as Plato's mythic and hypothetical constructs of communities are concerned with the relevance of utopian ideas in the present case of fourth-century Athens, Tolkien's utopianism inevitably looks to the present of his legendarium, despite the 'backward-looking' lapsarian narrative. Númenor might be an almost lost legend by the time of the War of the Ring in the Third Age, but the values which constructed this once-great utopia are still cherished and fought for by a handful of characters, such as Gondorian Faramir and Arnorian Aragorn, modern men whose virtues have been moulded out of the ancient utopia of Númenor.

Faramir is, in fact, an excellent example of a character living in a stage of late decline in Gondor and who is defined by the Platonic virtues which reach all the way back to Númenor-Atlantis: 'a king of old',[221] Denethor mockingly, but also with unintentional precision, terms him. Thus, one might observe the political moderation of *utopia Númenórea* in the hero: in opposition to his war-like, hybristic brother and father, Faramir argues in favour of a more balanced dispersion of Gondorian troops across the frontlines and against a singular, excessive military aggression against Mordor – one mighty, fatal, hybristic push to reclaim Osgiliath.[222] Númenórean piety and human, ontological moderation: Faramir is a devout character, and the only hero in *The Lord of the Rings* to actually 'pray', looking west not just to Númenor but to 'that which is beyond Elvenhome and will ever be'.[223] Númenórean material moderation and asceticism: the furnishings of Faramir's secret hideout in Ithilien, 'plain and unadorned for the most part',[224] complement his unassuming character, a man of moderate appetite, which is also reflected through his rejection of the most powerful material object in Middle-earth, the One Ring. And sophocracy: Faramir is, of course, a wise leader, which Aragorn acknowledges by making him the Prince of Ithilien at the end of the story;[225] his wisdom is, in addition, acknowledged through his love of Gandalf, the archetypal wise wizard, and through his knowledge of elvish language, like ancient Númenórean kings.[226]

Tellingly, these are the words which Faramir uses to describe his love for Gondor and Minas Tirith: 'I love only that which they defend: the city of the men of Númenor; and I would have her loved for her memory, her ancientry, her beauty, and her present wisdom. Not feared, save as men may fear the dignity of a man, old and wise'.[227] The combination of 'ancientry' with 'present wisdom' is particularly noteworthy. In other words, Númenor might be an ancient fallen paradise, but the ideals and the enacted virtues of individual men which rendered it utopian are still championed in the present ages of Middle-earth by characters such as Faramir, who is the character most associated with Númenor in the Third Age. The notion that lapsarian narratives interlink with narratives of restoration, that the lost utopian past can be reborn in the present-future, gains sharper relief in the subsequent section.

## The fall and Augustan restoration of Roman Gondor

In contrast to the Germanic sphere of Rohan,[228] there is not much doubt among Tolkien scholars that the country of Gondor is an ancient-world construct.[229] As is typical of Tolkien's mythmaking technique, though, the writer seems to assemble a hotchpotch of different cultures to make his own 'ancient-world' culture in Middle-earth. The monumental architecture, material symbols such as the crown, and the mortuary culture of Gondor recall ancient Egypt.[230] Tolkien's analogous cartographic positioning of Southern Gondor, the *apparently* impregnable fortifications of Minas Tirith and the battles and troop movements which take place before the walls might suggest a Trojan aspect to this civilization.[231] Then again, seven-walled Minas Tirith might recall seven-gated Thebes, the seven circles of Persian Ecbatana, or triple-defended Constantinople.[232] But the strongest source for Tolkien's reconstruction of Gondor, and particularly Minas Tirith, must be ancient Rome.[233]

Resemblances are manifold. Cartography: Tolkien's analogous placement of Minas Tirith in Italy (Florence, though, not Rome);[234] architecture: the typically Roman stone buildings and organized road networks of Gondor, as viewed by a 'post-classical' hobbit such as Pippin;[235] imperialism: both Gondor and Rome are initially very successful militaristic states;[236] cultural imperialism: Gondor practices forms of acculturation by educating and integrating vassal states such as Rohan, a process reminiscent of Romanization;[237] military: like Rome, Gondor maintains foreign 'cohorts' in its armies;[238] national 'myth': a small group of pious exiles flees from their fallen city (Troy/Númenor) on ships and arrives on foreign shores to found a new dynasty (Rome/Gondor). Amid these parallels, a key element which connects Tolkien's Gondor to our inherited imaginations of Rome is the overarching narrative of apparently interminable decline: 'Perhaps most obviously, both Rome and Gondor experience decadence and decline'.[239] This decline is evident in Appendix A to *The Lord of the Rings*, in the section 'Gondor and the Heirs of Anárion', wherein Tolkien chronicles the rise, fall and near collapse of the southern kingdom: from having reached the 'summit of its power',[240] there is a long narrative of slow decline or 'decay',[241] of the 'waning strength of Gondor',[242] during which the kingdom narrowly avoids collapse on several occasions.[243] In a sense, one could argue that Gondor decays from its very founding as a continuation of the civilizational decline which saw the collapse of paradisical Númenor.[244]

By the time of *The Lord of the Rings* in the late Third Age, Gondor is only a shadow of its former self. The political boundaries of the empire have shrunk, which can be compared to the gradual loss of Roman provinces across the Mediterranean in the fourth and fifth century CE, and there are numerous signs of this territorial reduction through Tolkien's epic fantasy. Whereas the southern kingdom's domain once stretched to the Falls of Rauros in the north, the Fellowship encounter no Gondorian soldiers along the Anduin river but only two lonely stone sentinels, the Argonath – giant statues of ancient Gondorian kings (Isildur and Anárion) and tokens of a glorious but symbolically 'petrified' past that is well removed from a declining present. This is not unsimilar to how post-classical travellers, such as the anonymous poet of the Old English 'The Ruin',[245] have remembered the collapse of Roman civilization through giant, but lonely ruins. In *The Lord of the Rings*, the personal focalization of characters such as Pippin, Gimli, Legolas and Boromir[246] is a constant reminder of the once-greatness of Gondor and its current decline.[247]

Elsewhere, on the eastern front, the once-beautiful capital of Osgiliath now lies in ruins and is a war zone; the shift of the capital to Minas Tirith, incidentally, recalls the fifth-century CE transition of the Roman capital from Rome to Ravenna.[248] Indeed, in the chapter 'Minas Tirith', 'Roman' Gondor seems to have already fragmented into an assortment of small, essentially independent kingdoms along the White Mountain (Lossarnach, Lamedon, Dol Amroth etc.),[249] with only Minas Tirith appearing like an imperial stronghold; this resembles the 'Langobardic principalities of Italy'[250] after the political collapse of the Western Roman Empire in the fifth century CE.[251] Yet such historical analogies must not be viewed as a perfect one-to-one correspondence (an 'allegorical reading')[252] since Tolkien creatively 're-chronicles' elements of Roman history. Thus, the 'Trojan' exiles of Númenor immediately establish two kingdoms in Middle-earth, Arnor in the west and Gondor in the east, with the former collapsing as a state more than a thousand years before the latter narrowly avoids collapse in *The Return of the King* (1955).[253] Such a dual, partitioned 'empire' clearly draws on the later division of the Roman Empire into the Western Empire and the Eastern or Byzantine Empire.[254] Scholars have, accordingly, noted aspects of the Byzantine decline of Constantinople in Gondor;[255] Tolkien himself wrote of the decline of Gondor to a 'decayed Middle Age, a kind of proud, venerable, but increasingly impotent Byzantium'.[256]

When Mordor attacks Gondor in the Siege of Minas Tirith and the Battle of Pelennor Fields, the catastrophic end appears nigh for the ancient kingdom. In fact, this final battle agglomerates several different enemies that threaten a typically 'Roman' collapse: Carthaginians, barbarians and Huns.[257] So, a 'Carthaginian' invading force has arrived from the far southern deserts ('Tunisian' Harad), with many of these 'savage', Orientalized Haradrim riding on oliphaunts, and so recalling the famous image of Hannibal crossing the Alps.[258] Towards the mythologized end of the Western Roman Empire in the fifth century CE, various 'barbarian' tribes, such as the Ostrogoths and Vandals, attacked Rome; likewise, in the Battle of Pelennor Fields, Tolkien's 'Roman' Gondorians are assailed by 'Easterlings with axes, and Variags of Khand, Southrons in scarlet, and out of Far Harad black men like half-trolls'.[259] Rome's most infamous enemy during this late imperial stage of decline were the Huns, led by Atilla, who fought against the Romans in the Battle of the Catalaunian Plains. Tolkien also presents a great army of horsemen in his battle on the plains,[260] but rewriting the inherited historiographical traditions, the Englishman surprises his readers with an unexpected, 'eucatastrophic' turn on real-world events:[261] these Huns are Rohirrim from an idealized Germanic north,[262] and they save a Roman Minas Tirith from being sacked.[263]

*The Lord of the Rings* can be read as a kind of medieval fairy tale in which the narrative of Roman decline is halted by post-classical, medieval or 'Anglo-Saxon' wanderers, such as the hobbits or the Rohirrim, and thus the great empire of Roman Gondor is restored.[264] One could follow Tolkien's own description of his story's conclusion here, of Gondor's restoration as reminiscent of 'the Holy Roman Empire',[265] which might render the new king, Aragorn, as analogous to a number of post-classical figures, such as Charlemagne[266] in history or King Arthur in myth, who were regarded as having restored Rome.[267] The restoration of a declining Rome was not, however, an exclusively post-classical or medieval narrative.[268] As Watts has shown, narratives of both Roman decline and Roman restoration are absolutely present in classical thought, most notably in the turbulent final years of the Roman Republic and the imperial restoration which ensues. Gondor has been creatively constructed by Tolkien, without identical chronological parallels,[269] to recall our collected classical and post-classical narratives of Roman decline, collapse and renewal. Important in this regard is the most Roman, even the 'most Virgilian [...] hero'[270] in Tolkien's work, Aragorn, whose 'destiny was not merely to help defeat Sauron or to rule a great kingdom but to serve as the agent of Gondor's renewal'.[271] While Ford regards Aragorn's Gondorian renewal as 'more a Germanic ideal than a Roman one because his kingdom incorporated the other peoples of the west',[272] Aragorn's renewal and his new utopia of Gondor are in fact characterized by strongly classical-Roman idealizations, which have not yet been fully identified (however much these ideals are *seen* from 'rewritten medieval perspectives' in Middle-earth).[273]

To start with, scholars have noted some passing parallels between Aragorn and Virgil's Aeneas:[274] both are 'exiles' from a fallen civilization (Troy and Númenor; like Faramir, Aragorn is often styled as a descendant of Númenor) who are called by fate to found a new dynasty; to achieve this, they must pass through ghostly underworlds (*Aeneid* VI; the Paths of the Dead) before being able to set up their future dynasty,[275] and both have to shirk the love of a foreign princess (Dido, Éowyn), with tragic repercussions, in order to marry their destined brides (Lavinia, Arwen) at the seat of imperial power.[276] The difference between the two heroes is that Aeneas is a (pre-)founder, a heroic figure in the foundation myths of Rome (Romulus being the actual mythical founder),[277] who would strictly be more analogous to Elendil in Tolkien's legendarium,[278] whereas Aragorn is the restorer or 'refounder' of Gondor. An analogous Roman restorer-figure can, nevertheless, be found for Aragorn. Virgil's mythologization of Aeneas in the *Aeneid* was closely related to ideas of Roman renewal towards the end of the first century BCE. The epic poet was rewriting the mythic Homeric character in a period in which Augustus was promoting a narrative that Roman decline had ended, thereby heralding a restoration under his rule as *princeps* ('first citizen'; also *imperator*); Virgil's Aeneas, thus, becomes a mythic forerunner to the historical Augustus, who is a kind of second Aeneas (or Romulus).[279] While Aragorn bears some resemblance to the mythical hero of Roman foundation myths, as a restorer-figure who resembles ancient Gondorian kings,[280] there are perhaps even more interesting parallels to be drawn with the Emperor Augustus (originally, Octavian) as restorer.

In comparing the narratives of restoration which halt decline under Augustus and Aragorn, we find that utopian visions seem to be shared in four broad respects: infrastructural restoration; institutional restoration; moral restoration; and broader geopolitical restoration.[281] The extent of this family of shared characteristics suggests that the New Gondor at the start of the Fourth Age can be conceptualized as a utopia or restored paradise which is strongly reminiscent of the idealization – and propagandizing – of an 'Augustan (Golden) Age' in Rome after a period of late Republican decline, as established by writers such as Horace, Virgil, Suetonius and Augustus himself in his own *Res Gestae* and other monumental projects – a 'program designed to emphasize that he had cured the disorder, violence and lawlessness of the later Republic'.[282] As previously discussed, narratives of Roman decline across the centuries were not just exercises in nostalgic, wishful thinking but always part of utopian dissections of the present, with the aim of restoring cherished values and ideals.[283] Likewise, in a Roman Gondor, there is a definite logical transition from different manifestations of decline to corresponding forms of restoration.

Firstly, then, the biographer Suetonius describes at length how Augustus' restored Rome is marked out by an infrastructural renewal since, apparently, the buildings of the Eternal City at the end of the Republican period of decline are no longer commensurate with its great status:[284]

> Aware that the city was architecturally unworthy of her position as capital of the Roman Empire, besides being vulnerable to fire and river floods, Augustus so improved her appearance that he could justifiably boast: 'I found Rome built of bricks; I leave her clothed in marble'. He also used as much foresight as could have possibly been provided in guarding against future disasters.[285]

In the subsequent passage, Suetonius lists the various public works which Augustus had built, including the *Forum Augustum* and temples to Mars,

Apollo and Jupiter; Suetonius also cites other independent construction projects which flourished during Augustus' reign.[286]

This characteristic Augustan renewal of Rome's *aedificia*, which 'could be interpreted as qualified utopian urban visions',[287] is received by Tolkien in his descriptions of infrastructural decline and subsequent restoration in Minas Tirith. Although Pippin 'gazed in wonder at the great stone city, vaster and more splendid than anything that he had dreamed of [. . .] it was in truth falling year by year into decay';[288] this is perhaps reflected by the 'dead tree'[289] which Pippin encounters and also by the lack of ornamentation in the great hall of Denethor.[290] Yet 'inspector Gimli', who like every dwarf is an expert in construction, is the key focalizer of Gondorian dilapidation, noting that 'the good stone-work [in Minas Tirith] is the older and was wrought in the first building'.[291] And Osgiliath provides a spectre of what Minas Tirith will look like if it collapses: 'that is the ruin of Osgiliath on either side of the Anduin, which our enemies took and burned long ago';[292] during the Siege of Gondor, 'Fires now raged unchecked in the first circle of the City',[293] and Minas Tirith totters on the brink of collapse.

Fortunately, a Tolkienian eucatastrophic rewriting of the fall of Rome ensures the survival of Minas Tirith, and once Aragorn becomes King Elessar, he turns like *princeps* Augustus to infrastructural renewal: 'In his time the City was made more fair than it had ever been, even in the days of its first glory; and it was filled with trees and fountains, and its gates were wrought of mithril and steel, and its streets were paved with white marble'.[294] There are several points of similarity with the Augustan programme of infrastructural renewal. First, like that of Suetonius' Augustus, Aragorn's rebuilding programme has a twofold aim: to strengthen the city against future calamities, with gates protected by 'mithril and steel', and to beautify it. On the latter, Jordan has noted how Aragorn's greenifying of the war-charred Minas Tirith recalls Augustus' commissioning of public gardens over previously 'putrid' spaces, relics of the civil wars.[295] However, the closest reception of urban-renewed Rome is surely in the parallel of, to paraphrase Suetonius, Aragorn finding a city in cold stone and leaving its 'Roman' streets in 'white marble'. Lastly, like the numerous independent commissions of public works which flourish during Augustus' reign, both Legolas and Gimli, as external contractors, imagine while walking through the streets of Minas Tirith how they might renew the architecture of the declining city; the dwarf says: 'I shall offer him [Aragorn] the service of the stonewrights of the Mountain, and we will make this a town to be proud of'.[296]

The infrastructural renewal of the *urbs* (city) – its beautification, strengthening, marmorization – is a spatial symbol for other forms of restoration which the reigns of Aragorn and Augustus bring about. They are both concerned with putting a check on the instability and violence which characterized the previous declining regimes and with reviving the *institutiones civitatis*. From a legal perspective, just as Augustus is often characterized by ancients, such as Ovid, and moderns alike as a notable law-maker in domestic justice, establishing norms and order after an anarchic period of violence,[297] Aragorn too is heralded as a law-maker in Gondor: this is apparent in his merciful judgement of the tricky case of Beregond, who is both guilty of murder and of preventing another's murder in the self-same act.[298] Moreover, providing a divine groundwork for human institutions, the two leaders return the state to a more pious entity through their religious observations. In the case of Augustus, his commissioning of temples is noteworthy, and the *princeps* of course later becomes deified in the Roman cultural imaginary,[299] while Aragorn is concerned with replanting the White Tree,[300] re-establishing Gondor's connection to the sacred West,[301] a connection also sealed through his marriage to the elf Arwen.[302] And both leaders are concerned with political reconciliation: they integrate the previous political regimes, Republican government[303] and Stewardship, into the restored autocratic or monarchic government.[304] In short, both leaders restore the *urbs* as a physical, legal, political and religious entity, checking a narrative of decline which had been observed through the physical decay of the city, acts of lawlessness, political instability and impiety.

Along with institutional restoration, the checking of social-moral decline, a 'moral dystopia'[305] which had been fashioned by violent wars and political instability, and the promotion of traditional family values, is also apparent in both reigns – in essence, a transition from a destructive to a *reproductive* (child-oriented) vision of society.[306] 'At the fall of the Republic and the start of the Principate, or early empire, the first emperor, Augustus [...], was so concerned at the tendency towards late marriage and childlessness among the Senatorial class that he enacted laws restricting the civil and political freedoms of those who were unmarried or childless.'[307] Equally, the idea that Minas Tirith is 'falling year by year into decay'[308] because of its depopulation is immediately noticeable to Pippin when he enters a city curiously devoid of families and children and only populated by fighting men:[309] 'there were always too few children in this city; but now there are none – save some young lads that will not depart',[310] says the soldier Beregond. The renewed Gondor of Aragorn restores an Augustan family-centred society to Minas Tirith: 'and all was healed and made good, and the houses were filled with men and women and the laughter of children, and no window was blind nor any courtyard empty'.[311] In combination with the references to family units here, the golden-age theme of natural fecundity – 'it was filled with trees and with fountains'[312] – adds to the wholesome picture of a community which has returned to its traditional reproductive role of looking after its children. Similar golden-age iconography can be found in Augustus' commissioned *Ara Pacis*, with its representations of fecundity and reproduction in nature – 'twin babies who clutch at the food and her [the goddess'] breast, and surrounded by grazing animals'[313] – being connotatively melded to the social stability and peace of the new Augustan Principate, in opposition to previous years of discord.[314]

Images of golden-age fertility can, on the other hand, lead to ambiguous notions of (Oriental) sumptuousness, immorality and decline, and thus Augustan iconography was careful to contain this renewed golden age within safe, controlled, imperial iconography and bounds, with the *Ara Pacis* being enclosed by 'Corinthian pilasters' and 'surmounted by orderly processions of senators, priests and imperial family members'.[315] The importance of gardens, as figures which constrain nature,[316] in Augustan renewal also adds to this moral constraint on excess natural profusion. Similarly, such an imperial constraint exists in Aragorn's renewed golden age, where the greenery is generally contained by infrastructure *inside* the stone city, by gardens and fountains, or is demarcated as defined, finite, bounded areas inside his greater realm, such as Ithilien, which becomes the garden of Faramir, and the Shire, as the garden of the hobbits. Aragorn's restored golden age thus enacts a typically Augustan moral paradigm, which restores traditional familial values and virtues of healthy reproduction, which are necessary after a long period of war and depopulation, while ensuring that such a return to pre-war bliss does not degenerate into sumptuousness through the ordered constraints of imperial iconography, infrastructure and political borders.

On the matter of political borders, the restorations of Augustus and Aragorn also have significant effects on the wider world outside the *urbs*. Suetonius summarizes how the Roman leader consolidated his political power through a number of wars: firstly, civil wars, most famously against Mark Anthony,[317] and secondly, wars against foreign nations, including Germans and Dacians.[318] In describing the latter wars with foreign powers, Suetonius draws on notions of *pax Romana* to characterize Augustus' military actions as wholly peacemaking in intent, as an end to a period of instability: '[He] pacified other tribes who gave trouble. Yet Augustus never wantonly invaded any country, and felt no temptation to increase the boundaries of the Empire or enhance his military glory; indeed, he made certain barbarian chieftains swear in the Temple of Avenging Mars that they would faithfully keep the peace for which they sued.'[319] So successful is Augustus' policy of pacification, *pax Augusta*, that faraway tribes such as the Indians and Scythians send envoys to the *princeps* in order to establish friendly diplomatic relations with the Roman people.[320]

Like Augustus, who has to confront the political instabilities of a late Republican sphere, Aragorn, before he is crowned as King Elessar, has to avoid a potential civil war erupting with Denethor, who represents the old political establishment, and of course to fight off the numerous external enemies who have been eating away at Gondor for centuries.[321] Aragorn's handling of Gondor's enemies is thoroughly Augustan in representing a kind of *pax Gondorea* across a vast empire: the War of the Ring is essentially aimed at stopping violence, and afterwards foreign powers from faraway lands, 'Indians' and 'Scythians', can enter into peaceful negotiations with the clement King Elessar: 'And embassies came from many lands and peoples, from the East and the South, and from the borders of Mirkwood, and from Dunland in the west. And the King pardoned the Easterlings that had given themselves up, and sent them away free, and he made peace with the people of Harad.'[322] This *pax Gondorea* also resembles its Roman counterpart in conscripting foreign nations and soldiers through oaths to maintain the collective peace; thus, Pippin, as an enlisted soldier, is jokingly – but truthfully – reminded by Aragorn that Anórien, which includes the Shire, is part of the greater Gondorian Empire.[323] In fact, just as *pax Augusta* involves the claiming of substantial territories in Europe for the purposes of maintaining the peace,[324] so too Aragorn's tour of his pacified provinces, which is a bit reminiscent of an occasionally iterant emperor such as Augustus[325] but more so of the wandering Hadrian, is a personal act of reclaiming lost territories, a graphic reminder of who the new emperor is.

Such a *pax Augusta/Gondorea*, importantly, allows the pastoral lands beyond the *urbs* to once again flourish, a return to a Saturnian image of paradise, a restored golden age. The problematic idea that Augustus' *aurea saecula* (golden age) combines two quite different, even antagonistic visions of utopia – an imperial *pax Romana* and, somehow equally, a return to a pastoral, Saturnian age of simple bliss and plenty – is captured by Trojan Anchises, who forecast the future *princeps* of Rome to his son Aeneas:[326] 'Augustus Caesar, son of the Deified, and founder of golden centuries once more in Latium, in those same lands where once Saturn reigned; he shall extend our dominion beyond the Garamantians and the Indians in a region which lies outside the path of the constellations.'[327] Aragorn also enacts this dual vision of a restored Gondorian Empire, in both imperial and pastoral terms. Like Virgil's Octavian/Augustus, who allows the shepherds of Arcadia in Virgil's *Eclogues* to go unharassed by marauding soldiers trying to claim their pastoral lands[328] and who will perhaps provide peace from the civil wars for the farmers of the *Georgics*,[329] Aragorn will ultimately ensure that the pastoral lands of the Shire, of the hobbits, are protected from the depredations of outsiders in his realm of Arnor,[330] and that the pastoral ideals of the hobbits, such as otium and *amicitia* (friendship), can be experienced once more.[331]

In summary, comparison of the renewals of Augustus and Aragorn reveals how lapsarian narratives of decline and fall are closely interconnected with utopian visions for the present and future, both in classical narratives and in Tolkien's writing. As with a Platonic Númenor, comparison has also revealed the complexity of utopian restoration projects, which involve a multifactorial redressing of declining elements to create infrastructural, legal, religious, political, moral, imperial and pastoral renewal in Rome and Gondor; in other words, Tolkien's narratives of decline are not simple nostalgic exercises but are quite explicit in their recognition of problems which need to be rectified and restored – they are utopian thought exercises.

Finally, some words of caution are needed here. First, while this section has focused on Augustan renewal in Aragorn's Gondor, other historic, mythic narratives of Roman renewal, such as those of Justinian, Charlemagne and

King Arthur, are not ruled out as *comparanda* for Aragorn's restored empire. Nevertheless, it is important to emphasize the paradigmatic imagination which Augustus' restoration has engendered in our inherited histories of *Roma* – 'this story of Rome's restoration was now woven into Augustus's new imperial political order'[332] – that, in other words, subsequent *principes* or emperors might model their restorations on Augustus'; moreover, outside of Roman historiographies, the very idea of an 'Augustan Golden Age' has become almost synonymous in the post-classical world with ideas of cultural renewal, particularly in 'France, England, and Saxony'.[333] Second, Tolkien's narratives of fall and restoration have, thus far, primarily been viewed as receiving and rewriting ancient narratives; however, it is important to recognize that these narratives are also embedded in the contexts and often problematic, even damaging ideological contests of their times of production, as we will investigate in the next section. Like many modern cultural productions, Tolkien's fiction reappropriates the motif of the 'fall of the ancient city' to articulate (anti-)modern desires in the realms of the political, the religious and the moral.

## Conclusion: The ancient city *must* fall

As Watts has shown in his discussion of narratives of Roman decline and fall, every generation has reworked this motif in new ways to fit its own historical contexts and utopian desires, from Enlightenment thinkers such as Montesquieu and Gibbon[334] to Fascist dictators such as Mussolini[335] to several modern US presidents.[336] In general, lapsarian narratives of a vernacular, even trivial kind are alive and well in the twenty-first century, whether one is talking about the decline of test cricket, of literacy levels or of Cheddar cheese,[337] and 'ancient decline' can easily become swept into modern discourses and appropriated as a present-tense ideological construct. Tolkien's 'ancient' falls, similarly, should be compared and contrasted with several other popular twentieth-century appropriations in cinema and fiction of the decline and fall of an ancient city, such Rome, Troy or Knossos. What modern ideals are these works trying to propagate by employing such lapsarian narratives? How is ancient decline used to endorse certain twentieth-century visions of political, national and religious or secular identity? And how do these representations resemble, or differ from, Tolkien's narratives?

Rome was a popular choice for cinematic fodder in Hollywood blockbusters of the 1950s, from *Quo Vadis* (1951) to Stanley Kubrick's *Spartacus* (1960);[338] and the *topos* of ancient Rome experienced a resurgence in the 'epic 2000s' with Ridley Scott's *Gladiator* (2000).[339] These three films, despite covering very different periods of Roman history, are all linked by the pervasive theme of decline and fall of a negatively constructed Rome.[340] A wicked Rome is generally epitomized by a political leader whose moral character is highly questionable, usually through his non-normative sexuality and materialist love of luxury: thus, in *Quo Vadis* Peter Ustinov's decadent, indulgent aesthete Nero, who reclines in profuse luxury and sings to his sycophantic audience; in *Spartacus*, Lawrence Olivier's bisexual, obscenely wealthy Crassus, whose love of 'snails and oysters' sends a more austere Antoninus running straight for the hills; and in *Gladiator*, Joaquin Phoenix's Commodus as a second Caligula, an incestuous sister-lover. That the behaviour of these leaders implies a decline from a morally healthy society, which cherishes material moderation, heteronormative sexuality and family ethics, is reinforced by their ever-declining mental pathologies: Nero, regarding himself as Apollo reborn, becomes increasingly delusional and disconnected from the political realities; Crassus screams in an irrational fit at the stoic Spartacus during an impromptu gladiator match; *Gladiator* depicts Commodus' paranoia, his distance from social reality, through his increasing spatial isolation in the imperial palace. With the moral, psychological decline of the leaders comes a decline in the civil mores of the Roman people, who enjoy watching Christians being slaughtered in the arena (*Quo Vadis*) or slave-gladiators being made to fight to the death (*Spartacus*; *Gladiator*). Finally, the collapse of Rome as a political entity is usually quite clearly hinted at in these films: the city is faced with starvation (*Gladiator*), is practically burned to the ground (*Quo Vadis*), its armies are almost defeated and its cities plundered (*Spartacus*). A declining ancient Rome *must* fall in these films.

But behind these lapsarian narratives lies an often thinly concealed utopian argument for a superior community with a better system of values: a traditional Christian society cherishing values such as mercy, forgiveness, self-sacrifice and love rather than the (almost literal) hell of Rome under the reign of Nero, the Antichrist (*Quo Vadis*); a liberal, democratic or republican society rather than a fascist oligarchy or autocracy (*Spartacus*; *Gladiator*). These 'ancient' narratives of decline are 'invented traditions'[341] with discernible 'modern overtones';[342] they are relevant to the ideological contestations and belief structures which are dominant in the twentieth century.[343] As Wyke states plainly in the case of a very modern Spartacus, '[l]ittle material is available from antiquity on the slave war led by Spartacus because the Roman elite, as the producers or consumers of ancient historiography, did not find slave rebellion a worthy subject for historical discourse'.[344] Stanley Kubrick's *Spartacus* was a modern story with a strong history of communist receptions in the first half of the twentieth century;[345] the film was based on Howard Fast's leftist, Marxist-inspired novelistic interpretation *Spartacus* (1951), which was blacklisted,[346] and the screenplay to the film was written by Dalton Trumbo, who had previously been blacklisted by Hollywood in the paranoid Cold War climate of 1950s America.[347] Kubrick's excellent film carefully navigates how it represents a potentially proto-modern Marxist class revolution by leaving itself open to diverse readings: from a critical-left perspective (the famous phrase 'I'm Spartacus' thus critiquing McCarthyist 'naming and shaming');[348] from the conservative, Christian right (a crucified Spartacus); and from the liberal centre (as a civil-rights narrative against the enslavement of black America).[349] Ultimately, the film endorses an American compound-message of 'anti-imperialism and democracy, abolition, and racial equality'.[350]

It is difficult not to view the fall and restoration of Rome in Ridley Scott's *Gladiator* as an allegory which endorses contemporary American ideals:[351] the narrative of Roman decline under the 'fascist' dictator Commodus and its restoration with a senatorial government generally endorses the historical American form of republican (representative) democracy;[352] American multicultural liberalism, of liberty to all races and creeds, is encapsulated by the final emancipation of the subjugated slaves at the end of the film, including Maximus' Numidian friend Juba; the benevolence of American imperialism, *pax Americana*, is represented by the heroic representation of Aurelius' subjugation of hostile Germanic tribes at the start of the film and by a kind of necessary *pax Romana* which Maximus, a Spaniard himself, has fought for.[353]

The fall of Rome, then, was a powerful narrative which twentieth-century cultural texts could re-employ for their own ideological purposes: communist, leftist, republican, democratic, Christian, neo-imperialist. Similarly, the legendary fall of Troy in Asia Minor also appealed to Hollywood, and consequently to the sub-genre of peplum (so-called 'sword-and-sandal') films, which were popular in Italy in the 1950s and 1960s, with films including *Helen of Troy* (1956) and *The Trojan War* (1961), and with a resurgence in the epic 2000s through Wolfgang Peterson's *Troy* (2004).[354] These films use the narrative device of the fall to engage with contemporary political or religious values. In *Helen of Troy*, the unusually positively presented Paris, who is about as Trojan-looking as one of the Beach Boys, while admiring his peaceful fellow Trojans and their insular community, insists on establishing international diplomacy with Greek city-states such as Sparta; this is a narrative of political realism and foreign interventionism after 'pacific' isolation which seems appropriate to post-Second World War America. Wolfgang Peterson's *Troy* adopts a bitingly modern, secular narrative, placing the fall of Troy in part on the shoulders of damaging religious thought: this time Troy falls because of the nefarious augury of the Trojan high priest Archeptolemus, who insists on an ill-timed assault on the Greek ships, which results in the accidental death of Patroclus and thus the reintegration of Achilles into the Greek army; Archeptolemus later persuades the religiously superstitious Priam to allow the Trojan Horse into the city.[355]

Conversely, as a modern Catholic thinker reacting against an increasingly secularizing modernity, Tolkien assesses a decline in religious observation as coinciding with civilizational fall and characterizes restoration as involving a return to an observation of the sacred. To this end, one might compare Tolkien's fall of Númenor with the fall of Neronian Rome in *Quo Vadis*.[356] *Quo Vadis* was one of a number of Hollywood productions in the 1950s that received financial and ideological support from the Vatican – a movement satirized in the Coen Brothers' *Hail Caesar* (2004) – which influenced its romantic depictions of an early, ultimately triumphant Christian community.[357] Such religiosity in 1950s Roman epic was also, of course, aimed at conservative national and political ends: being 'of immense relevance to conservative America's self-portrayal during the Cold War era as the defender of the Faith against the godlessness of Communism'.[358] *Quo Vadis* depicts an early, 'underground' Christian church in Rome led by St Peter, which emerges during the extravagant, immoral and thus declining reign of Nero, as 'Antichrist'.[359] When the *Romani populi* are not pleased with Nero's aesthetic decision to burn Rome to the ground in order to create his utopian architectural project of a

New Rome, visualized as a literally hellish, pagan dystopia in Christian terms, the Roman emperor uses the Christians as scapegoats for the catastrophe, putting them to death in the arena to appease the pagan masses. Ultimately, Nero's plan cannot 'extinguish' the decline of the city, with the uprising of the common Romans and his own death marking the (temporary) fall of Rome through civil war. At the end of the film, the escape from the falling ancient city by the romantically inclined martyrs, the hero Marcus Vicinius and the heroine Lygia, signals a Christian fairy tale, a Tolkienian eucatastrophe at the end of a classical fall, with Vicinius having been converted to Christianity through his love of Lygia.[360] This Christian eucatastrophe is repeated in Kubrick's *Spartacus*, though more tragically, with Varinia departing on the Appian Way from a Rome which seems in terminal decline, denoted by the suicide of the 'last' noble Republican Roman (Gracchus), and with Spartacus' crucifixion being an obvious precursor to the Roman crucifixion of Jesus Christ.[361]

In the late histories of Tolkien's Númenor, there is a struggle between two denominations. The powerful and the majority, led by King Ar-Pharazôn, have slipped into a form of misotheism, rejecting the true divine forces of the Valar and the creator;[362] subsequently, they dig up the sacred White Tree,[363] abandon their friendship with the elves, who are their connection with the sacred West, and ultimately make war upon the Valar. This misotheistic community seems to embody a Christian characterization of a pagan, ancient-world society since they build a domed temple to the Satanic figure of Sauron, wherein they practise dark rites.[364] In contrast, the aptly named 'Faithful'[365] are a pious community in hiding, rather like the early Christians represented in *Quo Vadis*,[366] since they are not permitted to dwell in the main Númenórean city of Armenelos;[367] and their actions are secretive, as represented by Isildur's night-time mission to steal a fruit from the White Tree.[368] Like the Christians in *Quo Vadis* who are falsely accused of starting the conflagration, the Faithful are subject to false charges of plotting against 'their kin, devising lies and poisons';[369] and like these persecuted Christians, the Faithful become martyrs who are tortured in Sauron's temple: 'with spilling of blood and torment and wickedness, men made sacrifice to Melkor [...]. And most often from among the Faithful they chose their victims'.[370]

As Númenor starts to resemble a Christian imagining of the hellish dystopia of Neronian Rome, Ar-Pharazôn, along with the Númenórean elite, correspondingly reveals many of the maligned moral qualities of twentieth-century Roman villains: Nero's god-complex,[371] Commodus' (and Caligula's) sexual incest,[372] Crassus' immense riches and military resources.[373] The psychological decline of the Númenórean leader is mapped onto the social and moral decline of a populace who are given over to luxury and debauchery.[374] Ultimately, like Christians evacuating from a cinematic Rome, the persecuted Faithful are forced to abandon a 'late Roman' Númenor to its downfall, fleeing in ships like Virgil's Trojans, under the pious 'Aeneidic' Elendil, before the island sinks below the seas like Plato's Atlantis.[375] Númenor is truly a classical palimpsest. These exiled Númenóreans appropriately establish a 'New Rome' in the form of Gondor at the start of the Third Age.

However, in Gondor too there is a narrative of religious decline, whereby the early 'Faithful' leaders such as Elendil yield to later 'pagan' rulers such as Denethor, who abandons the moral ways of the Faithful Númenóreans and takes part in pagan rituals. This is most clearly demonstrated when Denethor declares his intention to his messengers to kill Faramir and himself: 'We will burn like heathen kings before ever a ship sailed hither from the West. The West has failed. Go back and burn.'[376] Tolkien's choice of the word 'heathen', the connotations of which have an undeniably strong Christian provenance, is remarkable here in a fantasy world which has often been regarded as avoiding overt references to religious institutions; Denethor is turning his back on the (divine, Christian) West by giving up hope – he does not appreciate the divine moment of eucatastrophe in Middle-earth, the joyful comedy of life which brings hope – and by partaking in the anti-Catholic, pagan–Roman behaviour of honourable suicide and cremation.[377] The restoration of Aragorn (and Faramir) marks a return to (Catholic) piety for the dying ancient city.

Was Tolkien's restored utopia of a quasi-Christian, Faithful community, along with the corresponding fall of the pagan ancient city, a response to his own contemporary contexts, as with Neronian Rome in *Quo Vadis*? It is difficult to say since Tolkien's contexts were often as much ancient and medieval as modern – his mind lived in the pre-modern; and allegory is, in any case, a dreaded word in Tolkien studies. Nevertheless, it might be pertinent to observe that Tolkien, as a 'religious conservative', was also concerned with the survival and defence of an apparently declining Catholic Church in the often volatile climates of the twentieth century. From a familial perspective, Tolkien felt from a young age an antipathy and social, financial ostracization on the part of

Protestant relatives towards his mother, who converted her two boys to Catholicism;[378] Tolkien recognized this as part of a broader marginalization which English Catholics felt under the more powerful influence of the Anglican Church of England.[379] There were also worrying 'pagan' situations on the international Cold War scene with what Tolkien regarded as attacks on Catholic Spaniards during the Spanish Civil War – one should recall here that Tolkien was kindly fostered by a Spanish priest from the age of twelve.[380]

In addition to the falls of Rome and Troy, the fall of 'Minoan' Knossos, along with other real and imagined Bronze-Age settlements in Crete, has been a frequent site of literary representation in the twentieth century: for instance, Nikos Kazantzakis' children's story *At the Palaces of Knossos* (probably written around 1940, published in Greek in 1981), Mary Renault's historical fiction *The King Must Die* (1958) and Moyra Caldecott's historical fantasy *The Lily and the Bull* (1979).[381] In these fictions, the fall of a Minoan city sometimes coincides with the fall of an historicized Atlantis, which is often placed on the Minoan 'colony' of Thera, as in Poul Anderson's science fiction *The Dancer from Atlantis* (1971)[382] and, in television, in the six-part *Doctor Who* serial 'The Time Monster' (1972). All these works are part of the broader modern mythmaking enterprise which has been referred to by scholars as 'Cretomania' – a kind of 'Neo-Minoanism' or 'Minoan revival' – since the archaeological discoveries and excavations at Knossos around 1900 and the canonization of 'the Minoan' by Sir Arthur Evans.[383]

Evans's reconstructed vision of Minoan Crete in his four-volume work *The Palace of Minos* (1921, 1928, 1930, 1935) provides some interesting parallels with Tolkien's legendary Númenor.[384] Both English mythmakers constructed a legendary, prehistoric, utopian island realm, which is inhabited by extraordinary seafarers who bring 'civilization' to mainland shores in Europe and Middle-earth.[385] There are some important differences, however, between their mythic visions of quasi-British 'nesothalassocratic' perfection, especially regarding the matter of decline and fall. Evans's vision of Minoan civilization is essentially progressive. This means that his utopians arrive at their golden age in the 'Late Minoan Age'[386] after a period of significant advancements and civilizational expansion (colonization, in post-colonial terms): Evans's Minoans were proto-modern, hyper-technocrats who excelled in the sciences and feats of engineering – 'the multiplicity of technical processes already mastered, the surprising advance in hydraulic and sanitary engineering [...] bear witness to a considerable measure of attainment in the domain of science';[387] his Minoans also enriched the Mediterranean culturally and economically through trade.[388] Evans is never exactly clear on the reasons for the 'gradual decline'[389] of his Minoans – internal unrest, an outside invasion,[390] the accident of natural disaster[391] or Oriental influences might all have played a part.[392] Perhaps it was never entirely clear to him how such a hypercivilized utopia could indeed collapse.

Tolkien, in contrast, is clear on the reasons for decline, and, unlike Evans's Minoans, his island people attain their golden age at the very start of their story before decline sets in: Tolkien's early Númenóreans are more like a Hesiodic people of the earth, living in harmony with nature and shunning technologies, and, moreover, they generally stay clear of seafaring – and sea trading – until much later on in their histories.[393] The adoption of sea trade and technology, through improved architecture and shipbuilding, actually precipitates decline and fall for Tolkien's islanders. In short, these two 'ancient' Occidental utopias are governed by two quite different generational worldviews in English culture: Evans's more expansive, progressive Victorianism and Tolkien's more reclusive, anti-modernist, post-imperial Edwardianism. The decline of a sea-trading Númenor is, in part, a criticism of British foreign intervention with the imperial, thalassocratic century coming to a close;[394] for Evans, brought up in an era when Britannia still ruled the seas, the civilizational impetus for foreign colonization by his Minoans is still framed in relatively positive terms. So too Evans's hyper-technological Minoans betray a nineteenth-century, progressive dream, whereas Tolkien's depiction of Númenórean decline represents the author's well-known, anti-modern distrust of technologies and the catastrophic damage of scientific advancements, doubtless revealed to the English writer, as to many of his more retrospective, anti-modern and anti-technology intellectual contemporaries (such as Robert Graves) through their experiences in the trenches during the First World War.

Evans's utopian stylization of his Minoans was only the start of a long 'Cretomaniac' movement in twentieth-century cultural productions, and other creative writers were far less positive about the ideal of Minoan Knossos. Nikos Kazantzakis' children's story *At the Palaces of Knossos* is wholly negative about Knossos. This Knossos, which was once perhaps a place of golden-age perfection,[395] is a tyrannical power which has managed to subdue most of the navigable coasts, but which is now declining towards collapse because of various failings: decadent aristocrats,[396] starving lower classes,[397] a capricious and violent king[398] and territorial losses. The seminal cause of decline in this Knossos, however, relates to Kazantzakis' own Cretan ideal of *eleftheria* (freedom), which is not possible in this repressive, authoritarian,[399] quasi-Ottoman[400] city of Knossos, a place which undermines all possibility of individual liberty.[401] Or, in Spenglerian terms, a decaying old 'civilization' needs to be superseded by a healthy young 'culture',[402] a young Bronze Age Athens, where people can enjoy unmitigated *eleftheria*,[403] and which forms the utopian counterpart to the declining Minoan Knossos. Kazantzakis' story becomes, on a more abstract level, an exploration of what freedom truly is. Superficially, it is represented through the physical freedom which Icarus seeks by virtue of his father's winged technology[404] and through Ariadne's dream for freedom of movement and travel, realized through her boarding Dionysus' ship[405] – but both of these freedoms prove to be false and destructive; rather, it is the youthful community of Athens which best exemplifies a utopia of *eleftheria*, as experienced by a blacksmith's son called Harris, a place where one can enjoy *free will*.[406]

Mary Renault repeats many of Kazantzakis' motifs in *The King Must Die*, a historical fiction which Tolkien very much enjoyed reading.[407] Her Knossos is suffering decline for similar reasons, such as burgeoning class revolts[408] and a waning of thalassocratic power, a weakness which a young Theseus soon recognizes;[409] Renault also adds a gender-religious element to the political decline of her Minoan Crete, as the Aegean is transitioning from a matriarchal to a patriarchal system of government; lastly, one notes that even King Minos himself is undergoing decay – quite literally, in fact, since he has leprosy.[410] Like Kazantzakis, Renault employs the 'fall of the city' motif to highlight certain ideals, which are epitomized in her narrative by the hero Theseus, who embodies liberal notions of free movement. Theseus' story is one of physical movement across different cultural boundaries during which he acquires a multicultural fellowship, including Athenians, Eleusinians, native Cretans and Amazons. He also advocates fluidity on the level of gender and sexual identity, tolerating the transvestism, homosexuality and lesbianism of his fellow 'Cranes', while he himself, despite being representative of a new patriarchal order in the Aegean, becomes a lithe bull-leaper and the pioneer of the Crane dance.

Theseus' dynamism, his desire to move between political, cultural, physical and gendered borders, is what sets apart his new Athenian political community from the stagnancy of a Knossian dystopia, which collapses in on itself.

The notion that dystopian ancient cities, such as a reimagined Knossos, decline and fall because of their own stagnancy, a lack of permeability and the repression of individual freedoms, are quite modern, liberal notions.[411] Tolkien too presents the dangers of cultural stagnancy and the necessity to maintain free movements as, in part, the reasons behind Númenor's eventual, necessary departure from its golden-age paradisical state. The actions of the Númenórean prince Aldarion in dedicating himself to shipbuilding are motivated by a political realism of the situation in the mainland of Middle-earth where the absolute evil of Sauron is getting a foothold again in unprotected lands and where the freedom of innocent people is being undermined.[412] Númenor cannot remain a stagnant, insular construct forever without ultimately harming itself and all 'the free people' of Middle-earth. It must enter into history, but by doing so the possibility of change is immediately awakened, and for a perfect community change is an anathema.[413] Aldarion's father, King Meneldur, meditates on the problematic stagnancy of his island kingdom, which must necessarily step out of its golden-age isolation and enter worldly affairs[414] – of course, movement and change can bring both positive and negative repercussions. The logic that isolated utopian communities can decline into dystopias and collapse because of their hermetic, xenophobic isolation and stagnancy and, consequently, that dynamism, change and diversity are xenophilic virtues to be apprehended, are behind both of Tolkien's stories of hobbits venturing out of the Shire and experiencing the wider world, as the subsequent chapter explores.

In summary, while Tolkien's narratives of declining ancient communities certainly receive and rewrite utopian thought exercises from antiquity, whether a Platonic Númenor or an Augustan Gondor, equally they must be contextualized in terms of the writer's own life and times. Comparative analysis with other twentieth century representations of this lapsarian narrative – the decline and fall of the ancient city – reveals a panoply of different modern concerns at play in Tolkien's writings: religious conservatism, anti-modernism, anti-technological thought, anti-imperialism and liberalism.

# 2

# Hospitality Narratives: The Ideal of the Home in an Odyssean *Hobbit*

## Introduction: Home, hospitality and Homer

In contrast to the grand geopolitical scale of *The Lord of the Rings*, Tolkien's *The Hobbit* represents place in more mundane, low-key terms; the recurring *topos* in the children's story is that of the simple home.[1] This is indicated by several of the chapter titles in the novel, which refer to a physical home or the parts thereof: 'Queer Lodgings', 'On the Doorstep', and 'Not at Home'.[2] It is also reflected by the plot of the tale. *The Hobbit* commences in Bilbo's comfortable home of Bag End, from which he reluctantly departs together with thirteen dwarven companions, under the leadership of their exiled king, Thorin Oakenshield, and the wizard Gandalf, on a quest to reclaim the dwarves' lost home, the Lonely Mountain (Erebor). During their adventures, the travellers encounter different varieties of home, across diverse cultures: the crude cave dwelling and makeshift outdoor kitchen of the trolls; the idyllic, tranquil home of the half-elf Elrond; the underground home of the goblins; the mead hall of the arctanthropic shapeshifter, a 'werebear' known as Beorn; the cave home of the elven king of Mirkwood; the great hall in Lake-town; and finally, the lost mountain home of the dwarves, now occupied by the dragon Smaug. The story concludes with Bilbo Baggins's return to Bag End.

Even when larger political communities are described – territories, kingdoms or towns, that is, homelands rather than homes – they are frequently referred to or focalized by Tolkien in small-scale, 'homely' terms. The elven dwelling in Rivendell, undoubtedly a substantial 'palatial' complex given the number of elves abiding there in *The Fellowship of the Ring* (1954),[3] is described in *The Hobbit* in terms of a single individual's home, 'the Last Homely House

West of the Mountains', which belongs to Elrond, '[t]he master of the house'.[4] The underground realm of the goblins below the Misty Mountains consists of an interweaving labyrinth of tunnels and holes, as the miserable Bilbo discovers when he is separated from his companions, who have been captured by these evil industrialists; nevertheless, when the Great Goblin confronts Thorin, one of the goblin slave drivers uses an ironically homely metaphor: '[w]e found them sheltering in our Front Porch'.[5] In Lake-town, again a substantial community, most of the action takes place primarily in 'one great hall',[6] not unlike Beorn's hall. The Lonely Mountain was once a great kingdom of dwarves, but in *The Hobbit* it is the home of a single individual, the monstrous dragon Smaug; it is later reclaimed and kept by little more than a dozen dwarves. Moreover, when trying to find a way into the mountain, Bilbo sits 'on the doorstep',[7] which is a reference to the chapter title; the usage of such home-like metaphors and metonymies, as the goblins' Front Porch, are apparent throughout the children's story.

In exploring the logic behind such a repetition of or emphasis on a certain fixed place or *topos* in a story, narratologists interested in spatial studies have provided us with some useful toolkits. In recent times they have moved past the traditional notion in literary studies that place functions as an inert backdrop to the more important story elements, such as plot, which embodies the temporal, dynamic art of novelistic writing, and character, the aspect given emphasis in dramatic narratives and theatre.[8] From a structural perspective, the arrangement, deployment or stylization of place in two different narratives can be as diverse as their representations of character.[9] But beyond such structural diversity, narratologists have also explored how place can contribute to the meaning of a work and what functions place can have in a narrative. For example, in her introduction to the narratological study of space, the classicist Irene de Jong suggests five different generic functions of place in a given narrative: thematic, mirroring or mimetic, symbolic, characterizing and psychologizing.[10]

In *The Hobbit*, one such function of space might be psychologizing: the journey of Bilbo Baggins from his 'womb-like' hobbit hole at Bag End might describe an individual's developmental journey, a rite of passage, from birth to experience to maturity.[11] Psychological interpretations of the children's book, such as those of Green,[12] have been a popular critical way of understanding the quest of *The Hobbit*, not as simply the type of 'exterior' quest in medieval romances and heroic sagas to slay a dragon, reclaim gold and return the absent king to his throne, but as an interior quest of personal change and development. From a spatial perspective, the cave has a long, multivalent metaphoric history in Western literary traditions, as Weinberg has shown,[13] and can, indeed, at times connote a womb-like site of rebirth, where the individual subsequently steps out into a greater experiential arena;[14] accordingly, Green's psychological analysis of *The Hobbit* gives emphasis to a 'Larger Landscape'.[15]

While Green's emphasis on open, unconfined space in that section of the story aptly occurring in 'Wilderland' is not wrong, his generalization does ignore several lengthy scenes which are based in homes, including Gollum's cave, Beorn's lodging, the elven cave home in Mirkwood, the great hall in Lake-town and Smaug's cave home. So many constricted 'cave-wombs', so many psychological rebirths? Tolkien was not only concerned with the value of grand arenas of the natural world, as the subsequent chapter discusses, but also with the value of that most mundane, quotidian, intrinsically human of places: the individual home, the *domus*, the *oikos*. This chapter moves away from psychological readings of the children's story to a new understanding of the role of place therein; to this end, a sixth function might be added to Irene de Jong's five narratological functions of space: the ethical.[16] What, a given narrative might ask, is a 'good-place', a *eu-topos*? And what is a 'bad-place', a *dys-topos*? In the genre of utopian literature, the question of eu-topianism is often asked exclusively with respect to the macroscopic *topos* of a society or broader community, usually set in 'nowhere' (ou-topia), a remote part of the world, whether in Plato's *Critias* or Thomas More's *Utopia*; yet the question of eu-topianism can also be posed with respect to the restricted, relatively small-scale, mundane *topos* of the home, and, for this purpose, the wealth of interdisciplinary scholarship on hospitality can be brought into conversation with the field of utopian studies.

What is a good home? And what is a bad home? These questions are embedded in a long narrative tradition which represents the sociopolitical, often religious[17] ritual of hospitality, as James Heffernan has discussed in his monograph *Hospitality and Treachery in Western Literature*.[18] Simply put, in such narratives, a home is judged to be good when appropriate hospitality, the tokens of which are culture-dependent, is demonstrated, and where there is a harmonious relationship between the host and the guest; a bad home is a place where various degrees and forms of inhospitality are evident, either on the part of the host, the guest, or both. The thematic importance of hospitality to *The Hobbit* can be observed from the outset in some of the chapter titles: 'An Unexpected Party' and 'A Warm Welcome' describe a host's reception of guests; 'Roast Mutton' and 'A Short Rest' describe components of a hospitality scene.[19]

This chapter explores the extent to which *The Hobbit* can be interpreted as a hospitality narrative, a tale which represents guest–host relationships and even adjudicates[20] on the ethical question of what makes a home a good place. A classical-reception framework is employed here to show that Tolkien's exploration of different imagined homes, from Bag End to the Lonely Mountain, is in part retrotopic, that he draws on narratives of places past for the sake of exploring ideals. In particular, Tolkien's hospitality narrative has its roots in, draws on and can be interpreted through the seminal, paradigmatic hospitality narrative in Western literature, the Homeric *Odyssey* – a work essentially concerned with excursions from *oikos* (home) to *oikos*. This is not to say that the ancient Greek epic provides the only means for understanding hospitality in *The Hobbit*; the general consensus in Tolkien studies is that the English writer drew on a hotchpotch of different sources in creating his own modern mythology out of the vast 'worldwide Cauldron of Story'.[21] In the case of Tolkien's writing of a hospitality narrative, several other cultural, literary traditions need to be acknowledged as sources: firstly, biblical scripture, in both the Old and the New Testament; secondly, Germanic and early medieval literature; thirdly, the nineteenth-century boom of fairy stories. Beside such inherited literary traditions, Tolkien's personal experiences of the *topos* of home have obvious relevance, as do his experiences in the Catholic Church.[22] Nevertheless, the lion's share of this chapter pertains to classical texts, more specifically the Homeric *Odyssey*, and using these as a definite source for Tolkien requires some justification before undertaking a further examination of what hospitality means in the case of the ancient epic and, subsequently, its reception in Tolkien.

Of all ancient Greek and Roman writers 'Homer' , as a literary figure and as an idea, simply seems to have mattered most to Tolkien (Virgil being a close second). The Englishman reflected on his early encounter with the ancient Greek *aoidos* (bard) as a kind of formative awakening in aesthetic taste: 'I was brought up in the Classics, and first discovered the sensation of literary pleasure in Homer;[23] this in contrast to modern English literature, which did not move his 'heart and head'.[24] At King Edward's School in Birmingham (1900–1911), Tolkien most likely had to read through unprepared passages of Homeric Greek, particularly the *Iliad* in 1908 and 1909,[25] and at some point he also seems to have read Chapman's translation of Homer's *Odyssey*,[26] since he compared his first encounter with Joseph Wright's *Primer of the Gothic Language* (1892) as entailing 'a sensation at least as full of delight as first looking into Chapman's Homer'.[27] At the University of Oxford, the syllabus included the study of Homer,[28] and Lewis Farnell gave lectures on the *Odyssey* to Tolkien's group in the Michaelmas Term of 1912.[29] During his subsequent Honour Moderations in 1913, Tolkien was examined on prepared translations from the Homeric poems and took 'a general paper on Greek and Latin grammar, literary criticism, and antiquities, including questions on Homer'.[30]

In his later recollections in his published letters, Tolkien makes occasional reference to 'Homer' or the 'Homeric': situating *The Lord of the Rings* in a mythic tradition which stems from Homer;[31] describing the men of the Second Age as living in a 'simple Homeric state';[32] and referring to the Rohirrim as 'heroic Homeric horsemen'.[33] Another interesting reference to Homer occurs in one of Tolkien's manuscripts. When Tolkien was sketching the plot of *The Return of the King*, he wrote in a different-coloured ink at the top of the draft page: 'Homeric catalogue. Forlong the Fat. The Folk of Lebennin'.[34] This represents his first imaginative reference, or the first captured on paper at least, for what became an important action sequence in 'Minas Tirith', the opening chapter of *The Return of the King*. The hobbit traveller Pippin, waiting outside the gates of the city, witnesses a procession of clans from the surrounding towns and communities of Gondor arriving at the capital city in order to buff up the defences before battle. It is intriguing that Tolkien's imagination was stimulated at this point in the creative process by a reference to a typical element of Homeric storytelling: the so-called 'Homeric catalogue'.[35]

Apart from Tolkien's own education, reflections and manuscript notes, a growing subfield of scholarship has addressed the reception of Homeric elements in Tolkien's creative fiction.[36] This chapter intersects with previous scholarship on Homeric influences in Tolkien's works in several respects: pointing to a narrative concerned not only with homecoming[37] but also with the ethical idea of the home; building on the Odyssean paradigms which Reckford noticed in the depiction of Bilbo Baggins as a hero and on the correspondence between individual scenes in the *Odyssey* and *The Hobbit*;[38] and, like Pezzini,[39] turning to the subtle representations of divine intervention in Tolkien's works which have their antecedent in Homeric epic – here, though, from an Odyssean rather than an Iliadic perspective.

Tolkien's formative background in and his receptions of Homer can help us understand and assess the Englishman's treatment of the central hospitality questions of *The Hobbit* – of what constitutes a good home and what a bad home – since the 'hospitality question' is also very much central to appreciating the narrative of the *Odyssey*, as scholars in Homeric studies have proven:[40] most famously, the Phaeacian sequence,[41] the Polyphemus episode,[42] and the return narrative (Books 13–24).[43] Taken together, such studies show the pervasiveness and cultural centrality of *xenia* (hospitality) to Homeric poetry, particularly the *Odyssey*, with its representation of early Greek society (what the ritual entails; its components), ethics (what is good and what is bad hospitality), religion (the divine authority behind the socio-ethical ritual), economics (the business of guest-friendship) and politics (hospitality and inter-community relations).

The sheer pervasiveness of the hospitality ritual in the Homeric *Odyssey* is illustrated by scholars such as Edwards and Reece, who have proven the typicality of hospitality scenes to the epic poem.[44] The 'typical scene', sometimes also dubbed a 'theme' in the Homeric poems,[45] describes a stock action sequence in the narrative, such as that of arming[46] or battle;[47] it is characterized by a limited, repeated set of elements, and these elements are quite often related in a fixed order, thus forming a pattern in the scene.[48] These typical scenes, along with formulae, character doublets and similes, are significant features in the oral meaning of the Homeric poems. Reece's critical engagement with *xenia* throughout his seminal work is based upon the study of repetitive 'elements'[49] within scenes of hospitality,[50] which render these scenes typical; he provides a list of twenty-five primary elements and seventeen subsidiary elements which reoccur in these scenes in the Homeric poems.[51] On the basis of this table of typical elements – such as the feast, the identification of names, the bathing sequence and the exchange of guest-gifts – Reece posits that there are twelve major hospitality scenes in the *Odyssey*.[52]

These scenes are not mere habitual social rituals, with various performed actions and speeches; they are imbued with ethical meaning in the *Odyssey*. The guest may pose the ethical question before the hospitality moment: 'Wretch that I am, whose land have I come to now? Are the people barbarous, arrogant and lawless? Are they hospitable [*philoxeinoi*] and godfearing?'[53] To these anxieties of the guest, a host such as Alcinous may respond with assurance of his or her benevolence as a host: '[w]e revere our guest [...] a man needs no great grasp of things to understand that a guest and suppliant is no less precious than a brother.'[54] Or, ominously, a host such as Polyphemus may declare his antipathy and disdain for guest-friendship, in both word and action.[55]

There are good, bad and ambiguous hospitality scenes in the poem, and scholars have endeavoured to weigh up the evidence in various respects and characterize the different ethical qualities of the hospitality scenes in the epic. For example, when the young Telemachus, Odysseus' son, ventures as a *xenos* (guest) to the shores of Pylos and the palace of Nestor (Book 3) and then, afterwards, further south to Sparta and the home of Menelaus, scholars have regarded these two hosts to be exemplary practitioners of hospitality.[56] Yet these benevolent welcomes are in stark contrast to the abuses of hospitality which scholars have observed in the behaviour of Penelope's suitors (paralleled by the ogre Polyphemus), who are the guests of Telemachus in Odysseus' home;[57] these suitor-guests[58] are quite literally eating Telemachus out of house and home[59] and are even plotting to kill him.[60]

Furthermore, in order to understand the directionality or didactics of hospitality ethics in the narrative, this 'hospitality question' must be read alongside the successful *nostos* (homecoming) plot structure of the epic poem.[61] Odysseus not only returns to his physical home on Ithaca but also 'wins out':[62] the hero gets his wife back, he is reunited with his son and he punishes the suitors – in short, as the rightful host he wins back the authority of his home from abusive guests.[63] While the severity of the violent vengeance at the end of the story is morally problematic for a modern reader of the archaic Greek poem,[64] in its own terms the *Odyssey* provides a definite punitive resolution to the ethical dilemma, the state of inhospitality which existed at the start of the poem. The story seems to track, from a broader structural perspective, an ethical progression:[65] from an initially unsatisfactory state of hospitality for an absent host, Odysseus, and for his naïve son, Telemachus, bearing witness to the destruction of his father's home at the hand of usurping guests, to a series of episodes in which different forms of reception – positive (Nestor), negative (Polyphemus) or somewhat ambiguous (Circe) – are represented to both Odysseus and Telemachus as travelling guests or *xenoi*, and, finally, to a resolution where the earlier crimes against the home are atoned for, in the second half of the epic poem.

As a final point on the subject of ethics, it is important to note that hospitality in the Homeric *Odyssey* is backed up by the divine protection of Zeus, and that, accordingly, the ritual is imbued with religious connotations. Hospitality represents an absolute ethics. Odysseus, having entered Polyphemus' cave, wishes to await his host in the hope of acquiring *xenia* (hospitality; and more specifically, guest-gifts).[66] Homeric *xenia* is not analogous to modern secular notions of 'hospitality', least of all the 'hospitality industry'. The host–guest relationship has a religious element to it, which Odysseus makes abundantly clear to Polyphemus.[67] They approach his knees in the ritualistic manner of religious suppliants seeking sanctuary.[68] The act of receiving guests and bestowing gifts upon them is described by Odysseus as the *xeinōn themis* (divine right of guests);[69] *themis* is often used in the Homeric corpus to refer to a universal moral law, often governed by a divine hand.[70] And, of course, Zeus is himself given the epithet *xeinios* (of the foreigner-guest)[71] and is charged with looking after the welfare of *xenoi* and *hiketai* (supplicants), and acting as their *epitimētōr* (avenger)[72] when wronged.[73] The relationship between host and guest transcends social ethics as it is ingrained with religious reverence, particularly to Zeus; its violation is considered a blasphemous crime, analogous to slaying a man who seeks sanctuary in a temple.[74]

The above outline of Homeric hospitality serves as a guiding framework for a new understanding of Tolkien's *The Hobbit*. Much more can of course be said about Homeric hospitality. In terms of politics ('foreign policy'), a *xenos* is both a guest and a foreigner, and the final section of this chapter explores the importance of foreignness – xenophilia (love of the stranger/foreigner) and xenophobia (fear of the stranger/foreigner) – to Tolkien's writings in general. From an economic perspective, hospitality was also clearly a practical business in archaic Greek society,[75] and a poorly calculated exchange of gifts, entailing a loss of monetary value in goods, is not advisable, as the episode of Glaucus and Diomedes in the *Iliad* reveals.[76]

In the following three sections, a reception-based reading of *The Hobbit* as a narrative of Homeric hospitality is provided. This reception can be seen on the level of repeated motifs (characters, actions, spatial details) in hospitality scenes, in line with approaches in comparative mythology and folklore; certainly, in the case of episodes such as that of the three trolls in the chapter 'Roast Mutton', comparative analysis reveals how classical reception framed these narratives. Yet the classical reception undertaken in this chapter is far more interested in comparing and contrasting the ethical scrutiny of these different hosting situations. What is a good home and what is a bad home? Moreover, as in the *Odyssey*, there is a plot movement in the *nostos* from an initially unsatisfactory state of hospitality to its ultimate resolution. The hospitality quest of *The Hobbit* can be divided into three parts: the first revealing the inadequacies of hosts and guests; the second affording the *xenoi* various paradigms of host situations in the wildlands; and the final part resolving the earlier inhospitalities. Lastly, Odyssean reception can also be found in the religious background to various hospitality scenes in the children's story, which posits benevolent hospitality as essentially absolute, as watched over by a magical, supernatural, even divine order.

## A comfortable host and abusive guests

Bag End, the home of Bilbo Baggins, sits inside a green hill, which looks over a beautiful garden, meadow and river. The interior of the house matches its paradisical landscape. Home, for the small inhabitant, 'means comfort'.[77] Thus, the entrance to the house has been carpeted and upholstered so as to make it a very 'comfortable tunnel';[78] its single-storied layout such that the hobbit does not have to exert himself climbing up and down stairs; whole rooms are designated as walk-in closets; and Bilbo's food supplies are plentiful in his many pantries.[79] As a host, Bilbo 'was fond of visitors'.[80] Such a benevolent reception of guests seems to be evident when Bilbo warmly greets an old man (Gandalf) who has approached his threshold.[81] Gandalf, however, at once unsettles the hobbit by responding with a riddle which deconstructs the host's proffered benevolent welcome: 'What do you mean? [...] Do you wish me a good morning, or mean that it is a good morning whether I want it or not; or that you feel good this morning; or that it is a morning to be good on?'[82]

Gandalf has astutely gauged what 'good' really connotes in Bilbo's outwardly hospitable welcome: namely, the hobbit's own personal comfort in his home ('that you feel good') and his disregard for guests who might disturb this goodness-comfort ('a good morning whether I want it or not'). Tellingly, Bilbo invites Gandalf to share in his present comforts, offering him a seat and a smoke of his own pipe; the prescriptive nature of comfort for Bilbo's guests becomes apparent when the hobbit says: 'There's no hurry, we have all day before us!'[83] The guest's rebuke is immediate. Gandalf has 'no time to blow smoke-rings'[84] and informs Bilbo that he is looking for someone to go with him on an adventure. Bilbo refuses his guest's request with increasing rudeness: first suggesting that the wizard has got the wrong address; then ignoring his guest; and finally flatly refusing hospitality by shutting his door in Gandalf's face.[85]

Bilbo's partial refusal of hospitality to Gandalf – he is still polite enough to invite him for tea the next day – lies in what the wizard represents, a disruption to the comfort of the home. Tolkien twice marks out this pivotal word: firstly, in Bilbo's panicked refusal of his guest's offer – '[I] have no use for adventures. Nasty disturbing uncomfortable things!';[86] second, through the narrator's observation that 'Bilbo got quite uncomfortable and even a little cross'[87] when his guest did not leave immediately. The key word for understanding Bilbo's relationship to his home, Bag End, and to the reception of others in this space is evidently: *comfort*. This emphasis on comfort, along with the material objects and physical description of Bag End, might connote a typically Victorian *domus dulcis domus* (home sweet home), 'the civilized atmosphere of a comfortable sitting room in an old manor house',[88] a place where a high-bred gentleman can be at peace, smoking a pipe,[89] munching on cakes, being free from any female influences[90] and removed from the lower-class necessity of work.[91] Despite the quintessentially Victorian, English homeliness of Bag End, there are certain parallels to be drawn with the Homeric *Odyssey*.

Although the narrative of Odysseus' adventures only commences in earnest in Book 5, the Ithacan hero is in fact the subject of the proem at the start of the *Odyssey*; Odysseus has been a guest of the immortal nymph Calypso, who has imprisoned the hero for seven years on her island of Ogygia and desires an immortal union with him.⁹² Like Bag End for a Victorian or Edwardian, Ogygia for a Greek 'means comfort': Calypso's hearth in her cave is kept warm by a 'great fire';⁹³ the whole island is filled with a woody fragrance;⁹⁴ Calypso's divine singing voice can be heard in her cave;⁹⁵ there are tokens of material luxury, such as the goddess' loom woven with gold thread,⁹⁶ and of natural beauty, such as forests, springs and meadows.⁹⁷ Even a god, 'if he came there, might gaze in wonder at the sight and might be the happier in heart',⁹⁸ which is precisely what Hermes does upon arriving there.⁹⁹ In her luxurious home, Calypso shows what appears to be exemplary hospitality to the messenger of the gods in a '"visit" type-scene',¹⁰⁰ allowing him a seat to rest on,¹⁰¹ proffering her assistance as hostess to her guest¹⁰² and offering him nectar and ambrosia.¹⁰³

Despite such tokens of hospitality, Calypso's hosting of Odysseus is deficient in some important respects.¹⁰⁴ Although Calypso has offered Odysseus the material comfort of her *locus amoenus* (pleasant or charming place)¹⁰⁵ as well as the 'spiritual comfort' of her realm by offering to make him her immortal spouse¹⁰⁶ and, consequently, removing him from the sufferings of the world,¹⁰⁷ she has not allowed him the opportunity to disturb this stagnant bliss by leaving her home, which means that the detained Odysseus, more a prisoner than a guest, 'does not enjoy his stay in this paradise'.¹⁰⁸ Only at the prompting of the Olympians does Calypso finally release Odysseus from his long-enforced stay.¹⁰⁹ Odysseus is critical of Calypso's hospitality. She has detained him for a long time against his will, which is contrary to the behaviour of a good host.¹¹⁰ Secondly, as an extension of this, she has tried to erase his very status as a *xenos* by inviting him to become a second host, her *posis* (husband), thus ignoring his desire to reach his own home.¹¹¹ Thirdly, in his later four-book-long speech to the Phaeacians (the so-called *Apologue*), Odysseus even downplays the material luxury of Calypso's home (and Circe's), preferring his own rugged island home of Ithaca, which is decidedly rough and tough, a hilly breeding-ground for hardy men and for herders of swine such as Eumaeus.¹¹²

Odysseus' criticisms of Calypso as a hostess are precisely the lessons in home and hospitality which Bilbo Baggins needs to learn in the course of *The Hobbit*: namely, that a guest should not be indefinitely delayed by a host (Bilbo declares to Gandalf 'we have all the day before us');¹¹³ that a guest should not merely be regarded as a mirror image of the host without his or her own desires (Bilbo encourages Gandalf to smoke a pipe on the front porch just like him);

and that a guest should not be forcibly 'married' into the comforts of the host's own home (to enjoy the paradisical luxury of Bag End). Towards the end of his journey, Bilbo Baggins learns to appreciate what Odysseus, as well as Gandalf, already knows: that the space of the home means more than eternal Calypso-like comfort and luxury, *piona oikon* (a fat home),[114] which a 'guest' must 'marry into' at the pleasure of the host; rather, it means a reciprocity between the separate desires of guest and host.

It is, furthermore, noteworthy from the religious perspective of the hospitality ritual that the inhospitalities of both hosts, Calypso and Bilbo, are conquered by supernatural agents. Calypso is forced to release Odysseus from the magical bounds of her realm because of the interventions of higher divinities: the combined machinations of Athena, Zeus and Hermes.[115] Gandalf is a wizard, and his bag of tricks for overcoming the reluctant host Bilbo includes both verbal magic, his riddled riposte which unsettles Bilbo's subtly inhospitable welcome, and real magic, a magical sign etched over the door of Bag End which will act as an invitation to Bag End on behalf of an unwitting host for thirteen dwarven guests. Even the very name 'Gandalf'[116] seems to have an otherworldly effect on the grumpy hobbit, triggering his 'Tookish' persona, his desire for adventure and fun – talk of goblins and dragons and fireworks – over his more bourgeois, stay-at-home 'Baggins' persona. In Tolkien's broader legendarium, it becomes apparent that Gandalf is more than a wizard in the fairy-tale sense: he is a kind of angelic spirit, who has come to Middle-earth from the heavenly Undying Lands; and, therefore, the 'magic' he employs is an indication of a divine or angelic governing hand.[117] Such an interpretation aligns Tolkien's work with the Homeric epic in providing a supernatural, even god-like authority behind an (in)hospitality scene. This will be a recurring feature of hospitality scenes in *The Hobbit*.

As a result of Gandalf's magical inducement, Bilbo is transformed into a host who is compliant to the demands of his unexpected guests: thirteen rather uncouth, nomadic dwarves. The dwarves, on the one hand, exhibit polite manners in formally announcing their names and pledging their 'service' to their host; on the other hand, they are far from ideal guests in their behaviour. In fact, the guest–host relationship between the dwarves and Bilbo resembles in certain respects another inhospitality situation at the start of the *Odyssey*, between the suitors and Telemachus. Both sets of guests are set on claiming a home: the suitors, while ostensibly competing for Penelope's hand, are also competing to supplant Odysseus, and thus Telemachus, as head of the *oikos*;[118] the dwarves are seeking to reclaim their lost home of Erebor from the dragon Smaug. These *xenoi*, aggressively seeking to establish themselves as hosts of a home once more, conversely threaten the sovereignty of their less experienced hosts.

This is represented in both stories through the metaphor of being eaten out of house and home. Bilbo begins to fear such a scenario through the excessive feasting of the visiting dwarves, which transforms him from a respectable, middle-class homeowner to a mere waiting servant. The dwarves poke fun at Bilbo's anxieties of his house, and his status as homeowner, being consumed and destroyed through playful poetry and song on broken crockery.[119] The suitors, with less humour than the characters in the children's story, threaten Odysseus' home through slaughtering and devouring their way through all of Telemachus' inherited livestock, a fact which the young Ithacan prince painfully comes to realize.[120] Significantly, Telemachus calls on Zeus, as the protector of *xenoi*, to punish these abuses of a host's hospitality.[121]

As abusive guests, the dwarves and the suitors also openly question the authority of their hosts. Bilbo's apparent expertise as 'professional burglar' for their expedition is a figure of mockery to Thorin Oakenshield, the leader of the dwarven company, who is openly dismissive of Bilbo's abilities.[122] Likewise, the suitors, especially Antinous, disparage the authority of Telemachus as master of his *oikos* when the young host has called an assembly in Book 2; the suitors even refuse to leave his property.[123] This verbal aggression to their host turns to physical aggression and violence in the case of the suitors, who plot to assassinate Telemachus.[124] The dwarven guests are more amicable in their treatment of their host Bilbo, since their lost home is not Bag End, after all. Still, the subsequent adventures show that the dwarves have no ethical qualms about risking Bilbo's life for the sake of achieving their own ends (reclaiming *their* home) against formidable opponents, the three trolls and the dragon Smaug; indeed, they even suggest leaving Bilbo for dead after their escape from the Misty Mountains.

Improper hospitality at the start of *The Hobbit* and the *Odyssey*, then, can be displayed both by hosts (Calypso and Bilbo) and by guests (the suitors and the dwarves). In the latter case, the guests pose the risk of the host losing sovereignty of the space of the home. This is emphasized in the case of Telemachus and Bilbo because they are represented as youthful (in the case of Bilbo through the metaphor of physical size) and inexperienced characters:[125] they have both been deprived of their fathers, the appropriate past models for one's authority as host; they both fail to properly assert their present authority as hosts; and they are both compelled by supernatural instigation, Athena and Gandalf respectively, to leave their homes and to go on journeys of future maturation, a necessary educational introduction to hospitality.[126] Thus, just as Athena helps to save Telemachus from the abuses of the suitors,[127] it is only through the supernatural intervention of the wizard, a mediatory force in the hospitality encounter, that a burgeoning disrespect for the host of Bag End is suppressed before a great rift develops between host and guests.[128]

## Wandering guests

The central journey of *The Hobbit*, after the company of fifteen departs from Bag End and before they arrive at Erebor, provides several different representations of hospitality – some malevolent, some benevolent, some ambiguous – when the travelling guests, the *xenoi*, seek out the welcome of various hosts. This journey in *The Hobbit*, through the aptly named Wilderland, is analogous to the adventures and receptions which the *xenos* Odysseus experiences during his wanderings (*Odyssey* 5–13) in the preternatural Mediterranean, removed from the here and now of Greek society. During these host situations, the *xenoi* learn what kinds of hospitality are entirely unacceptable, what kinds are ideal (even too ideal for a mortal), and what kind of behaviour – namely, reciprocity – is needed to navigate ambiguous or complex hospitality situations.

The first 'hosts' encountered in *The Hobbit* are three anthropophagous trolls. Bilbo, acting as a scout for the hungry, sodden dwarves, finds a fire and a makeshift 'kitchen' in a forest clearing, which is occupied by three giants. Bilbo tries in vain to steal something from the huge hosts, is captured along with all the dwarves, and is finally rescued by Gandalf. The scene owes quite a bit to Norse mythology[129] as well as to Scandinavian fairy tales popularized in the nineteenth century;[130] however, the reception of the Homeric *Cyclopeia* in the

*Odyssey* (Book 9) is just as significant a source.[131] In the tradition of comparative folklore studies, one might cite the following common motifs:

(i) The travellers (thirteen in the *Odyssey*; fifteen in *The Hobbit*) find the giants' homes in the wilderness, surrounded by wild mountains or hills.[132]
(ii) The travellers must pass over a watery boundary (the sea, a river) to reach the giants.[133]
(iii) The giants' homes are situated on a heavily wooded hill.[134]
(iv) There is a visual sign of the homes through smoke or fire.[135]
(v) Mountains are focalized as 'uncivilized' places.[136]
(vi) The theft of live sheep or cooked sheep ('Roast Mutton') is contemplated.[137]
(vii) The giants are reckless in their consumption of alcohol.[138]
(viii) The giants are culinary figures, primitive chefs.[139]
(ix) A hero tries to placate the giants by tempting them with food[140] or wine.[141]
(x) A hero pokes a flaming branch or stave into a giant's eye.[142]
(xi) The guests are trapped, caught and eaten or otherwise prepared as food.[143]
(xii) The giants are defeated through linguistic trickery by a hero.[144]
(xiii) The giants are cave dwellers.[145]
(xiv) The cave door is blocked by a large stone which the travellers cannot move through physical force.[146]
(xv) The cave is full of food and dead remains.[147]
(xvi) Powerful, 'magical' weapons are found inside the cave.[148]
(xvii) The travellers plunder food from the cave.[149]

In the *Cyclopeia*, several typical elements of an ideal Homeric hospitality scene have been inverted or perverted such that the episode might be thought of as a parody of the ritual.[150] Polyphemus rejects Odysseus' request that the host honour Zeus *xeinios*;[151] the guests are not served food but become food;[152] and the sardonic *xeinēion* (guest-gift) of the ogre host is to eat Odysseus last of all.[153] The fault does not lie solely with the host, however. The Greek visitors do not behave as proper guests, entering his home and eating his food without his permission[154] and suggesting the theft of Polyphemus' livestock.[155]

'Roast Mutton' can be read as a parody of the hospitality tale reminiscent of the Polyphemus encounter. The dwarves waver between notions of hospitality and theft, between being guests or raiders. When they look at the trolls' fire, it is focalized as 'a reddish comfortable-looking light'.[156] Comfort is a marker of home in Tolkien's novel. The dwarves also anticipate provisions and shelter: 'anything was better than little supper, less breakfast, and wet clothes all night'.[157] And yet the dwarves are highly suspicious, like Odysseus' men, and favour the possibility of theft, nominating Bilbo as their 'burglar'[158] to investigate, and Bilbo does try, unsuccessfully, to pick the pocket of the troll William. While the *Cyclopeia* and 'Roast Mutton' are notable for their inhospitable hosts, the guests are also violating reception norms by favouring theft and ignoring guest procedures.

Acts of eating and food are central to hospitality narratives in the *Odyssey*[159] and also in Tolkien's work. In both narratives there is an eating paradox: the travellers expect to be given 'mutton' by their host(s) or, at worst, to steal mutton or live sheep;[160] their hosts, however, have little interest in animal flesh, preferring the flesh of their guests. A simple pastoralist, Polyphemus humanizes his flock, tenderly addressing his chief ram, and he shows no interest in devouring his livestock.[161] In a similar vein, one of Tolkien's trolls expresses no great delight in eating sheep, declaring, '[m]utton yesterday, mutton today, and blimey, if it don't look like mutton again tomorrer'.[162] The culinary-minded giants turn their guests into their preferred meal, and in so doing they animalize their guests: the Ithacans are compared to puppies when they are killed,[163] while Bilbo is regarded as a 'nassty little rabbit'.[164] Naturally in a modern children's tale such as *The Hobbit*,[165] there is no actual eating of the guests as there is in the *Odyssey*,[166] but the dinner preparation sequence of the hospitality scene, and thus their imagined consumption, is extended.[167]

The outrageous violation of hospitality is punished. In the *Odyssey*, Polyphemus is blinded by the Greeks and robbed of his sheep; in *The Hobbit*, the three trolls are turned to stone, a motif from Norse mythology, and their cave plunder is redistributed. However, prior to their petrification at the hands of Gandalf, there is a battle sequence which resembles another famous Homeric scene, when Odysseus and his men heat up the tip of a wooden stake and plunge it into the ogre's eye.[168] In *The Hobbit*, Thorin brandishes a branch and manages to injure one of the trolls, Bert, with its fiery end.[169] In addition to physical assault, the punishment of the giants is also brought about through verbal trickery in each story. Odysseus announces himself under a fake title to Polyphemus, '*Outis*'[170] (Nobody), which will cause the ogre to declare to his fellow Cyclopes that 'Nobody is attacking me',[171] thus ensuring that he, once blinded, cannot obtain the help of his neighbours to defeat Odysseus. Gandalf, having returned from his earlier scouting, uses a flexible range of vocal abilities to mimic the voices of the three trolls, causing them to bicker until sunset, which petrifies them.[172] Thus a potentially fatal breach in normal guest–host relations is assuaged by the 'divine' Gandalf. Throughout *The Hobbit*, this religious background to hospitality scenes is apparent: Gandalf (and later his protégé, Bilbo) employs different brands of 'magic' – real wizardry ('staff magic') as well as the clever, 'Odyssean' use of linguistic tricks ('verbal magic') – in order to negotiate potentially inhospitable homes.

The following hospitality scene in *The Hobbit* takes place at Elrond's home and closely resembles the Ithacans' guest-stay with Aeolus on his island-palace. A number of similarities are apparent between the respective episodes. Both occur immediately after the encounter with the gigantic man-eaters, with the travellers in a state of despondency: the Greeks are mourning their companions,[173] while the dwarves are in no mood for singing songs.[174] The homes of these two rulers are magically isolated, fairy-tale places, removed from the here and now of the outside world: it is no facile task to find Elrond's home, tucked in a hidden mountain valley, requiring the astute guidance of Gandalf;[175] the location of the Aeolian isle is geographically vague, and this 'nowhereness' is accentuated by its description as a 'floating isle'.[176] Both hosts boast a quasi-divine status. Thus, they have god-like powers over the natural world: Aeolus is the master of winds,[177] and Elrond has power over the waters which flow around Rivendell.[178] They also display a connection to the gods: Elrond through his being an immortal (half-)elf and thus having access to the Undying Lands; Aeolus through his ties with Zeus who rendered him 'king of the winds'.[179]

The quasi-divine status of these hosts, in combination with the nowhereness of their residences – their *ou-topian* removal from typical earthly realms and homes – means that the *xenoi* can enjoy a hypercivilized form of hospitality. The Greeks are given ideal hospitality for an entire month by Aeolus,[180] and presumably the fare and entertainment are rich since Aeolus' family enjoys 'countless dainties [...] and through the daytime the hall is rich with savoury smells and murmurous with the sound of music'.[181] Similarly idealized forms of hospitality are experienced by Bilbo in Elrond's home: '[h]is house was perfect, whether you like food, or sleep, or work, or storytelling, or singing, or just sitting and thinking best, or a pleasant mixture of them all';[182] like the Greeks, the travelling company enjoys this welcome reception for a lengthy time, 'fourteen days at least'.[183] The benevolence of these hosts is extended to their guest-gifts: Aeolus provides the Greeks with a bag filled with all the unfavourable winds to ensure that they return home to Ithaca promptly;[184] Elrond generously replenishes the dwarven supplies for their journey,[185] but he also offers something more valuable, 'the best advice'[186] for their planning of their journey home, and, accordingly, he helps decipher their magical rune map, explaining how the dwarves can enter their ancestral home through a hidden door. His Aeolian guest-gift is to assist the homecoming of his guests.

What is also noteworthy in both the Aeolian and Rivendell scenes is that both homes are marked out as distinctly temporary, ephemeral abodes; such hypercivilized hospitality is only available to the respective guests for a limited period of time. This is indicated by the short narrative time of the reception scenes: in the *Odyssey*, the actual hospitality scene in Aeolus' house lasts approximately fifteen lines;[187] in *The Hobbit*, the stay in Elrond's home last about five pages.[188] Such short narrative time is in marked contrast to the long story time in both stories (one month, two weeks), which nevertheless still feels quite insufficient to Bilbo.[189] Rivendell is, as the chapter title declares, 'A Short Rest' – it cannot be experienced as a lengthy, even permanent home for a guest, 'for ever and ever'.[190] Aeolus' isle is also 'a short rest', an ephemeral pit stop. When the Greeks return a second time, after they have foolishly opened the bag of winds and have been jettisoned back to the island, Odysseus expects the hospitality of Aeolus – but he is out of luck; Aeolus denies the continued blessing of his divine home from the hero: 'Away from this island, away at once, most despicable of creatures! I am forbidden to welcome here or to help send elsewhere a man whom the blessed gods abhor'.[191]

The brevity of these hypercivilized forms of hospitality is, in part, meant to reflect that all good guest-stays are necessarily limited in time – the converse would be the permanence of Ogygian hospitality where the *xenos* is no longer truly a guest by definition. The shortness of the respective stays is also, though, an indication that these two homes, of Aeolus and Elrond, are representative of a level of quasi-divine existence which transcends the normal experiences and sufferings of mortals. Odysseus' acceptance of the 'quick fix' of Aeolus' divine guest-gift, the bag of winds, represents a misguided attempt to circumvent the mortal experiences of the exiled *xenos* – the wanderings and the sufferings which are part of his *nostos* and, indeed, which make up his heroic identity as Odysseus, 'the man of pain'.[192] The perfective Aeolian reception of Elrond connotes, for Tolkien, a timeless, divine paradise-home beyond the limits of the mortal world. In *The Lord of the Rings*, Rivendell is a kind of senescent waiting room to heaven: when Bilbo gives up the One Ring to Frodo and experiences the rapid process of ageing which will lead to his death,[193] his decision is to stay at Rivendell until the end of the story, when he will be transported to Arda's closest approximation to 'heaven', the Edenic Undying Lands. In *The Hobbit*, Bilbo cannot stay for 'a long rest' in this quasi-divine paradise of Rivendell because he is still a mortal with experiences before him, and being a mortal in Tolkien's literary imagination means always being a kind of *xenos* – *anthrōpos xenoios*: '[b]ut the sons of Men die indeed, and leave the world [Arda]; wherefore they are called the Guests, or the Strangers'.[194] A mortal, for Tolkien, is a travelling guest who navigates between the stagnant idealism of utopia in the form of the temporary home – which is what Bilbo learns Bag End really is – and the dynamic idealism of the road and journeying, of new experiences and struggles.[195]

In the case of Tolkien's idealization of this *anthrōpos xenoios*, the influence of his own personal experiences and his love of the Catholic Church must be given emphasis. In a letter to his son Christopher, Tolkien fashions postlapsarian man, kicked out from Eden, as essentially an exile, a guest without an absolute home.[196] The good Christian remembers with nostalgia the paradise-home which God had given to man and realizes that the current state of affairs on earth is ephemeral; it is not a fixed home. The exiled guest, knowing that he can never reclaim Eden, or even the nostalgic homes of his past, views the present home always as transitory, at best a reflection of an ideal home-*topos*. Yet the closest manifestation of this ideal of true paradise-home is, for Tolkien, the Catholic Church, as Rivendell is in Middle-earth; the relationship between man and the Catholic Church is one of hospitality: for the exiled guest to come periodically to the place of worship, the proxy home of the Host, as a guest and to receive the Blessed Sacrament, a hospitality ritual which Tolkien, in several of his letters, highlights as essential to the Catholic faith.[197] Tolkien may also have appreciated the Christian sacredness of hospitality not only because of his fundamentally Edenic, Genesiac understanding of scripture[198] but also because of his own personal experiences. Tolkien's formative years were marked by a constant displacement, where what was considered the safe space of home was taken away from him: from 1892 to 1904, Tolkien had experienced at least nine different homes. Tolkien's love of the Catholic Church has been seen by biographer Humphrey Carpenter as an act of transference of love at the death of his mother;[199] equally, though, the young Ronald Tolkien's fondness for the faith might have been nourished by the kind hospitality of Father Frances Morgan, the Catholic priest who, under no obligation, provided a second home and upbringing for Tolkien and his brother. Tolkien twice praises this 'charity' of Father Morgan.[200]

To return to *The Hobbit*: after their departure from Elrond's home, the company of fifteen passes through the 'Front Porch' of the goblins and through the underground networks of these proto-industrialists. It is once again through the magic of Gandalf that the dwarves are freed from the goblins, who wish to enslave Thorin's company; and it is likewise through magic, a powerful ring with the ability to render its wearer invisible, that Bilbo escapes from the clutches of the hobbit-like creature Gollum. The company subsequently escapes from the Misty Mountains, is pursued by goblins and wolves towards the brink of destruction, and is rescued from a precipitous, fire-engulfing death by the timely advent of the eagles.

The next major hospitality scene occurs outside the home of Beorn, a shapeshifting bear-host who is 'not known for his hospitality'[201] – hence the chapter title 'Queer Lodgings'. In its physical appearance, Beorn's hall is suggestive of a generalized Germanic dwelling[202] and of a 'mead-hall' culture, with the associated hospitality rituals:[203] thus, the dwarven guests 'sat long at the table with their wooden drinking-bowls filled with mead'.[204] Beorn, characterized as a grim northerner, is also a mead-maker and a beekeeper.[205] In contrast to this Germanic libation and welcome, the offering of wine in a hospitality scene would carry both Catholic and classical connotations.[206] Wine is the staple drink in 'Roman' Gondor, and wine is what the host Faramir, as a man of the ancient world, offers to his guests, Frodo and Sam, in Hennuth

Anun.²⁰⁷ Northern, even Beowulfian the hospitality scene in Beorn's house may be,²⁰⁸ but there are some parallels to be drawn with the Scherian, Aeaean and Thrinacian sequences during Odysseus' wanderings.

Between the hypo-civilized trolls and the hypercivilized elves, Beorn is a more ambiguous host; he demonstrates both friendly or hospitable and hostile attitudes towards guests. Gandalf warns the dwarves and Bilbo: 'You must all be very polite when I introduce you. [...] [A]nd you *must* be careful not to annoy him, or heaven knows what will happen. He can be appalling when he is angry, though he is kind enough if humoured. Still I warn you he gets angry easily'.²⁰⁹ Beorn's hostile character is a direct feature of his arctanthropic nature, his essential wildness, in that he can transform into a bear and can tear his guests to pieces;²¹⁰ yet, the gruff man can also exhibit the friendly behaviour of a Germanic warrior-lord: hearty food, good mead, comfortable sleeping quarters in his wooden lodge and even guest-gifts in the form of beasts of burden which help the company on their voyage to Mirkwood, their next destination. This liminal display of hospitality, fluctuating between hearty friendliness and violent hostility, is reflected by his physical abilities to shapeshift, to cross boundaries and switch identities. The scene at Beorn's lodgings reveals the fragility and liminality of hospitality scenes in *The Hobbit*, which more often than not tread an ambiguous middle ground between Cyclopean hypo-civilization and Aeolian hyper-civilization, between hostility and hospitality, as is evident in the episodes in Mirkwood and Lake-town.

Such ambiguous guest-friendship is also apparent in the Homeric *Odyssey*.²¹¹ In Book 5, Odysseus arrives at Scheria, the land of the Phaeacians. Some critics, such as Rose, Most and Reece, have observed traces of inhospitality, particularly in the initial books of the Phaeacian sequence (*Odyssey* 5–8).²¹² Such tokens of inhospitality include both Nausicaa's and Athena's warnings to Odysseus of the xenophobic townspeople;²¹³ the elevated power which Arete holds as queen²¹⁴ and, consequently, her initial reluctance to welcome Odysseus openly;²¹⁵ Alcinous' violation of the proper etiquette of *xenia*;²¹⁶ the rudeness of the Phaeacian princes, Euryalus and Laodamas, during the athletic games;²¹⁷ possible delays by the Phaeacians in helping their *xenos* Odysseus return home;²¹⁸ and the threat of a marriage union between Odysseus and the king's daughter, Nausicaa, which could derail Odysseus' homecoming entirely.²¹⁹ Yet the Phaeacians have also been regarded as ideal hosts by many critics.²²⁰ In contrast to their apparent xenophobia, other parts of the Phaeacian sequence illustrate their famous history of transporting *xenoi* home;²²¹ and after years of wanderings, it is indeed the Phaeacians who ultimately expedite Odysseus' *nostos*,²²² which they achieve with remarkable ease.²²³

The problem of Phaeacian (in)hospitality is a complex, unresolved problem in Homeric studies, and it might point to textual incongruencies which arise from the amalgamation of different plots in the original oral composition of the poem.²²⁴ One interesting line of interpretation has tracked a progression in the Phaeacian narrative, from Book 5 to 13, from initial tokens of inhospitality to the gradual realization of exemplary hospitality by the hosts on Scheria.²²⁵ In such interpretations, Odysseus' role as a guest in mediating the ambiguous guest–host situation and in earning proper hospitality is often cited: he impresses the Phaeacians with his athletic feats,²²⁶ he placates Queen Arete's doubts²²⁷ and, most importantly, he tells a great story in his *Apologue* (*Odyssey* 9–12) – the so-called 'stranger's stratagem'.²²⁸ Glenn Most argues that the structure of the *Apologue* places certain episodes in symmetrical alignment with one another and so tends to give weight to the thematic similarities of these episodes; in particular, he says, the structure draws attention to the threat of a host delaying his guest for too long and to a host who turns his guest into food.²²⁹ The storytelling of the *Apologue*, depicting negative reversals of *xenia*, accordingly helps Odysseus as a guest to strategically moderate the ambiguity of his own reception among his hosts, the Phaeacians, and to ensure proper hospitality is granted. Odysseus' storytelling is ultimately so effective that it has a quite magical effect on his listening audience: when there is a pause in storytelling, the Phaeacian listeners seem entirely spellbound, rapt with silent *kēlēthmō* (enchantment).²³⁰

Intriguingly, there is a similar employment of the stranger's stratagem outside the home of Beorn, which moves the scene from initial signs of hostility to more benevolent forms of guest-friendship. Like Odysseus, Gandalf employs the enchanting device of storytelling in order to navigate a way through an ambiguous reception moment, where the xenophobic attitude of their host is immediately clear: "'Who are you and what do you want?" he [Beorn] asked gruffly, standing in front of them and towering tall above Gandalf."²³¹ The wizard, in reply, uses the art of storytelling to gradually entice the bear-man to admit more and more of the company into his lodgings. At first arriving only with the unthreatening Bilbo, Gandalf tells Beorn the exciting story of their wanderings over the Misty Mountains, with the number of the company in this internally narrated story slowly increasing: from a 'friend or two'[232] to 'a troop'[233] to the full 'fifteen'.[234] Beorn's potential inhospitality at receiving so many guests – dwarven guests, moreover, a race he dislikes – is alleviated by his Phaeacian fascination with Gandalf's storytelling; like King Alcinous, Beorn is spellbound by the tale, by the magical effect of the wizard's words, and he must hear the story to its end.

Gandalf's storytelling has the function not only of acquiring immediate entrance into Beorn's home but also of alerting the bear-man to negative reversals of hospitality, or to aggressive behaviour in general, which the company has received on their way to his home: 'we were attacked by the evil goblins [...] There was a terrible storm; the stone-giants were out hurling rocks, and at the head of the pass we took refuge in a cave, the hobbit and I and several of our companions'.[235] As in Odysseus' *Apologue*, Gandalf is using the stranger's stratagem, providing negative examples of improper reception, the unwelcoming cave of the goblins (like the one of Polyphemus), to persuade the host to display the proper forms of hospitality required in polite society and to resolve the potentially ambiguous reception situation. Gandalf's story works: Beorn provides the company with guest-gifts, ponies to ferry them along their journey home, just as the Phaeacians help ferry Odysseus home on their magical ship. Furthermore, the notion that a guest, in order to win a host's hospitality, has to give something, which in this case is nothing less than a great story – which also doubles as 'news of the world', a valuable 'host-gift' in a pre-modern system of information exchange[236] – is part and parcel of the system of reciprocity which underpins guest–host situations in both the *Odyssey* and *The Hobbit*.

The ambiguity of the Beorn sequence also mirrors another hospitality scene in Odysseus' *Apologue*: the Ithacans' stay in the home of Circe in Aeaea. Like Beorn, Circe is an ambiguous host.[237] She is at first unfriendly, imprisoning the trespassing Greeks[238] before Odysseus uses the suggested trickery of Hermes (a divine presence, again, for resolving an inhospitable situation) to subdue the witch and to ensure her exemplary guest-friendship:[239] the ample food and drink of her home, rest for an entire year (although also connoting a delay in the *nostos*), and guidance for the rest of Odysseus' voyage.[240] The natural quality of Circe's home also suggests comparison with Beorn's home: while the tough man can transform himself into animal form,[241] Circe employs her shapeshifting magic on others, transforming a dozen of the Greeks into pigs;[242] and while Beorn has tamed horses and other animals to act as his attendants,[243] Circe has tamed wolves and lions, which lie outside her home.[244] In these hospitality scenes, then, the ambiguity of the receptions also reveals an intersection of the human sphere, where hospitality is the norm, and the non-human sphere of nature,[245] the wild, where the potential danger of this alterity is realized through its removal from social customs such as hospitality.

In Tolkien's narrative, it is Gandalf who acts as a bridge between the companions and the (super-)natural world; in the Homeric epic, Odysseus is a necessary mediator between his men and the supernatural – their divine hosts, Aeolus, Circe and, indirectly, Helios. Thus, on Helios' island of Thrinacia, Odysseus warns his men, unsuccessfully, against slaying the sacred cattle of the sun god;[246] Gandalf, with a better result, cautions the dwarves against stealing Beorn's loaned ponies.[247] In both episodes transgressions against 'sacred' animals which are guarded over by supernatural hosts will quickly turn the guests into enemies of a host. Like Odysseus who has a connection to a divine sphere, with agents such as Circe and Teiresias,[248] the wizard moderates the inherent ambiguity of hospitality scenes, ensuring that the potential hostility of hosts is mitigated, and that guests do not step over the limits imposed upon them and turn into thieves. Through the ethical guidance of Gandalf, *The Hobbit* emphasizes the essential reciprocity of the hospitality ritual, the delicate balance required between the interests of host and guest.

After 'Queer Lodgings', the following (in)hospitality scene in *The Hobbit* occurs when the travellers, minus Gandalf, reach the elven cave-palace after journeying through the dangerous natural world of Mirkwood. This ambiguous scene of host-reception has some parallels, again, with the Aeaean sequence on Circe's island. In both narratives, the travellers have to move through forests to arrive at the homes of the hosts,[249] who are immortal (elves and a goddess). On the way through the woodland, both Thorin and Odysseus encounter a deer or stag and kill the animal.[250] Bilbo climbs a high tree to get a view of the surrounding forest;[251] Odysseus scouts out the wooded Aeaea from the vantage point of a hill.[252] Finally, the characters are tempted into approaching the immortal beings: in the case of the dwarves, they are lured by the feasting of a party of elves,[253] whereas Odysseus' men are attracted first by Circe's enchanting singing and are then compelled to stay through the food which she offers them.[254] Odysseus' men, transfigured into swine, are locked in a pig pen, while the dwarves are also, ultimately, imprisoned by the elven king.

Glenn Most points to two kinds of inhospitalities that are apparent in Odysseus' wanderings:[255] first, anthropophagy, the inversion of offering food to the guest by the host, in the cases of Polyphemus and the Laestrygonian king Antiphates; second, the threat of terminal delay of the guest in the host's home, of losing or forgetting about the *nostos*,[256] in the cases of Circe (one year)[257] and Calypso (seven years).[258] Equally, *The Hobbit* represents these two fears for travellers: anthropophagy in the cases of the trolls, Gollum and the spiders in Mirkwood; and terminal delay, most clearly in their Circean imprisonment in the cave home of the elven king. '[H]e ordered the dwarves each to be put in a separate cell and to be given food and drink, but not to be allowed to pass the doors of their little prisons, until one at least of them was willing to tell him all he wanted to know'.[259]

The cause for this inhospitality does not lie entirely on the shoulders of the elven host, however; in ambiguous cases of guest-hosting in *The Hobbit*, such as that of the Mirkwood elves,[260] Tolkien frequently shows a failure to partake in reciprocal relations on the part of the guests. One can compare the Mirkwood imprisonment scene[261] to the positively resolved hospitality scene with Beorn: in the latter, Gandalf was able to offer the 'gift' of storytelling, of news of the world, to Beorn; in the former case, without the magical mediating influence of Gandalf, or even his protégé Bilbo, the dwarves provide their elven host with no information to reciprocate his offers of hospitality, of room and board.[262] In benevolent hospitality scenes in the *Odyssey*, such as in the palace of Nestor,[263] the host's expectation of news of some kind, and thus information, is endemic to a positive hospitality scene.[264] To be clear, the dwarves do not reciprocate with information for the elven king because such information would pose a threat to their selfish desire to reclaim all of their lost gold in the Lonely Mountain for themselves;[265] the failure of the dwarves to observe the necessary reciprocity of guests in Mirkwood will, accordingly, later be reflected in their failures as selfish hosts of their reclaimed home, the Lonely Mountain, in the final part of the story.

Finally, in order to rescue their imprisoned companions from the unfriendly hosts, Odysseus and Bilbo are compelled to draw on supernatural aid. Hermes provides Odysseus with the means to defeat Circe, a precious plant called moly, which will render the hero immune to Circe's potion;[266] Bilbo can only enter the hidden realm of the woodland elves on account of his new magic ring, which becomes a supernatural surrogate in Gandalf's absence and thus a means of resolving an inhospitable situation.[267] Bilbo's actual solution to escape from the elven cave-palace is reminiscent of another moment of Odyssean subtlety: to escape Polyphemus' cave the Ithacans ride out into the open, tied to the bellies of the ogre's sheep; the dwarves ride out of the elven kingdom inside empty wine barrels.[268]

## Returning home

In Lake-town, Thorin publicly proclaims himself to be the exiled king of the dwarves, which, in combination with legends of his return, ensures his popularity and the calculated, economic hospitality of the Master of Lake-town, who provides the company with boats, beasts of burden and provisions for their expedition to the Lonely Mountain. Both the *Odyssey* and *The Hobbit* conclude with a return narrative which shares some broad parallels in plot. The kings (Odysseus; Thorin Oakenshield) aim to reclaim their homes which have been usurped by greedy supplanter-hosts who consume the wealth of the exiled hosts (the suitors; the dragon Smaug); the usurping hosts are subsequently shot and killed by arrows to seal the resolution of their inhospitalities.[269] This scene of vengeance and punishment, however, leads to civil unrest: in the *Odyssey*, the neighbouring families of the suitors take up arms against Odysseus in retaliation for the slaughter;[270] in *The Hobbit*, the men of Lake-town, whose settlement has been destroyed through the violent onset of the dragon, besiege the dwarven home and demand financial recompense for their losses.[271] In both stories, an imminent battle between neighbours is averted: in the Greek epic, it is Athena herself, the goddess, who declares the strife over,[272] prompted by Zeus' thunderbolt; in the children's story, it is Gandalf, again adopting a quasi-divine role with 'a voice like thunder',[273] who instructs the dwarves, men and elves to put aside their common difficulties to unite against a common foe – the army of goblins and wolves.[274] Peace is restored between neighbours.

Yet such broad plot parallels between the two stories overlook the many failures of the dwarves in the return narrative. To start with, as a dispossessed host, Thorin is no Odysseus; he has no clever, 'polymetic'[275] plan to get rid of the dragon-host and to reclaim his ancestral halls, apart from merely turning to Bilbo for help.[276] Fortunately, during his rite of passage, the hobbit has grown sufficiently to adopt the role of the wizard, using magic, both real and verbal, to oust Smaug: firstly, Bilbo uses his ring to become invisible and talk in the presence of the dragon; secondly, he employs riddles to try his luck at finding some weakness in his foe – which he does in noticing a bare patch in the worm's armour, a revelation which will lead to the dragon's destruction at the hands of Bard. After Bilbo has helped to get rid of the imposter host, Smaug, Thorin Oakenshield, as restored king and host of the Lonely Mountain, is reluctant to take the advice of the wise raven Roäc: '[w]e [i.e. the ravens] would see peace once more among dwarves and men and elves after the long desolation; but it may cost you dear in gold'.[277] Thorin's response is self-serving and xenophobic: to secure his home, to turn it into an impregnable fortress, to keep his riches safe, and to send word to other dwarves, residing in the Iron Hills, to come to their aid in preparation for war.[278]

Thorin's conception of hospitality is solipsistic: home for Thorin is a storage pit for his own wealth – not all that different, ironically, from the Lonely Mountain's previous greedy, unwelcoming landlord, Smaug.[279] While Bilbo has at this point of the story learned the value of reciprocity in ensuring amiable relations between hosts and guests – notably, he offers his own share in the treasure, the Arkenstone, to resolve tensions – Thorin treats Bard and the people of Lake-town as 'foes and thieves'[280] rather than as destitute refugees and needy guests. Thorin's behaviour represents a fundamental breach in reciprocity laws in the hospitality story: he stubbornly refuses to pay the price for their returned home, which only materialized courtesy of the actions of their guest, Bard, and he ignores the plight of the destitute, homeless guests, although the men of Lake-town had earlier hosted the dwarves. Thorin's hubristic rejection of these beggared guests can be compared to the confrontational response of the suitors to Odysseus, concealed in the raiment of a beggar. Both the dwarves and the suitors, in effect, have gained their homes through the destruction of others' property: the former through the destruction of Lake-town by unleashing the dragon; the latter by squatting in Odysseus' *oikos*. Yet both parties are immune to the needs of guests who would impose upon their unjustly gained wealth and resources, and these hosts even threaten violence – Thorin shoots an arrow as a warning shot to Bard's herald,[281] while Antinous, one of the suitors, throws a chair at the disguised Odysseus.[282]

Ultimately, it takes a battle against a common enemy and the death of their leader, Thorin, for the dwarves to change their attitudes. They atone for their earlier behaviour after the battle, paying shares of their treasure to their guests.[283] The real moral progression of the novel, however, comes through the unlikely hero, Bilbo Baggins. Upon his return from his many adventures, the hobbit's home is no longer a place of solitary comfort, into which a guest – so long as he is not troublesome – may be invited; to the contrary, it is open to travellers far and wide.[284] Such a reception is not welcomed by his xenophobic neighbours, for whom Bilbo has lost his respectability, but 'he did not mind'.[285]

In sum, reading *The Hobbit* in conjunction with the *Odyssey* helps to re-evaluate our understanding of Tolkien's children's story: not simply a heroic quest of dragon-slaying or treasure-finding, nor a geopolitical quest,[286] nor even a psychological quest into adulthood,[287] but an ethical quest, centred on the social, religious institution of the home and the relationship between hosts and guests. As a hospitality narrative, *The Hobbit* can be divided into three stages, each of which draws on different ethical paradigms of guest-friendship from the *Odyssey*. In the first stage, the inadequacies of Bilbo as a host are made evident: he reveals himself to Gandalf as an Ogygian host, who only cares for guests in as much as they can marry into his comfortable existence; at the same time, the hobbit is also an extremely naïve, Telemachian host, who loses control of his house in interactions with the suitor-like dwarven guests. In the second, 'educational' stage of the story, the *xenoi* endure various kinds of reception by hosts: a malevolent, parodic 'guest-welcome' at the hands of Cyclopean trolls; hypercivilized, divine hospitality from Aeolian Elrond; and ambiguous receptions in the house of Phaeacian Beorn and among the Circean wood elves. All these models of hospitality reveal different lessons in *xenia*: the malevolent inhospitality scenes illustrate through parodic inversion – eating guests and incarcerating them – the standard social protocol required in hospitality scenes, namely, the proper feeding of guests and speeding them on their way; the benevolent hospitality scenes are necessarily ephemeral, alluding to a state of affairs when man – *anthrōpos xenios* by nature – is no longer a guest-traveller but resides in the heavenly beyond, in Tolkien's Christian vision; the ambiguous hospitality scenes, most importantly, provide situations which point to the essential reciprocity needed in guest–host relationships, for example, the exchange of information or necessary supplies (for refugees). In the final stage of *The Hobbit*, the characters respond to this instruction as travelling *xenoi*, in that they ultimately provide ideal models of hospitality, particularly Bilbo Baggins, who becomes decidedly xenophilic.

Tolkien's reception of the *Odyssey* is reflected not only in his broadly structuring his tale towards a positive realization of *xenia* and exploring specific manifestations of good and bad guest–host behaviour (in other words, it is an ethical journey) but also in the religious background to hospitality scenes. Hospitality in the *Odyssey* is watched over by Zeus *xeinios*, as Odysseus makes clear in the Polyphemus episode.[288] Many problematic hospitality situations are resolved with the help of Olympian divinities: through direct intervention, Zeus, Athena and Hermes combine their authority to ensure that Odysseus is allowed to escape from the Ogygian prison of Calypso;[289] Athena, taking anthropomorphic form, acts as a suitable M/mentor to Telemachus in his struggles against the suitors;[290] Aeolus, a quasi-divine being himself, provides the travelling *xenoi* with ideal hospitality;[291] Hermes helps Odysseus overcome the initial inhospitalities of Circe by providing him with a series of tricks to match those of the witch;[292] Athena uses her divine craft to ensure that Odysseus is favourably received among the Phaeacians;[293] and the goddess is responsible, at the end of the epic, for the harmonious resolution of the strife between neighbours.[294] From an anthropological perspective, Bruce Louden has shown how the majority of guest–host situations in the *Odyssey* indicate traces, to varying degrees, of theoxenies – that is, scenes depicting a god arriving as a guest in disguise;[295] the potential for any guest to be a divinity is what, according to Louden, gives Homeric *xenia* its sacred quality.[296]

Tolkien's religious backgrounding of the hospitality ritual is just as marked, revealing a supernatural authority which mediates host–guest situations. Improper hospitality scenes are almost always resolved by an implementation of magic, mainly through its personification in the form of the wizard Gandalf, who is also a divine being, one of the *istari*, in Tolkien's legendarium. Gandalf tricks Bilbo into giving up his solipsistic attitude towards home; the wizard makes sure the dwarves are respectful enough of Bilbo as a host; the trolls are defeated by his verbal gymnastics; the wizard guides the company into the hidden safe haven of Elrond's Homely House; the goblins' enslavement of the dwarves in their underground caverns is halted by a burst of real magic from the wizard's staff; the haughty Beorn is made amenable to his guests through Gandalf's strategic storytelling; and, importantly, it is Gandalf himself who directs the attention of men, dwarves and elves away from their mutual destruction and towards a common foe.

The 'magic' which Gandalf employs can be real otherworldly magic, represented by the instrumental power of his staff, but also a kind of verbal magic – the power of words. In employing words as one of his magical tools, a means to win over or defeat hosts, Gandalf is not too different from the crafty, polymetic Odysseus, who employs verbal trickery to defeat Polyphemus[297] and whose entire speech in the *Apologue* is itself a form of verbal enchantment, an argumentative exercise to ensure the hospitality of the Phaeacians.[298] Bilbo Baggins learns from Gandalf in employing these two kinds of magic to overcome inimical receptions: for example, he uses the real magic of an invisibility ring as well as the power of words, in the form of riddles, to get the better of the usurper-host Smaug. The success of Bilbo Baggins in the latter half of the novel is predicated upon his education from the 'divine figure' of Gandalf, who has shown the hobbit how different kinds of magic can be employed to his success in mediating inhospitable situations. Similarly, Odysseus' ability as a polymetic hero, his skill in *mētis* (cunning, shrewdness) and *doloi* (tricks, stratagems),[299] connects him to the Greek goddess of wisdom and civilization; Athena later claims that the hero's prowess in tricks would even surpass that of a god,[300] not insignificant praise, considering that Athena herself is a goddess known for her many wiles.[301] It is Odysseus' capacity to excel in *dolos* which ensures so close a tie with his patron goddess.

## Conclusion: Xenophilic writing

It is worth pointing out that *xenoi* in the Homeric poems are usually defined as both guests and foreigners.[302] This characteristic of 'foreignness' is embedded in the very denotation of *xenos* in the Homeric poem,[303] whereas the English word 'guest' need not imply any foreign quality. Throughout Odyssean hospitality scenes, interactions are marked out by a distinction between not only a homeowner and his visitor but also a local person or population and a foreign person or traveller:[304] between Nestor the Pylian or Menelaus the Spartan and Telemachus the Ithacan; between the Phaeacians from Scheria and Odysseus from Ithaca; between Odysseus and the 'hosts' he encounters on his journeys through foreign lands; between Eumaeus the Ithacan and the disguised Odysseus as a pseudo-Cretan; even the majority of Penelope's suitors, Telemachus' irreverent guests, come not from Ithaca but from the neighbouring islands.[305]

Likewise, Tolkien's form of eu-topianism in *The Hobbit*, directed towards the *topos* of the home, leads to a broader ideal of *xenophilia*: love not only thine guest-neighbour but thine complete foreigner. This Homeric sense of *xenos* as foreigner-guest is shared by Tolkien's Bilbo Baggins. But beyond his children's work, the tension between xenophobia and xenophilia is also evident across Tolkien's other writings: between characters who have a tendency towards stagnancy, provincialism and a suspicion of foreigners and characters who display a love of travel, diversity, fellowship (which means for Tolkien friendship across cultural barriers), intercultural experiences and, simply, the symbolic value of the road. Like *The Hobbit*, Tolkien's other masterwork, *The Lord of the Rings*, displays a movement from initial forms of xenophobia and cultural insularism towards xenophilia.

At the start of the epic fantasy, the hobbits as a collective community are generally distrustful of outsiders and the world beyond; such provincialism is articulated often by the traditional, pastoral, 'cabbages and potatoes'[306] wisdom of Sam's father, Gaffer Gamgee. The hobbits are an insular community. An outsider such as Gandalf is generally treated with suspicion by locals (apart from his fireworks); Frodo and Bilbo, regarded as travellers and elf-friends, are 'both cracked';[307] and even an entire hobbit community such as Buckland is regarded as 'queer' by other hobbits because of its liminal position, because it lies on the eastern frontier of the Shire.[308] The events of *The Lord of the Rings* show such a cultural insularity to be an inherent weakness in a pre-modern world which is undergoing geopolitical expansion, which is modernizing – transitioning from the Third Age to the Fourth Age, entailing the dominion of men. Because of their pervasive xenophobia, hobbits (along with the equally provincial Bree-landers) are unable to distinguish between entirely benevolent *xenoi* such as Gandalf or Aragorn(also known as Strider) and malevolent *xenoi* such as Saruman's ruffians. As Sam first observes in the Mirror of Galadriel[309] and as the hobbits later realize when they return to 'the Scouring of the Shire',[310] the insularity of the hobbit community has left it vulnerable to the depredations of the corrupted wizard Saruman, whose industrializing objectives threaten to destroy this pastoral landscape and the rural lifestyle of the inhabitants.

The turning point from a xenophobic to a xenophilic community occurs with the return of the four hobbit heroes at the end of *The Lord of the Rings*. While the heroes still maintain their essential hobbit identity, they have also integrated into other cultures, wearing 'strange gear':[311] Merry has become a rider of Rohan, and Pippin a soldier of Gondor. They are notably characterized as 'travellers',[312] returning to the Shire on ponies, laden with travel gear and finds from their journeys. Their foreign experiences as *xenoi* ensure that these four hobbits, in particular Merry and Pippin, who have been in the wars, appear as commanding adults compared to the child-like inhabitants of the Shire, and that they can easily overthrow Saruman's ruffians and restore peace to the Shire: '[t]he ruffians gave back. Scaring Bree-land peasants, and bullying bewildered hobbits, had been their work. Fearless hobbits with bright swords and grim faces were a great surprise.'[313] But the new peace in the Shire will be different to that which reigned before, exemplified by the new leadership of Merry and Pippin, styled as travellers – 'riding by with their mail-shirts so bright and their shields so splendid, laughing and singing songs of far away'[314] – and whose connection to the lands beyond is realized through their choice of Gondor as their final resting place.[315] Under this 'merry' leadership, the hobbit community, taking its place in a wider 'community of nations', has become xenophilic: the Shire has become a protectorate of Gondor.

Tolkien's sense of xenophilia throughout his writings would certainly have been inherited from a wide array of cultural influences (Germanic, medieval and Christian texts), personal experiences and beliefs (Catholicism and his own sense of exile), and political ideals (his opposition to the homogenizing effects of globalization and the integration of mass, Anglo-American culture);[316] however, judging by the Odyssean template of hospitality in *The Hobbit*, a classical, specifically ancient Greek influence is not to be discounted. In his essay 'English and Welsh', Tolkien even regarded his formative encounter with the Greek language as an exciting encounter with the foreign: 'part of the attraction [of learning Greek] was antiquity and alien remoteness (from me): it did not touch home'.[317] Greek is the realm for the linguistic *xenos*.

Throughout the twentieth century, xenophilic writing, whether in literature or in philosophy, has drawn heavily on paradigms from ancient Greece: thus, in modernist fiction, James Joyce's *Ulysses* (1922), like Tolkien's children's story, uses the Homeric *Odyssey* as a framework for appreciating various hospitality scenes in Stephen Daedalus' Dublin; in semi-autobiographic travel writings, such as Henry Miller's *The Colossus of Maroussi* (1941) and Lawrence Durrell's *The Greek Islands* (1978),[318] modern Greece, as a landscape of memory, has become idealized to the Anglocentric reading public as the land of hospitality for the wandering *xenos*; and perhaps the most influential philosophical work on the topic of hospitality and xenophilia in the past half century has been Jacques Derrida's *Of Hospitality* (1998),[319] which repeatedly draws on ancient Greek exempla to illustrate his discussion.

How does Tolkien measure up within this modern, Greek-inspired, twentieth-century tradition of xenophilic writings? How do the questions and problems which Tolkien raises on hospitality intersect with those of other modernist and postmodernist thinkers and writers? This is certainly a question for further research; in the tradition of comparative literature studies, however, some preliminary remarks might be made on Tolkien's 'philosophy of xenophilia' by juxtaposing his thought with that of Derrida, who introduces a number of hospitality dilemmas of modernity, while at the same time looking back retrospectively at ancient Greece. In *Of Hospitality*, the French philosopher immediately draws on ancient Greek thought, particularly the dialogues of Plato and the tragedies of Sophocles,[320] to introduce some central paradoxes presented by the 'foreigner question'.[321] Through scrutiny of selected passages, Derrida provides us with a host of dilemmas which the hospitality situation introduces, including, but not limited to, problems of integration,[322] of conditionality[323] and of politicization of private space.[324]

Drawing on the interlocutor Socrates' simile of feeling 'like a foreigner or *xenos*' in the confusing, alien home of the law courts, which is presented in Plato's *The Apology of Socrates*,[325] Derrida brings up the problem of integration as a paradox which challenges the very existence of the *xenos*, threatening to 'hostify' the guest.[326] The necessity to understand language, according to Derrida, already implies that a degree of integration is required from the outset. This process of hostifying goes beyond mere language: it involves integration into a given culture's legal system as well as 'its limits, norms, policing, etc.'[327] To paraphrase Derrida, hospitality, by definition, assumes a relationship between a 'host' and a 'guest'; yet when the host assimilates the guest, forcing this individual into changing such that he or she would be more compliant with the host's culture – including language, customs, legal structures, mores – he or she then ceases to be a *xenos* or 'foreigner' (the hospitality paradox).[328] The essential 'otherness' of the *xenos*, the foreigner-guest, is being eroded; he or she is forced to 'hostify'.

At the start of Tolkien's children's story, Bilbo Baggins clearly demonstrates such a host's desire for integration by never enquiring of his guest's particular needs during the entirety of their interaction; any problematic demands the guest may have are deliberately passed over, and his visitor, Gandalf, is encouraged to become a nameless 'second' host: the mirror image of Bilbo, standing at the front porch and smoking a pipe. From this perspective, one can observe the shrewdness of Gandalf's deconstruction of the host's 'Good morning',[329] wherein the hobbit's address is shown to involve a prescriptive element: Bilbo's guests better not have a bad morning – not if they expect to be welcomed in his home. Bilbo's movement away from such a monocultural model of the host is reflected at the end of the story by his being shunned by his more xenophobic or provincial hobbit neighbours, who cannot understand the porousness of his threshold for different foreigners: he 'had the honour of dwarves, wizards, and all such folk as ever passed that way; but he was no longer quite respectable'.[330] At the start of *The Lord of the Rings*, Bilbo is generally regarded as 'queer' in his manners – he has become 'an other' – which makes him less acceptable to the social norms of the Shire community.

Tolkien's Bilbo represents a positive movement away from the xenophobic tendencies of integration and towards an identity defined by a readiness to engage with the foreign, with the strange other. It is doubtful, though, whether Tolkien's idealization of xenophilia, the embracing of the foreign, in *The Hobbit* reaches what Jacques Derrida terms 'absolute', 'just' or 'unconditional hospitality'.[331] According to the French philosopher, the Greeks generally distinguished between the class of *xenos* (the accepted foreigner) and the absolute other or *barbaros*. To the first of these hospitality was given, based on the recognition that it implied a network of mutual interests, such as political and legal rights, a reciprocity which was extended beyond the individual to a broader relationship between families, dynasties and larger communities; for the second category of absolute foreigner or barbarian, no hospitality was possible.[332] In his postmodern attitude to deconstructing power structures, Derrida, moving beyond the gift economy of the ancient world, and even beyond Immanuel Kant's essentially conditional sense of cosmopolitan hospitality,[333] seems to nurture the ideals of an 'absolute hospitality': 'that I open up my home and that I give [...] to the absolute, unknown, anonymous other, [...] without asking of them either reciprocity (entering into a pact) or even their names'.[334]

In contrast, in Tolkien's texts, reciprocity or mutual exchange is very much the virtue which solidifies the relationship of conditional hospitality, between host and guest, locals and foreigners throughout his stories. This is evident throughout the various travels of the dwarven company, where Gandalf acts as a mediatory figure between the two parties: for example, in the house of Beorn, the wizard ensures that the guests get what they want (room, board, helpful gifts) and that the host gets what he wants (information, polite guests, a short stay). Even Bilbo Baggins and his dwarven compatriots, old chums by the end of their adventures, must observe the formalities of reciprocity at the end of their journey: the polite exchange of corresponding offers of food. Thus, Balin offers Bilbo the hospitality of their home if he chooses to visit the dwarves again,[335] and to this offer Bilbo naturally reciprocates: 'If ever you are passing my way [...] don't wait to knock! Tea is at four; but any of you are welcome at any time.'[336]

The limiting, adversative phrase 'but any of you' implies that there are, conversely, some individuals who are not welcome at Bag End. Such unwelcome individuals are generally those who pose a risk to the economy of reciprocity: most obviously, in *The Lord of the Rings*, agents of evil, such as Ringwraiths and the ruffians of Saruman, but also simple hobbits, who find themselves incurring the sarcastic rebukes of the owner of Bag End for their failure to observe reciprocity or, conversely, for their indulging in 'a spot of absolute hospitality'. In *The Fellowship of the Ring*, after Bilbo has handed over the keys of Bag End to Frodo, having made up his mind to give up his ring and travel to Rivendell, he leaves behind an assortment of labelled gifts for past visitors of his home.[337] These labels contain Bilbo's caustic wit for those past guests who had indulged a little too much in Bilbo's hospitality, who had forgone the polite limits of conditionality and reciprocity.[338] In a sense, through his sarcastic words, Bilbo is trying to stabilize the necessary reciprocity of the hospitality situation through social shame, in place of unlikely material returns.

There are several reasons why Tolkien endorses a conditional, reciprocal model of hospitality rather than Derrida's absolute hospitality. Firstly, this conditionality is simply a generic convention of hospitality writing in literature, which requires some kind of conflict in the case of the home, between friendliness and treachery;[339] the idealizations of a philosophical tract, such as Derrida's, can be broached in literature but never represented completely. Secondly, this conditionality arises because Tolkien is not a postmodernist in the Derrida mould, with a tendency to sceptically relativize all relations with respect to positions of power. Tolkien's ethical worldbuilding is not limited to the ideal of hospitality, which for Derrida is an ethical absolute, and shows a clear Christian belief in the categories of good and evil (whether the evil be Augustinian or Manichaean).[340] In short, in Tolkien's world, there are simply agents one would not open one's door to, or through whose doors one would not pass, because to do so would be to invite certain destruction. Destruction for Tolkien is the principle of evil which opposes, in a Taoist-like balance, divine creativity as the principle of good; in Derrida's postmodernist ethical framework, which is divorced from notions of absolute good and evil, such destruction is possible but never certain. Reciprocity, in Tolkien's hospitality scenes, is simply the most significant way in which characters demonstrate their ethical allegiance to the universal good – that they will not try to destroy the other.

Lastly, comparative readings of Tolkien's xenophilic writings with Derrida's treatise also bring up the distinctly modern problem of the state's control over the private space of the home and thus of the hospitality ritual, which is realized, for example, by expanding technologies: 'shared technology makes it impossible for the two spaces [private and state] and the two types of structure to be mutually impermeable.'[341] In Tolkien's *The Lord of the Rings*, the potential for modernization – new technologies, new systems of control – to alter the nature of hobbit hospitality is represented in the penultimate chapter 'The Scouring of the Shire'. Saruman, under the new persona of 'Sharkey', has closed down all the local pubs and inns, which made up the traditional, local 'hospitality industry'; he has stockpiled huge resources of food and drink to the detriment of all other inhabitants of the Shire, who thus no longer have the means to act as private hosts; and he has therefore prevented the four hobbit *xenoi* from receiving their anticipated warm welcome at home.[342] Saruman has also instituted a secret police to monitor the movements of all individuals and to maintain curfews on individuals homes.[343] Lastly, in some cases, he has even possessed individual homes, such as Lotho Baggins' at Bag End, turning a once host into a hostage in his own home.[344] Saruman has essentially politicized hospitality into an oppressive state-controlled enterprise, turning the ritual into a state organ by centralizing the power of host responsibilities at the revamped Bag End and by denying others the legal rights and economic possibility to entertain guests.

In a sense, Tolkien's turn to the ancient world, whether Greek, Christian or Germanic, for providing a paradigm for guest-friendship in *The Hobbit* and *The Lord of the Rings* represents a generally anti-modern desire for the individual to reclaim an autonomy over a home space, and thus the right to express xenophilia, which is rapidly disintegrating in the technocratic modern world, where systems of control endorse and confirm state-based hospitality.[345] Tolkien does provide more benevolent examples of state-based hospitality, in the form of the 'northern commonwealth of nations' evident at the end of *The Hobbit*[346] and the commonwealth of Gondor, Rohan and the Shire (Eriador) at the end of *The Lord of the Rings*;[347] yet, these are generally characterized as permitting the free movement of individuals, 'comings and goings',[348] in contrast to the 'Scoured Shire' of Saruman, which reveals how new technologies and systems of control can entirely eradicate hospitality as an individual ritual. Importantly, this danger, for Tolkien, is not simply a threat to his sense of classical liberalism and individualism, which are well documented features in his literary thought, but also to the religious background of the hospitality ritual. For Tolkien, man is a kind of *anthrōpos xenios*, always an exiled guest from the original paradisical home of God; the ritual of guest-friendship in the individual home thus becomes a subtle religious observance. At the end of *The Lord of the Rings*, Saruman's absolute centralization and concretization of state hospitality represents a move to transfer authority for hospitality from what is essentially the divine onto the shoulders of the state.

# 3

# Sublime Narratives: Classical Transcendence in Nature and beyond in *The Fellowship of the Ring*

## Introduction: Understanding the natural world in *The Lord of the Rings*

*The Lord of the Rings* is a work which is fascinated with exploring the natural world.[1] The sheer breadth of the different ecosystems (pastoral lands, forests, mountainous terrain, flatlands, deserts, the sea, riverscape, the underground) and the descriptive depth of individual intrusions into each respective part of Middle-earth (Tolkien's 'Niggle-like' focus on tree and leaf) have yielded a vast amount of scholarship which has addressed the importance of the natural world in *The Lord of the Rings*, and in Tolkien's broader oeuvre, and the possible meanings behind the pervasive representations of nature in Tolkien's Middle-earth. At the risk of essentializing numerous studies into tendentious categories, this introduction identifies four distinct scholarly approaches to understanding the natural world in Tolkien's epic: environmental or ecocritical readings, symbolic interpretations, theological readings and primary-belief readings.[2] Subsequently a fifth, literary-based approach for understanding the role of nature in *The Fellowship of the Ring* is suggested, which interprets nature as sublime or transcendent. Such a natural sublime draws on a rich literary history in modern, romantic, Christian and, importantly, classical texts; ancient literature provided Tolkien with some powerful motifs and ideas through which his own natural sublime was expressed, most memorably in his Ovidian, Orphic Old Forest. The connection between the experience of the sublime and the ancient world is cemented in the concluding section of this chapter, in which characters are shown to have transformative encounters not only in nature but also among 'classical' ruins in Middle-earth.

The anthropocentric sense of the human domain having an effect on or, more broadly, a relationship with the natural world is behind a large, growing amount of ecocritical scholarship[3] dealing with representations of the environment in Tolkien's works.[4] Ecocritics such as Campbell tend to foreground their analyses of *The Lord of the Rings* through biographic exposition on the life and dendrophilic thoughts of Tolkien.[5] Humphrey Carpenter's biography is the most influential text in this regard,[6] providing a romantic undertone to Tolkien's short-lived stay (1896–1900) in the rural hamlet of Sarehole, a lush-green isolated paradise,[7] which provided the young brothers Ronald (J.R.R.) and Hilary Tolkien with plenty of adventures and misdemeanours,[8] and which also had a 'deep and permanent [effect on J.R.R. Tolkien]. Just at the age when his imagination was opening out, he found himself in the English countryside'.[9] Tolkien's subsequent removal from this pastoral bliss marked his return to the dreary urban landscape of Birmingham,[10] a transition of place which is realized in emotional terms: 'Ronald was [...] desperately forlorn at being severed from the Sarehole countryside'.[11]

This personal, emotional transition from a natural environment to the urban is often contextualized by Tolkien scholars in terms of broader processes of industrialization and environmental destruction occurring at the time in England, more specifically, in the West Midlands.[12] Curry views Tolkien's environmentalism as a reaction to a 'war on life',[13] placing the usurpation of the natural world by urban settlements in a broader global context, involving biodiversity reduction, deforestation, wetland desiccation, sea pollution and species extinction.[14] Tolkien seems to have been quite conscious and critical of such environmental destruction occurring on a mass industrial scale; in a letter to the *Daily Telegraph*, the English writer wrote in emotional tones of 'the destruction, torture and murder of trees', 'the savage sound of the electric saw'.[15] Against such reckless destruction, Tolkien frequently styled himself a friend of the natural world, confessing a love, in one interview, for 'good water, stones and elm trees and small, quiet rivers and so on and of course rustic people';[16] and dendrophilia is certainly well attested in his published correspondences: 'in all my works I take the part of trees as against all their enemies'.[17] Given such flora-friendly sentiments,[18] his idyllic, rural upbringing and his antipathy to a 'machine-driven' modernity,[19] several scholars have unsurprisingly analyzed Tolkien's works, *The Lord of the Rings* in particular, as an environmental, anti-industrial epic and Tolkien as a 'visionary environmentalist'.[20]

There are strong textual indications for regarding *The Lord of the Rings* as an environmental epic, concerned with negative and positive interactions between the human and natural worlds;[21] in Manichaean terms, deforestation and desertification are perpetrated by the forces of evil, and environmental resistance-fighting and integration are exhibited by 'the good guys'. Curry notes how *The Lord of the Rings* represents a 'war on trees' in Middle-earth.[22] Thus, the anthropomorphic tree-being Treebeard mourns the shrinking territory of his once-great Fangorn Forest, 'from here to the Mountains of Lune',[23] and fears 'the withering of all woods';[24] the wrath of this oldest ent is directed most at orcs, who are 'felling trees – good trees',[25] and at the powerful wizard Saruman, who is behind the deforestation of Fangorn.[26] Consequently, the destruction of Saruman's Isengard at the hands of the ents and the annihilation of the Isengard soldiers, the Uruk-hai, by mysterious moving trees called huorns, could represent an environmentally positivist narrative of nature fighting back.[27] Tolkien's eco-conscious text also provides some apocalyptic visions of deforested lands which become 'desolate places',[28] devoid of green leaf, clean water and, ultimately, life[29] – places marked by significant appellations such as the Brown Lands, the Dead Marshes, and Mordor, which is 'ruinous and dead, a desert burned and choked'.[30] In 'The Scouring of the Shire', Saruman, as recently installed overlord of the Shire, starts to chop down trees indiscriminately in the pastoral greenscape, on a mission to Mordor-fy the land[31] or to turn it into 'an industrial state [which is ...] understood as abhorrent and unacceptable'.[32] Saruman is defeated by the hobbits, and his destructive deeds are undone by the gardener Samwise Gamgee, who manages to reforest the Shire.[33] As the 'green heroes' of this environmental epic, the hobbits assimilate with their environment:[34] they share many characteristics with it, becoming people of the soil, and their agrarian landscape informs their ethnic characteristics, economic activities, lifestyle, nomenclature, forms of heroism and even their disposition.[35] Such assimilation or integration of positive protagonists with their environment is reflected by other benevolent individuals in the epic, such as Goldberry, Tom Bombadil and Treebeard, as well as by ethnic groups, such as the elves as forest-people and the dwarves as mountain people.[36]

Ecocritical readings of Tolkien's writing are, however, complicated by a number of issues: their uneasy placement in the modern genre of environmentalist writings; the differences between Tolkien's writings and their later cultural receptions; and the complicated representations of nature in *The Lord of the Rings* itself. Firstly, Tolkien scholars have urged caution in terming both the author and his works 'environmentalist' in the contemporary sense of 'radical greens'.[37] Problems in aligning *The Lord of the Rings* with this genre include the lack of clear claims for direct political or social 'policy' change in Tolkien's writings[38] and his Christian understanding of the role of men as stewards of nature.[39] Secondly, one should also reflect on the differences between the original stories and their cultural receptions, appropriations and often simplifications, whether by the hippy, anti-establishment, youth-activist movements of the 1960s and 1970s;[40] by visual depictions of a dendrophilic Tolkien in mass media;[41] by Peter Jackson's filmic adaptations of the novels;[42] or by scholars themselves.[43] Thirdly, Tolkien's text itself poses some conundrums for positivist interpretations; his environmental vision is 'complicated, contradictory, and deserves more careful scrutiny'.[44] Particularly problematic is the depiction of the Old Forest and the 'evil'[45] tree Old Man Willow in *The Fellowship of the Ring*, intending to hurt, kill and totally destroy the four hobbits who must journey through this terrain.[46] The Old Forest, along with Mirkwood, its precursor in *The Hobbit*, is in some senses the 'standard fairy-tale dark wood on the order of those in "Snow White" and "Hansel and Gretel"'.[47]

Contradictions in Tolkien's eco-vision may also have arisen simply because the natural world serves other equally important, non-environmental functions in *The Lord of the Rings*, such as its symbolic or connotative function. Michael Brisbois refers to this as 'imaginary nature' in Middle-earth, which 'allows us to perceive the hidden meanings behind the natural images and events of the novel'.[48] Plants and trees, for example, 'bear a rich symbolism in his [Tolkien's] fiction',[49] which might well draw on a deep heritage of intercultural meaning across a broader Indo-European context.[50] On a comparative reading of arboreal symbolism, Reckford notes how Virgil and Tolkien share fundamental themes such as 'change, loss, sadness, uncertainty, and suffering',[51] which are articulated 'poetically, in the way they look at trees'.[52] Such symbolism is often highly specific:[53] for example, birch trees are 'associated with beauty and sanctity'[54] and beech trees 'with innocence and healing'.[55] Outside of internal systems of signification in his worldbuilding, Tolkien also used arboreal metaphors to reflect metapoetically on his creative process;[56] thus, a frequent Tolkienian metaphor revolves around leaves and leaf-moulds.[57]

Mountains are a frequent obstacle over which (Caradhras), under which (Moria), and alongside which (the White Mountains) characters have to navigate. While specific mountains may have specific connotations in the story,[58] from a general perspective mountains become culturally imbued with 'Palaeolithic' notions of the dangerously primitive or primordial.[59] The Fellowship, for instance, encounters the looming menace of the ancient mountain peak called Caradhras, an older evil than Sauron perhaps, which threatens to destroy the company through the sudden onset of a blizzard.[60] Caradhras's status as a dangerous, primitive nature entity is further realized through his 'throwing' rocks at the Fellowship;[61] this motif is more clearly anthropomorphized in *The Hobbit*, where Bilbo sees the stone-giants launching rocks at each other.[62] This image of giants recklessly casting stones in the mountains seems to recall a trope common to classical mythology: that of Polyphemus, the Laestrygonians, and Otus and Ephialtes[63] – all representative of primitive, pre-Olympian forms of behaviour.[64]

In this brief tour of different scholarly interpretations of the natural world in *The Lord of the Rings*, the apparent Christian or Catholic character of Tolkien's lands, which is implicated in the very cosmogony of Arda in the 'Ainulindalë' and 'Valaquenta', cannot be neglected.[65] According to Birzer, Tolkien 'thought that the natural world was a gift from God and that man was obligated to act as its steward'.[66] Birzer quotes a passage from one of Tolkien's last pieces of unpublished writing, 'The New Shadow', in which two characters debate ethical notions of how humans should use, or exploit, the natural world, thus underlining the Christian view of man's inheritance of nature from divine creation and his necessary stewardship, his caretaking of nature.[67] In this view of this passage, nature is not an ethical good in itself but rather an objective product of divine creation for the benefit of man which should be used by men in moderation and with divine reverence.[68]

There are many examples in Tolkien's writings of benevolent stewards who tend and cultivate nature, such as Samwise Gamgee in the Shire, Treebeard in Fangorn and Faramir in Ithilien; gardening is almost an act of faith for them. Sam is a heroic gardener, one who briefly puts down his spade to take up the sword; his triumph at the end of *The Lord of the Rings* is the replanting of the Shire, which he manages through the quasi-divine, elvish assistance of Galadriel, also a gardener, of the ordered elvish paradise of Lothlórien.[69] The seed of the mallorn tree that Galadriel gives him links Sam's stewardship of the Shire, as mayor-gardener at the end of the story, to her stewardship of Lothlórien and, ultimately, to the trees of Tol Eressëa near Valinor, an elven 'Garden of Eden' in the far west.[70] In Valinor itself, the two great trees Telperion and Laurelin were established by the Vala Yavanna, a Demeter-like figure, and reflect the original light of creation,[71] thus explicitly linking holy, revered nature (trees) with the divine.[72] In opposition to such good 'Christian' stewards, the orcs can only destroy nature – never tending or cultivating anything which grows; Tolkien's orcs are perversions of divine creation, ruinations of the original elves by the Satanic Melkor. The orcs destroy nature not because they hate nature *itself* but because this attack represents a Melkorian-Sauronian war on divine creation.[73]

A fourth scholarly approach to understanding the natural world in *The Lord of the Rings* may broadly be termed 'primary-belief' readings: such analyses shirk the symbolic quality of Tolkien's representations of nature and, instead, highlight the apparent naturalism (the close attention to detail, the individual differences) and realism (the scientific functioning, the workings) of, for example, flowers, trees, mountains and cosmic bodies.[74] 'Real nature' in Middle-earth, and in the wider world of Arda, can be observed in several respects:[75] objects such as trees are described in fine, naturalistic detail, 'graphic intensity',[76] with regard to, for example, 'colors, textures, shapes, and seasonal variations';[77] familiar, real-world natural phenomena such as seasonal changes, the lunar phases,[78] geological processes,[79] and material objects function in a scientifically realistic way in Middle-earth;[80] Tolkien furnishes his spatial world with an onomastic depth, a quantity and etymological intricacy of place names as rich as that of our own world; and real-world environmental problems such as deforestation can be detected in Middle-earth. Tolkien's interest in allowing nature to speak for itself and to exist in its own terms, which is now a feature of contemporary post-humanist narratives of the natural world,[81] rather than treating nature as subordinately representational to human culture, is such that he even 'ontologizes' trees in *The Lord of the Rings*,[82] creating a 'nonhuman consciousness',[83] a species of tree-like beings called ents, who not only walk and talk but also have their own histories, language and beliefs.

On the basis of past scholarship, *The Lord of the Rings* can be read as an environmental treatise which explores retrospective visions of conservationism and preservationism, an essentially (anti-)modernist text reacting against processes such as industrialization, natural catastrophe and the growing autonomy of the technocratic Anthropocene; as a scientifically realistic and naturalistic text, the highly descriptive epic allows for a hermetic immersion into the natural world through its linguistic and taxonomical depth, which can, subsequently, help the reader escape into a post-humanist view of the natural world, allowing nature to 'speak for itself', although, conversely, nature in the story does seem to be trapped by human systems of symbolization, such that objects of the environment can connote abstract ideas of primitivity, beauty and so on; and as a Christian text, the epic embeds the natural world within a greater ethical landscape which promotes benevolent, moderated attitudes to nature through ideals of stewardship and which fashions reverence to the natural world as, foundationally, divine reverence.

To these functions of the natural world in Tolkien's epic, this chapter adds a fifth: the transformative, transcendental *sublime* narrative experiences which intradiegetic characters – and extradiegetic readers[84] – are afforded when entering into and existing within certain natural places. There has been a rich literary (representational) and philosophical (critical) tradition of exploring the sublime as a phenomenological experience in texts,[85] whether the classical sublime in the ancient world, as famously theorized by Longinus;[86] the Christian sublime in late classical and medieval texts;[87] the various sublimes speculated by John Dennis, Joseph Addison, Edmund Burke and Immanuel Kant in the early modern period;[88] or the romantic sublime in the British poetry of Wordsworth, Byron and company.[89] Some words of caution are necessary here before proceeding further. As James Porter has recently observed in his ground-breaking work of scholarship, and of critical thinking, the 'sublime' is no facile term to define, being heavily loaded with different philosophical, cultural and historical implications,[90] and one should be cautious of providing a generic, one-size-fits-all definition.[91] As a phenomenon, it seems to be composed of different parts: a sublime object or space as a trigger, sublime emotions or affects such as 'shock, awe, and terror',[92] and sublime transcendence.[93] Thus, the sublime can be found in different objects or spaces, whether in the mountains, lakes and forests of the natural world, in 'great art', such as the written form of poetry itself, or in the archaeological ruins of the past. The sublime can stimulate an array of different emotions, depending on the individual, varying between the positive and negative sublime, productive and destructive experiences.[94] And the sublime may, or may not, have different 'outputs' on the experiencer, whether material or immaterial, under which one might understand moral,[95] spiritual or metaphysical realizations.[96]

J.R.R. Tolkien's *The Fellowship of the Ring* is an integral part of this long narrative tradition in Western literary texts of representing the sublime, particularly in the dense forests of the natural world (here called the 'sylvan sublime') but also beyond this sphere (as the conclusion explores). In Tolkien's narratives of the sylvan sublime, transcendental, transformative awakening experiences are provided to the individual subject; these experiences help move the subject beyond his or her immediate, familiar, mundane, essentially 'known' world towards an understanding of some abstract idea[97] or even towards experiencing the supra-human divine in itself (the immaterial sublime), as well as, somewhat tautologically, towards a greater understanding of the splendour of the material world itself in all its infinitude, profusion and fecundity (the material sublime).[98] As with the general directionality of Tolkien's literary utopianism towards building a reimagined past (despite signs of ou-topian novelty), this chapter explores how Tolkien's sublime narratives are often retrotopian: they receive and rewrite similar sublime narrative encounters in pre-modern, ancient texts. Thus, Tolkien's immaterial sublime in his sylvan narratives receives and rewrites an ancient ideal of Orphism, although embedding it essentially in Christian thought, while the material sublime receives Ovidian notions of the dangerous profusion and diversity of the material world. By reading *The Fellowship of the Ring* alongside selected classical writings, the 'utopian' or perfective aspect of the natural world in the English writer's works can be viewed from a different perspective: not as an objectively demarcated environmental or ecological paradise, an ecotopia, but as a subjective paradise. Nature becomes 'utopian' – sublime – because of the transformative experience it can offer to the individual subject; conversely, this transcendent quality of nature is also partnered by a dangerous, dark, potentially fatal aspect of the human experience of the natural environment.[99]

This focus on the classical world does not imply that Tolkien's sublime narratives were not informed by his other inherited literary traditions (in medieval, Christian, romantic and Edwardian texts); the study of one leaf of Tolkien's compost does not preclude that of others, nor does it imply a singular dominance. Thus, this chapter illustrates how Tolkien rewrites certain classical motifs in his sublime narratives through the insertion of Christian, anti-modernist (anti-Nietzschean) ideas in the spiritual basis of the sylvan sublime; secondly, the conclusion of this chapter, which moves away from a focus on the natural world, reveals how Tolkien views and rewrites the classical past with romantic overtones, as in his Númenórean sublime, which views the classical world itself as sublime.[100]

It is true that the natural sublime, at least in modern British literature, is often commonly associated with the works of the romantics, such as Wordsworth and Coleridge;[101] thus, in his discussion of Tolkien's 'fantasy sublime' in the natural landscapes of Faërie, Sander places Tolkien firmly in such a romantic tradition.[102] Yet the popular tendency to conflate the development of the natural sublime with the genesis of the romantic movement in the early modern period – and, in parallel, to track a linear development from a sublime style in ancient texts to a sublime 'natural' experience in modern texts[103] – is essentially erroneous.[104] Classical texts as well as Christian texts from Late Antiquity or the early medieval period, whether theoretical treatises on the sublime or literary representations of the sublime, can draw attention to the importance of experiencing the natural world as a sublime object.[105] Indeed, in order to describe how a budding writer can reach the sublime style, Longinus, in his treatise *On the Sublime*, employs powerful metaphors from nature – of thunderbolts, lightning, great fires and rivers – to describe the reading of 'sublime works of art', such as those of Demosthenes, Cicero and Plato.[106] The impression seems to be first nature, then art. James Porter thus argues for primacy of the sublime experience in nature for Longinus and the ancients,[107] irrespective of what exact word was used to stand for the *sublime*;[108] Porter also argues that the ancient tradition of sublime representations in literature almost certainly did not originate with Longinus in the first century CE, and his analysis of sublime representations, accordingly, covers works by Homer, Lucretius, Lucan and Augustine, among others.[109] This chapter adds Ovid to the conversation. Furthermore, whether the sublime object was found in literary style or in experiences represented in literary narratives, it could bring forth sublime emotions[110] for the ancients, and even transcendence, for example, in the form of ethical development or of proximity to the divine.[111]

## The Christian sublime in 'Three is Company'

From a topographic perspective, *The Fellowship of the Ring* gradually transitions from a pastoral landscape – the rolling green hills, scattered trees and pleasant byways of Hobbiton and the inhabited lands of the Shire – towards dense, at times almost impenetrable forest. The first of these forests occurs still within the Shire itself, a place appropriately called Woody End, near the town of Wood-hall (again marking the spatial shift), where the three travelling hobbits encounter a party of elves under the leadership of Gildor. This woodland experience in 'Three is Company' provides a precursor to the 'sylvan sublime' which the hobbits later realize in the chapters 'The Old Forest' and 'In the House of Tom Bombadil'. Indeed, a passage in the earlier narrative provides one of Tolkien's clearer expressions of this sublime, when the trio of hobbits are invited farther into the woodland by Gildor in order to spend the night with the elves.[112]

This forest, as the sublime object of contemplation, becomes the appropriate natural arena in which the sublime phenomenon is triggered for the hobbits. Tolkien first places an emphasis on their relative distance from this sylvan space, which is geographically removed by its length ('some miles') and height ('on the hills') from the hobbits as observers; the three young travellers will, indeed, have to travel a long, tiring distance in order to reach their sylvan object of sublime contemplation and revelation – their 'W/woody E/end'.[113] Such relative dimensional differences in magnitude are typical physical tokens in the contemplation of sublime objects across many literary and philosophical traditions;[114] English philosopher Edmund Burke, for instance, in his *A Philosophical Enquiry into the Sublime and Beautiful* (1757),[115] draws attention to the category of 'vastness' from the perspective of the viewer as his lists of different aspects of the sublime – 'Greatness of dimension, is a powerful cause of the sublime. [. . .] Extension is either in length, height, or depth'.[116] Burke also introduces another visual category which is relevant to Tolkien's above narrative, that of 'obscurity';[117] in other words, the sublime feeling of awe, which Burke often equates with 'terror', is heightened by a writer 'by the force of a judicious obscurity',[118] by visual indistinctness. In Tolkien's narrative, visual obscurity is conveyed by the shadowy, faint lighting available to the observers and also by the increasing density of the woodlands.[119] This combination of a perceptual difference in magnitude and obscurity seems key to Tolkien's articulation of the natural sublime; beside such journeys into dense forests which are distant from civilization, an awe-inspiring mountain peak such as Caradhras is focalized by the members of the Fellowship as great in height[120] from their perspective (magnitude) while its peak is concealed in cloud (obscurity).[121] This image seems to pick up Coleridge's articulation of the sublime object, where the clouded-over concealment of the mountaintop renders it sublime from the removed, subjective position of the observer.[122]

Importantly, as the hobbits move further into the distant, 'denser' forest as sublime object, towards the 'End' of their 'Woody' experience, Sam experiences the highly characteristic sublime emotion of ambiguous awe or wonder – 'an expression on his face half of fear and half of astonished joy'.[123] Sam is fearful, to be clear, because he is transgressing a dangerous boundary between the accustomed experience of his pastoral life in the Shire and the extraordinary, transformative experience which this new, natural, sylvan *topos* will allow for. Yet unlike the Old Forest, where the dangerous, fatal, terrible aspect of the sublime is far more evident, the elves in 'Three is Company' prevent anything very dangerous happening to the hobbits as they approach the middle of the woods – beyond the soporific Pippin almost stumbling to the ground on a few occasions, although even this is mitigated through the elvish presence.

Along with other natural spaces such as mountains and rivers in Tolkien's writing, entrance into the forest frequently entails sublime transformation, where some revelation or epiphany enables the characters to transcend their previous selves – 'the crossing [of the border] always leaves a person changed. [...] Tolkien's forests [...] are barriers that have to be crossed, but the crossing itself, and the encounters made during it, transforms'.[124] The revelation or epiphany which the hobbits realize during their sylvan experience among the elves seems twofold, to use Porter's dual distinction: a sense of nature's own perfection (the material sublime) and the spiritual feeling of divine presence (the immaterial sublime).[125] On the former, Pippin, a bathetic-minded character, realizes the material sublime through his dog-like stomach. Nature is quantitatively diverse in the different 'fruits' it can provide to Pippin (white bread, fruits, a cool draught) as well as qualitatively rich in providing a depth of material experience hitherto unknown to the hobbit; such a depth is reinforced by similes which bring up ideal snapshots of the natural world (a garden, a fountain, a summer afternoon).[126] Similarly, Sam, true to his profession, experiences nature as profusely fertile and fecund: 'if I could grow apples like that, I would call myself a gardener'.[127]

In Tolkien's theological worldview, however, the material sublime must inevitably be secondary to an immaterial or spiritual sublime; thus, Sam, in spite of being impressed by the fruits offered to the hobbits in the woods, is more stunned by the elves themselves.[128] The awakening which the three hobbits experience is, to a large degree, signified by the very presence of the elves, beings who represent the spiritual plane of the divine, or, more technically in Tolkien's myths, the semi-divine. Within this sublime of divine recognition, Sam's captivation by elven 'singing'[129] is understandable given the association of 'angelic' singing and music with divine creation in Tolkien's cosmogony.[130] One notes, moreover, the attention throughout the elven-forest narrative to lightness in the description of the elves, generally connoting a kind of divine essence in Tolkien's legendarium.[131] Such lightness is given a clearly supernatural, almost cosmogonic character in the passage from 'Three is Company': a kind of moonlight seems to 'shimmer' around the elves as they walk past the hobbits, although they are not carrying any torches.[132]

Clearly, Tolkien's articulation of the sublime lies, at least partly, within the Christian and classical traditions of sublime narratives, where the end or cognitive goal of the epiphany is the very realization of God by the subjective observer or, in modified forms, of a divine, creative essence, symbolized by lightness and music.[133] That Tolkien's sublime is substantially Christian is confirmed by the writer's choice of the word 'joy' as the positive affect which Sam experiences among the elves in the forest: 'an expression on his face [...] half of astonished joy'.[134] In one letter, Tolkien defines 'Joy' as a particularly Christian feeling which comes from an appreciation of what lies beyond the walls of necessity – that is, earthly, material pursuits of 'happiness' – a gospel truth that is best represented by the sudden happy ending (*eucatastrophe*) of fairy stories.[135] In contrast to an emotional affect such as 'merriness', which is a pervasive term in *The Lord of the Rings* for describing positive feelings resulting from social exchanges and good fellowship, characters typically experience 'joy' in the epic when all hope is lost and their death and destruction seems nigh, such as the sudden elation Pippin feels at the Battle of the Black Gate of Mordor or Bilbo at the Battle of the Five Armies,[136] moments which are often signified symbolically through the 'divine', deus-ex-machina arrival of eagles in Tolkien's narrative. The implication of the experience of joy at such moments is that there is something beyond the human plane, and that sublime realization, as Sam also experiences among the elves in Woody End, brings intense 'joy'.

## The Ovidian perils and material sublime of the Old Forest

The next, more detailed example of a sylvan sublime in *The Fellowship of the Ring* occurs after Frodo, Sam and Pippin have crossed the Brandywine river, have met up with their friend Merry in Buckland and have decided to avoid the threat of the Black Riders by taking a detour through the Old Forest. In this case, Tolkien's representation of the sylvan sublime may not only have been inspired by his Christianity – a divine revelation entailing images of bright light, angelic singing, cosmogonic references to celestial objects, the concept of joy – but may also have received and rewritten certain classical, Graeco-Roman narratives. Tolkien, incidentally, is not the first writer in post-classical traditions to draw on the spatial archetype of the ancient forest as a place where the dangerous sublime could be found. Edmund Burke, in his detailed, taxonomized list of different causes of the sublime, which he equates often with terror in its affective manifestations,[137] employs an ancient sylvan paradigm in order to illustrate the importance of the quality of 'obscurity' to the sublime: 'For this purpose too [that is, for conveying the sublime mystery of a divine object of worship] the druids performed all their ceremonies in the bosom of the darkest woods, and in the shade of the oldest and most spreading oaks'.[138] Later, in his rather idiosyncratic discussion of the categories of 'Smell' and 'Taste', Burke again employs an ancient sylvan image to explain the ambiguous sublime sense of awe as simultaneously sacred and horrifying. '[T]his passage of Virgil [is not] without sublimity, where the stench of the vapour in Albunea conspires so happily with the sacred horror and gloominess of that prophetic forest'.[139]

'And so the concerned king goes to the oracle of his ancestors, prophetic forest god, for signs; and he consults the gods of the sacred groves at the mouth of the Tiber, and he worships at the most holy spring of the forests; and so he scourges the evil spirits and the fierce powers of the goddess Malaria.'[140]

Burke's idea that 'the sublime [...] comes upon us in the gloomy forest'[141] of the ancient world was probably also received by Nietzsche in *The Birth of Tragedy* (1872),[142] where his concepts of the Apolline and Dionysiac seem to match with Burke's concepts of the beautiful and the sublime.[143] Nietzsche, thus, defines his Dionysiac in sublime terms when he writes: 'Dionysiac music in particular induced feelings of awe and terror';[144] Nietzsche's sublime-Dionysiac is dangerous in that it can consume the individual into primitive oneness, yet it also provides a transcendent experience through ecstatic experience, so helping the inspired to enjoy life – the material world, nature – to an immeasurable degree.[145] Nietzsche uses different classical spheres to help the reader visualize the sublime-Dionysiac, such as a dangerous realm of Titans, but at its root the sylvan spatial symbol seems to resonate deepest when Nietzsche encapsulates what the Dionysiac stands for, and why the Apolline as a kind of willed concealment is necessary: 'in short the entire philosophy of the god of the woods, along with its mythical examples [...] the Greeks repeatedly overcame all this, or at least veiled and concealed it'.[146]

Whether or not Tolkien was familiar with the sublime ideas in these specific works of Burke and Nietzsche – he probably was not[147] – he was certainly familiar with their ancient source material. To that end, the *Metamorphoses* of the Roman, 'Augustan' poet Ovid (*c.* 43 BCE to 17/18 CE) becomes an important primary ancient source for Tolkien. The Englishman was most likely familiar with a good range of Ovid's works, and had probably translated some of the Latin during his school years, since he mentions the poet in one letter: 'I never learned Finnish well enough to do more than plod through a bit of the original, like a schoolboy with Ovid'.[148] The citation is not trivial since Tolkien rarely cites other ancient writers in his *Letters* apart from Virgil and Homer.[149] Tolkien certainly consulted Ovid's *Metamorphoses* at least once, most likely *Shakespeare's Ovid: Being Arthur Golding's Translation of the Metamorphoses* (1904),[150] since in his essay 'Sigelwara Land' (1932), on the etymology of the Old English Word for 'Ethiopians', he cites the story of Phaethon in the Ovidian epic.[151] Given this background knowledge, some scholars have undertaken comparative studies which explore the influence of narratives from Ovid's *Metamorphoses* on various episodes across Tolkien's legendarium: for example, the story of Pyramus and Thisbe (*Metamorphoses* 4) as rewritten in Tolkien's tragic, self-referential love story of Beren and Lúthien;[152] or the various myths of Orpheus (*Metamorphoses* 10, 11) and their reflection in the character arcs of Lúthien, Treebeard and Tom Bombadil.[153]

From a broader perspective, the choice of Ovid's *Metamorphoses* for a study in the reception aesthetics of post-classical or classical-inspired landscapes, whether in Tolkien or in other canonical English writers since the early modern period (from John Milton to Alexander Pope), is not trivial.[154] Rather than focusing on one particular Ovidian episode in the *Metamorphoses* as a singular source for Tolkien's representation of the four hobbits' journey through the Old Forest, this analysis draws on a general, oft-repeated sylvan motif in the *Metamorphoses* (with some variations, of course).[155] Segal notes 'the recurrence of an almost stereotypic sylvan scenery. A secluded grove, quiet water, shade, coolness, soft grass, sometimes rocks or caverns, are the usual attributes.'[156] In short, human characters move deep into a forest, a grove (a relatively small, often sacred woodland) or some other tree-clad space; this is true, in particular, of Ovid's 'Theban narrative' or 'Thebaid',[157] where 'the action takes place for the most part outside the city walls in an alluring landscape or *locus amoenus*; its basic elements of tree and water seem to offer protection'.[158] Subsequently, these wandering human characters behold a god, some other supernatural beings or divine representatives in a woodland glade or forest clearing.[159] While allowing mortals the 'sublime opportunity' to come face to face with the higher ontological level of the divine engenders characteristic reverence, and while there are indeed potential boons to these paradisical experiences in *loci amoeni*, such as the material sublimity of nature – if only for the extradiegetic reader rather than for the unfortunate intradiegetic character – such sylvan encounters in Ovid's narrative are fraught with very real peril for the unfortunate mortals; 'the idyllic landscape becomes the site for unexpected violence'.[160] Importantly for Segal, Ovid's sylvan spaces are 'the ancestors of the dangerous wild wood of later literature',[161] from Dante to Ariosto to Shakespeare.

In Ovid's retelling of the tragic foundation myths of the Greek city-state of Thebes, there are a series of these sylvan episodes. First, Cadmus, the founding hero of Thebes, sends his men into 'an ancient forest [*silva vetus*] undefiled /by axe or saw', in the 'heart' of which they find 'a wealth of water' as well as a deadly 'snake'.[162] The narrative aptly blends the sublime emotions of positive and negative awe, that is, sacred reverence and terror. On the one hand, the lush spring the proto-Thebans find in the glade, the clearing in the middle of the forest, is suggestive of the typical *locus amoenus* in Ovid's narrative where a god or nymph lives; in fact, the grove does, indirectly, belong to Mars, and its sacred character is confirmed by the fact that Cadmus' men are on a pious mission to find water for a ritual to Zeus for the founding of their city.[163] On the other hand, there is the matter of the terrifying snake. The men feel the 'awful' terror which is so characteristic of the sublime (at least in Burke's imaginative treatise), being *attonitos*:[164] 'horror struck, they quaked / in shock and terror'.[165] The snake proceeds to destroy the men through the bite of its fang, its crushing coil and its venomous breath.[166]

From this template in the grove of Mars' snake, the other sylvan narratives in Ovid's 'Thebaid' follow a similar pattern, notwithstanding some individual variations on the theme. The Theban Actaeon, after a successful hunting trip through the 'lonely woods' (*devia lustra*),[167] happens upon a spring of the goddess Diana (Artemis) deep in the forest, even witnessing the nude virgin goddess herself, who then transforms the unlucky, transgressive Theban prince into a stag, soon to be devoured by his own pack of hunting dogs.[168] Narcissus, who like Actaeon was hunting deer, encounters the nymph Echo in a forest (*silva*);[169] this sad tale of unrequited love ends in the deluded 'suicide' of Narcissus (falling in love with his own reflection) at a pool in another forest glade[170] and the permanent disembodying of Echo (becoming a mere echo).[171] The royal heir Pentheus, having been deceived by the god Bacchus, travels into the same kind of eerie dendral space (without a watery spring this time), with 'the encircling forest, half-way up' and to a 'clearing, bare of trees, / open and in full view from every side',[172] and here Pentheus dares to witness the Maenadic mysteries, at which point he is spotted and duly dismembered by his mother and fellow besotted Theban women.[173] Variations on this sylvan motif can be found in other Ovidian narratives in the epic: for example, Atalanta and Hippomenes veer into a 'woody forest' (*nemorosis silvis*),[174] where they unknowingly enter and defile a sanctuary of the goddess Cybele, the Great Mother, after which they are transformed into lions.[175]

In *The Fellowship of the Ring*, the adventure of the four hobbits into the Old Forest seems to inherit a good deal from this woodland motif which is so characteristic of the *Metamorphoses*.[176] To begin with, in both the Ovidian narratives and Tolkien's Old Forest sequence, the looming danger of the woodlands is foreshadowed as characters stand on the very threshold or just before they enter the sylvan area – a narrative element which can, in truth, be compressed in shorter Ovidian episodes.[177] Important in this regard is the antiquity of the woodlands. This oldness is manifest, for instance, in the *silva vetus* (old or ancient forest)[178] that surrounds the glade of Mars' serpent, and antiquity is also implied in the forest where the 'ancient [*prisca*] holy shrine' of Cybele lies, 'with wooden statues of the gods of old [*veterum deorum*]';[179] the very name of Tolkien's Old Forest declares its antiquity, but its senectitude is soon revealed to the hobbits through the shaggy, unkempt description of the trees immediately inside – 'all the stems were green or grey with moss and slime, shaggy growths', some of which are 'bent, twisted, leaning, squat [...] gnarled and branched',[180] and whose chief representative is *Old* Man Willow. These narrative references to a great age are not mere biological descriptions of aged flora but in fact point to the danger for human or hobbit agents in approaching a sphere which has long denied human encroachment, which is, in other words, a *primitive* milieu – both pre- and anti-human. Accordingly, Ovid hints at the inappropriateness of the *silva vetus* of Mars for the human intruders when he writes that it was 'undefiled by axe'[181] and when he, conversely, draws attention to the dense (*densus*), overgrown natural flora around a grotto in the glade,[182] which is a feature also of the dense (*densa*) forested valley around Diana's glade.[183] Similarly, Tolkien's forest appears incredibly dense to the hobbits when they first wander inside after going through the tunnel-gate;[184] and even though the hobbit community of Buckland had once hacked away some of the invading forest,[185] the hobbits cannot immediately detect any sign of human order in the forest – a clearing or a path.[186] In both Ovid and Tolkien the ancient forest, densely treed and untouched by human ordering (axe-work), is a dangerous place for human intruders to wander into.

In Ovid's short episodes, of course, it does not take long for the tokens of danger to be actualized into real terror: Cadmus' horrified men encounter and are destroyed by the monstrous snake of Mars; Atalanta and her suitor are turned into lions by the Great Mother. In the Graeco-Roman imagination, such ancient places in the wilderness, whether forests or mountainscapes (the two are often combined in ancient thought),[187] were generally associated with the danger of encountering primitive, even pre-Olympian, or violent deities, 'the gods of old' or, otherwise, Titanic, monstrous beasts which haunted such landscapes.[188] Tolkien's characters are also, ultimately, threatened with destruction from a kind of 'god of old'; however, unlike Ovid's intradiegetic characters who through tragic irony usually do not realize the tokens of primitive danger as they approach their forests, Tolkien's characters, rather like Ovid's extradiegetic readers, are well aware of the danger of the Old Forest before they pass over its boundary. Indeed, its very name seems to breed terror among the hobbits for what lies within the sublime forest – particularly in their Buckland friend Fredegar 'Fatty' Bolger. Repeating the name 'Old Forest' three times in three successive speeches,[189] he shows the requisite sublime terror which this *silva vetus* breeds on the hobbits before even venturing within: expressions of fear and horror, references to nightmares and even recourse to irrational superstition. This irrational, supernatural, even numinous fear of the forest, which again intersects with the Ovidian motif of the forest as a place of old gods, primitive monsters and even, indeed, of walking trees in the case of the Orpheus story,[190] is later referenced more fully by Merry in discussing the queerness of the Old Forest, which involves watching, talking and walking trees that mean to harm strangers.[191]

Once the intruders have pressed into the primitive forest in spite of dangerous warning signs, they experience a certain spatial disorientation.[192] Ovid writes of Actaeon's having had no fault in his subsequent transformation and death other than losing his way;[193] the Theban, presumably separated from his hunting comrades, inadvertently stumbled upon Diana's sacred spring, 'idly wandering / through unknown clearings of the forest'.[194] So too, in Tolkien's narrative, is the Old Forest a place of geographic bewilderment.[195] Frodo asks Merry to make sure that they find the forest path, that they do not lose one another and that they do not forget where the Hedge lies (their entrance to the Old Forest);[196] yet they struggle to locate a path,[197] and once they have located one, they soon lose it, having 'lost all clear sense of direction'.[198] In both narratives there is a sense of some outside force which facilitates this dislocation, bent on the very destruction of the wanderers: Ovid writes of how 'the Fates guided'[199] Actaeon into the hidden realm of Diana; so too the hobbits, while aiming to head northwards and back to the Bree-road, 'were being headed off, and were simply following a course chosen for them – eastwards and southwards, into the heart of the Forest and not out of it'.[200] To match the spatial disorientation, the Ovidian forest is also a place of bafflement for the senses. Actaeon tries to speak but cannot articulate any human sound, which is understandable given his metamorphosis,[201] while Echo, lost in the woods, is limited to the mere repetition of the noises of others.[202] Pippin, oppressed by the sense of the singular malevolence of the forest, hemming them in, cries out to the trees not to hurt them, but his voice is soon drowned out so that not even an echo is heard,[203] while Merry recommends silence.[204]

The journeys through the forests in the Ovidian narratives conclude with the mortal's unwitting, ill-fated arrival in some pristine forest clearing or watery glade. These clearings are typically described as clandestine places that lie deep within, or in the very centre of, the forests; thus, Diana's haunt lies within 'a valley clothed in hanging woods / of pine and cypress [...] Deep in its farthest combe, framed by the woods'.[205] Another essential spatial detail in these Ovidian episodes is the presence of a *fons* (spring) or some waterway in the glade:[206] the 'wealth of water' in the grove of Mars' snake,[207] the spring of Diana[208] and the spring in which Narcissus has his fateful encounter.[209] Likewise, Tolkien's narrative reproduces these spatial details: the so-called Withywindle valley is hidden deep in the forest, in 'the queerest part of the whole wood – the centre from which all the queerness comes',[210] far removed from the roads and civilization, which the hobbits yearn for; it is also hidden from the hobbits' perspective – 'they could see little but mists over the damp and deep-cut valley'.[211] The discovery of a powerful water source, the Withywindle river, situated in the open glade in the middle of the forest, also reflects a common element in the Ovidian motif.[212]

Thus far, the parallel narratives in Tolkien and Ovid seem to suggest a sublime sylvan experience in quite Burkean terms, receiving the ancient forest as a place of danger, the primitive, and terror, where humans are not welcome, where intruders lose their geographic and perceptual bearings as they head inevitably, through the control of an external force beyond their power, into the central, hidden glade of the grove or forest. But there is more to both narratives than mere danger and terror. An important characteristic of these hidden forest glades in Ovidian narratives is a sense of the material sublime, the 'evanescent beauty',[213] which the entrance into these forbidden places ephemerally affords the intradiegetic characters and, more so, the extradiegetic readers – a vision of nature as, in different respects, pristine, lush, richly diverse, abundant. Each glade is a *locus amoenus*.[214] The glade in the Actaeon episode is described thus:

> a limpid [*perlucidus*] spring
> Flowed lightly babbling into a wide pool,
> Its waters girdled with a grassy sward.
> Here, tired after the hunt, the goddess loved
> Her nymphs to bathe her with the water's balm.[215]

A picture of pristine, pure, unspoilt nature is evident here: one notes the references to the transparency (*perlucidus*) of the water and the 'virgin limbs' (*virgineos artus*)[216] of the chaste goddess Diana as well as the action of bathing (*liquido perfundere rore*).[217] Ovidian nature is also lush and profusive, associated with 'generation and sexuality'.[218] This has been seen already through the density of the woodlands surrounding the glades, and there are references to green, grassy swards which border the spring in both the Actaeon and Narcissus episode: 'grass grew around it [the spring], by the water fed, / and trees to shield it from the warming sun';[219] Segal regards the glade of Mars' serpent as 'one of ostensible fruitfulness with its abundant water'.[220] Lastly, a key feature of the Ovidian universe is a lust for natural diversity – 'its constituent elements [...] admitting of infinite variations of details':[221] for example, the 'forest of trees' surrounding Orpheus, including poplars, oaks, laurels, firs, willows and many other kinds;[222] or even, though a narrative of dark humour, the many types of dog breeds which hunt their master Actaeon.[223]

When Tolkien's four hobbits enter into the deep, hidden glade of the Withywindle valley, they emerge from the dark, ancient forest into a kind of *locus amoenus*, a delightful picture of nature, for the hobbits to experience the material sublime in its different aspects.[224] Important here is the change in lighting, from the gloom of the forest canopy into a sunlit space.[225] Nature is lush and overgrown here; there are Ovidian-like swards of grass which stretch to the water source: 'a wide space of grass and reeds'; 'the long grasses'; 'everywhere the reeds were lush and tall'.[226] Like the purifying springs in the Ovidian tales, the Withywindle seems to lure Frodo into bathing himself: he feels a compelling desire for cool water.[227]

Yet in both the Ovidian and Tolkienian narratives, this material sublime is essentially deceptive – there is only a fleeting chance for characters to experience, for example, diversity, profundity and cleansing purity in the natural world and, by extension, to realize human ideals such as 'peace, relaxation, and refinement'[228] or 'an inner world of free desires' in Ovid's narrative,[229] or 'peace'[230] in Tolkien's.[231] The sylvan experience is mingled with destruction and violence for the intruders. In Ovid, it is the very water of the glade which Diana uses to turn Actaeon into a stag, while the pool which Narcissus discovers effectively destroys him. '[T]he hallmark of Ovid's grove of Diana, where Actaeon will meet an untimely fate, is [...] deception [...] With its garden décor Ovid's *locus amoenus* makes a deceptive appeal to contemporary sensibilities.'[232] In Tolkien's narrative, likewise, there is a strong sense of the natural environment trying to deceive the hobbits – to lull them into a soporific, comfortable, warm state – only for their destruction to follow. Hence, Frodo's desire to bathe his feet in the water of the river almost leads to his drowning. Particularly important for Tolkien in this deceptive *locus amoenus* of the forest clearing is the heating effect of the sun and the apparently welcoming, soporific warmth the glade provides;[233] interestingly, the narrative contrast in Tolkien between the darkness of the forest as a place of concealment (from the Black Riders) and the exposure of a sunny clearing as a place of unexpected danger has resonances in several episodes of Ovid's *Metamorphoses* too: both hunters and virgins seek 'protection in the uterine comfort of the dark forest', yet subsequent exposure to '[t]he sun frequently is suggestive of danger, a source of violence and destruction'.[234] This 'sublime' tension of the sylvan, grove-glade landscape – as both dangerous, perilous,[235] deceptive, lethal places for mortals, entailing rape, transformation and death, and also as sites where the natural world can be witnessed by intruding mortals as thriving in immeasurable profundity, diversity, immaculateness and, certainly, sheer beauty – might be regarded as typically Ovidian.[236]

The 'end' of Ovid's sylvan sublime, the necessary transformative experience, apart from viewing nature in hitherto unappreciated ways, also entails being in the presence of some kind of divinity or divine representative;[237] the Ovidian forest glade is a numinous space where Diana, Cybele, Mars (through his terrifying monstrous snake) or Bacchus (through his Maenadic worshippers) might be found or at least felt in spirit, along with lesser nymphs and supernatural entities. Unlike Christian traditions of divine revelation, these classical gods are primitive and violent in their inclinations and send terror and destruction upon mortal intruders: '[d]ivinity itself, as Ovid represents it, is an enigmatic and essentially ugly force, working its will on mortals after the fashion of venatic lust'.[238] Tolkien's elves in 'Three is Company' certainly reflect the divine revelation of the Christian sublime moment; on the other hand, if this comparative reading of Tolkien and Ovid might be extended, it is quite possible to see the anthropomorphic tree Old Man Willow as the kind of 'divine appearance' in the forest glade which is so characteristic of the *Metamorphoses* narratives. Unlike the other trees of the Old Forest who may or may not actually move and be sentient, since this depends on the hobbits' fearful focalization, Old Man Willow possesses definite independent agency: he moves his branches, manipulates his trunk and apparently talks to the hobbits.[239] Like Ovidian goddesses and nymphs who enchant and protect their hidden sylvan realms with their divine powers,[240] the 'grey thirsty spirit' that is Old Man Willow 'drew power out of the earth' such that he has nearly the whole of the Old Forest under his 'dominion'.[241]

Moreover, the ways in which Old Man Willow goes about his business, in using his power to try to destroy the lives of the four trespassing hobbits, has Ovidian parallels. Frodo, in falling asleep and almost drowning in the Withywindle river, seems to 'echo' the fates of both Narcissus, who, being tired from the heat and needing to rest by the forest spring,[242] meets his end at the *fons*, and Arethusa, who dipping her feet in a calm stream and setting her clothing 'on a curved willow branch',[243] is accosted and pursued by a river god, Alpheus – not drowning ultimately, but becoming a *fons* herself.[244] Merry and Pippin seem to suffer from the typically Ovidian fate of 'metamorphosis', of turning into flora; in being trapped within the bark of Old Man Willow, which gradually encapsulates more and more of their bodies, they seem to recall the tragic fate of Myrrha who is dendrified: 'And now the growing tree had tightly swathed / her swelling womb, had overlapped her breasts, / ready to wrap her neck. She [...] / buried her face and forehead in the bark'.[245] In opposition to the destruction which Old Man Willow oversees, Sam, not yet admitting defeat, comes to a decision which is not without precedent in classical writings, from Ovid's Erysichthon who cuts down the sacred tree in Ceres' grove with an axe[246] to Lucan's Caesar who cuts down the sacred grove outside Marseille;[247]

Sam, thus, pontificates whether they have 'an axe among [their] luggage'[248] with which to counter Old Man Willow. Once Frodo admits that they only have 'a little hatchet for chopping firewood',[249] Sam turns to his next course of attack: fire. Like Ovidian forests, the Old Forest powerfully resists all human, or hobbit, attempts to colonize its territory – to chop down branches and burn it; Sam's attempts to impose his 'Promethean will' (axe and fire) on Old Man Willow come to nothing. A similar idea is represented throughout Ovid's *Metamorphoses*, where the landscapes are 'protected from physical change'[250] because of the governance of the gods.[251]

## Tom Bombadil as Orphic guide to the sylvan sublime

The dark, destructive, numinous Ovidian characteristic of the ancient forest, in all its overwhelming materiality, does not, however, conquer the four hobbits in Tolkien's narrative. To this end, it is worth noting that the hobbits actually encounter two 'gods' in this sylvan sublime. Old Man Willow, the quasi-divine figure of destruction, meets his match in the timely arrival of a new 'god' to save the hobbits: Tom Bombadil.[252] Tom has been a source of scholarly contestation in Tolkien studies. As a figure designed by Tolkien as a deliberate enigma or anomaly,[253] his status remains unclear within Tolkien's otherwise well-structured, taxonomized ontological hierarchies, from Ilúvatar to Valar to elves to dwarves to men.[254] Yet, interestingly, in line with the Ovidian motif of finding a god in the central glade of the sacred grove, some scholars have interpreted Tom as some form of deity: a possible incarnation of the almighty Ilúvatar himself, who represents the Christian God; one of the Valar, analogous to Graeco-Roman deities in the extent of their power rather than in their mechanisms of power;[255] or a Maia, a powerful, incarnated spirit from the Undying Lands, such as Gandalf.[256] Whether this enigmatic figure can be provided with a more precise 'divine' identity remains doubtful, but there is little doubt that the role he adopts in the narrative forest motif at least *resembles* that of a god, or otherwise a kind of nature spirit.[257]

While Tolkien's Tom Bombadil is quite unlike the type of violent, primitive gods which are encountered in the Ovidian forest narratives, he does, in fact, resemble a certain Greek mythic figure, not a god *per se* but a prophet and a bard, who in some traditions had divine parentage (Apollo, the muse Calliope), who was associated with divine mysteries, and who possessed god-like powers in some respects: Orpheus.[258] Orpheus, who is mentioned in various Greek and Roman literary texts, including Virgil, features in Books 10 and 11 of Ovid's *Metamorphoses*: the former is concerned with the tragic death of the bard's wife Eurydice and, subsequently, Orpheus' failed attempt to rescue her from the underworld, after which his musical mourning of her death is so powerful that it attracts an audience of trees, which then becomes a vehicle for further episodic narratives of 'dendrification'; the latter book recounts the violent death of Orpheus at the hands of Maenads.

Tolkien was certainly familiar with the Orphic mythic cycle; in classical texts his most likely source materials were the *Georgics* of Virgil and Ovid's *Metamorphoses*,[259] and in post-classical texts the medieval lay *Sir Orfeo*.[260] In his *Letters*, Tolkien even terms the 'story of Lúthien and Beren', which was probably his most beloved, certainly his most personal, self-referential story that reflected his own love for his wife Edith Tolkien,[261] 'a kind of Orpheus-legend in reverse, but one of Pity not of Inexorability'.[262] Several scholars have examined the influences of the classical Orpheus story on Tolkien's love story of Lúthien and Beren,[263] including narratives of musical enchantment in various underworlds, of lovers being united after a grim death or of the natural world being enchanted through song; yet the differences from the classical paradigm are as important as the similarities, and Tolkien's reversed, rewritten version of the myth reflects both his Christian worldview – centred on 'Pity' rather than on the 'Inexorability' of a classical, 'Homeric' eschatology – as well as a modern sensibility in reversing gender roles, with Orpheus being feminized in the form of Lúthien.

As Peter Sundt has suggested, Tom Bombadil is another strong candidate for an Orphic figure in Middle-earth, with a unique triangulation of three roles:[264] 'lover, musician, and nature pacifier'.[265] Tom is devoted to his wife Goldberry, his actions are frequently accompanied and enhanced by music and he has a special connection with the natural world, both fauna and flora. Thus, like Orpheus whose wife Eurydice is associated with the Naiads,[266] the nymphs of rivers, springs and other waters, Tom Bombadil is married to Goldberry, who is described as the River's daughter,[267] whose 'gown rustled softly like the wind in the flowering borders of a river'.[268] The Tom–Goldberry romance is essentially a happy, fairy-tale one without any of the tragic elements of Eurydice's death, her near resurrection when Orpheus voyages into the underworld and Orpheus' fatal glance backwards. However, elements of a katabatic journey are evident in Tom's rescue of the four hobbits from a type of underworld – the underground, haunted, necrotic den of a barrow-wight;[269] this rescue, moreover, is aided through Tom's musical poetry, which seems to have the Orphic ability to move stones.[270] The usage of music to conquer an underworld setting and restoring to life those seemingly doomed to a dismal fate are characteristically Orphic.

Lastly, in tandem with his roles as a lover and a musician, the Orphism of Tom is reflected through his ability to charm and tame nature. The Ovidian Orpheus enchants trees with his music:

> But when the bard,
> The heaven-born bard, sat there and touched his strings,
> Shade came in plenty. Every tree was there:
> Dodona's holy durmast, poplars once
> The Sun's sad daughters, oaks with lofty leaves,
> Soft limes, the virgin laurel and the beech.[271]

In Tolkien's narrative, Tom threatens Old Man Willow 'to sing a wind up and blow leaf and branch away';[272] subsequently, Tom 'put his mouth to the crack and began singing into it in a low voice',[273] the result of which is Old Man Willow's allowing Merry and Pippin to escape their 'Myrrhan' entrapment and for the tree to return to a dormant state. Tom, apparently, communicates not only with flora but also with fauna; Sundt notes that 'Tom's return with the ponies [after the barrow episode] is also reminiscent of Orpheus' magical control over nature'.[274] Perhaps Tolkien was equally influenced in the latter depiction of accompanying fauna by a frequent motif in late Renaissance art which depicted Orpheus as animal tamer, usually seated below a tree: for example, Roelant Savery's *Orpheus Charming the Animals with his Music* (1610), Jacob Hoefnagel's *Orpheus Charming the Animals* (1613), or Nicolaes de Bruyn's *Orpheus Charming Animals* (c. 1625).[275]

If Tom Bombadil can be regarded as some manner of god-like, Orphic figure in the Ovid-inherited motif of the narrative journey into the heart of the forest, it is worth pondering how the hobbits experience a kind of sublime transcendence in their sylvan encounter with Tom. It is clear that the Old Forest encounter with Tom adheres to some of the defining attributes of the sublime. One typical, generic marker of the sublime is the state of cognitive disorientation and disturbance which the hobbits feel when they first encounter this enigmatic figure:[276] Tom's forestscape seems 'unreal', and the hobbits feel as if they are moving through a 'dream' from which they will never awake.[277] This theme of being in a state of dreamlike disorientation, which the hobbits already experienced in their 'negative sublime' confrontation with Old Man Willow,[278] is continued during their stay in the house of Tom Bombadil, where in a unique sequence of narratives Tolkien spells out the dreams which three of the hobbits, excepting the log-like Sam, experienced in the home.[279] In this space of alterity, simple questions of identity (who is Tom Bombadil?) and normal worldly mechanics (the invisibility effect of the Ring) are suspended. The cognitive disorientation which the hobbits experience in Tom's forest-home is the necessary precursor to the sublime transcendence this location and an Orphic Tom will offer them. This transcendence is, interestingly, both material and immaterial.

In the hobbit's brief stay with Tom Bombadil they *learn* to appreciate nature in a breadth (the sheer diversity of nature) and, more so, a depth (the inner workings of each part of nature) they have not hitherto understood:[280]

> He [Tom] told them tales of bees and flowers, the ways of trees, and the strange creatures of the Forest, about the evil things and good things, things friendly and unfriendly, cruel things and kind things, and secrets hidden under branches. As they listened they began to understand the lives of the Forest, apart from themselves, indeed to feel themselves as the strangers where all other things were at home.[281]

Tom resembles a kind of Orphic guide to the material sublime of the forest for the hobbits. It is through the focalization of the Thracian bard, after all, that the Ovidian reader is introduced to the long catalogue of different trees (the breadth of nature), which are strangely animate (the unexpected depths and workings) and which literally form a forest ('shade') around Orpheus and the reader; moreover, Orpheus acts as a dendrophilic guide and as an intradiegetic poet-narrator, through whom Ovid sings about various tragic love tales which end in metamorphoses into plants or trees: those of Cyparissus, Ganymede,

Hyacinth, Myrrha and Adonis (Book 10 of the *Metamorphoses*).[282] One might well say of the Ovidian Orpheus, then, that, like his sylvan descendant Tom, he 'knows the ways of trees' and 'the lives of the forest' – the depths and breadths of the material world of the forest. Yet this deep sylvan knowledge given to the hobbits by Tom, as that given by Orpheus to the reader, does not exclude danger – 'evil things', 'cruel things' – to anthropocentric entities who encroach upon this dendral space.[283] This idea in both Tolkien and Ovid is itself a precursor to modern post-humanist imaginings of a natural sublime, which must be understood on its own terms[284] and is not necessarily conducive to the egocentric, 'Kantian' ambitions of human agents, seeking their own self-serving human enlightenment in the woods.[285]

Tom not only preaches and narrates the material wonder of nature as narrator-guide but demonstrates it too. Thus, in a realization of nature's plenty, he offers the quartet of guests a diverse assortment of wholesome natural foodstuffs, including cream and honey and butter and cheese and berries.[286] This focus on diversity and amplitude in nature is also characteristically Ovidian; Hinds writes of the 'very amplitude of the grove' that Orpheus literally summons and of how such amplitude is a characteristic Ovidian legacy 'to later traditions of landscape descriptions'.[287] In such displays of nature's bounty, moreover, Tom often communicates in his characteristic Orphic mode; talking about nature, 'his voice would turn to song, and he would get out of his chair and dance about'.[288] As a guide to the material sublime, Tom is described in terms that suggest he is assimilated wholly into his surroundings, a personification of nature's goodness: 'charging through grass and rushes like a cow going down to drink',[289] 'his face was red as a ripe apple',[290] and 'he carried on a large leaf as on a tray a small pile of white water-lilies'.[291] In his very being, Tom embodies some of the defining attributes of the material sublime in nature: its vigorousness, fecundity and bounty. In assimilating such a vision of nature into his own being, Tom Bombadil is not unlike another Graeco-Roman figure to be found in the wilds: Bacchus,[292] from whom vines spontaneously spring and around whom nature blossoms with fecundity and profusion. Incidentally, Tom is perhaps similar to Bacchus in other respects: in his short, unassuming stature; in his propensity to laughter and merriness; in his occasional capriciousness; in his liminal ontological status, between the divine and human; and in his lack of concern for the affairs of the outside political world, the *polis*, in Graeco-Roman terms.[293]

Through the guidance of an Orphic Tom, the four hobbits experience not only the material sublime but also the immaterial or spiritual sublime, just as they did with the angelic elves in the chapter 'Three is Company'. In the Old Forest, in short, the hobbits are provided with a microcosm of Tolkien's constructed universe where divine creativity and order ultimately conquer destruction and chaos; such a theological, Christian revelation is apparent through a *combination* of spatial, natural and musical metaphors, which draw on classical narratives. Important in this regard is the idea of a contest between two rival types of music in a natural setting, with one type of music veering towards order and beauty and the other towards destruction. Such a musical contest might well draw on an Ovidian passage from the *Metamorphoses* which describes the death of Orpheus, during a contest between 'Orphic' and 'Maenadic' music (or 'Apolline' and 'Dionysiac' music in Nietzschean terms):

> While Orpheus sang his minstrel's songs and charmed
> The rocks and woods and creatures of the wild
> To follow, suddenly, as he swept his strings
> In concord with his song, a frenzied band
> Of Thracian women, wearing skins of beasts,
> From some high ridge of ground caught sight of him.
> 'Look!' shouted one of them, tossing her hair
> That floated in the breeze, 'Look, there he is,
> The man who scorns us!' and she threw her lance
> Full in Apollo's minstrel's face, but, tipped
> With leaves, it left a bruise but drew no blood.
> Another hurled a stone; that, in mid air,
> Was vanquished by the strains of voice and lyre
> And grovelled at his [Orpheus'] feet, as if to ask
> Pardon for frenzy's daring. Even so
> The reckless onslaught swelled; their fury knew
> No bounds; stark madness reigned. And still his singing
> Would have charmed every weapon, but the huge
> Clamour, the drums, the curving Phrygian fifes,
> Hand-clapping, Bacchic screaming drowned the lyre.
> And then at last, his song unheard, his blood
> Reddened the stones.[294]

First, from a formal perspective, it is clear that Ovid is describing two quite different types of music: Orpheus' music is melodic rather than harmonic or polyphonic since his singing is accompanied by a single instrument which is being plucked, the 'lyre', and he strives, moreover, for concordance between voice and strings; the Maenadic music, conversely, is polyphonic, characterized by a mixture between drums, multiple voices, hands being clapped, woodwind instruments, 'fifes' and through the pejorative reference to 'screaming' – or *ululatus* (howling).[295] Their music seems to be opposed to the concordance of Orpheus' lyre-playing and to veer towards disharmony. The differences of these two types of music are not evaluated neutrally in Ovid, in formal terms of musical composition, but are, importantly, associated with a contest between Orphic order and Maenadic destruction in the natural world: Orpheus' music is aimed at taming the 'wild' (*ferarum*),[296] controlling the elements (arresting stones), and preventing violence; the Maenads' music is associated with the violence of weapons and blood, of losing the rationality of the mind (*insanaque*: madness)[297] and of destroying the life of nature-bard Orpheus and his tamed animals – 'the Maenads first pounced on / the countless birds still spellbound by his song'.[298] Finally, in the Ovidian contest between the Orphic and the Maenadic music, the latter triumphs (though not without later retribution from Bacchus).[299]

As a side note on the cultural reception of this Ovidian musical contest, it is difficult not to see the influence of such a passage on the thought of German philosopher and classicist Friedrich Nietzsche, especially in his discussion of the Dionysiac and Apolline in *The Birth of Tragedy*. Nietzsche appropriated the symbolic resonances of the Greek gods Dionysus and Apollo into a pair of juxtaposing aesthetic forces which an artist draws upon, the Dionysiac and the Apolline;[300] every artist, according to Nietzsche, is 'either an Apolline dream artist or a Dionysiac ecstatic artist or else [...] a dream artist and an ecstatic artist at the same time'.[301] The inspired Dionysiac artist loses control of individuality and becomes one with the contradictory, fertile, essentially destructive or chaotic genius of nature – musically, Nietzsche associates this aesthetic state with the uproar of complex harmonies and heavy rhythms, festive music; alternately, the Apolline artist favours controlled melody and is defined by the recourse to order and rationality in his art.[302]

The contest between Dionysiac and Apolline music (and other aesthetic forms) for Nietzsche is not limited to the aesthetic plane but points to an existential, ontological battle. The Dionysiac stems from a true belief in the essential chaos of the universe, the sense of a governing entropy which will consume individuality and destroy everything, and which can only be alleviated by the imposition of sheer human will (the Apolline), an essential illusion in the absence of a real god, in an objective universal sense; thus, Nietzsche writes that 'the highest impact of Apolline culture [...] must always overthrow a realm of Titans and slay monsters, and [...] emerge triumphant over a terrible abyss in its contemplation of the world',[303] and that the 'primal Oneness, eternally suffering and contradictory, also needs the delightful vision, the pleasurable illusion for its constant redemption'.[304] In Nietzsche's anti-theist modernism, the Apolline melody must be sustained by the will of the human musician alone over and above the ever-pervasive, universal, destructive polyphony of the Dionysiac.

In his Christian worldbuilding, however, Tolkien reworks the Ovidian idea of a musical contest between Orphic and Maenadic song – or Apolline and Dionysiac in Nietzsche's terms. Unlike Ovid's *Metamorphoses*, where the Orphic melody is drowned out by the Maenadic, or Nietzsche's *The Death of Tragedy*, where the Apolline is only an illusion to the destructive Dionysiac, Tolkien musical cosmogony in *The Silmarillion* points to the superiority and the substratal truth of the 'Orphic' form:

> And it seemed that there were two musics progressing at one time before the seat of Ilúvatar, and they were utterly at variance. The one was deep and wide and beautiful, but slow and blended with immeasurable sorrow, from which its beauty chiefly came. The other had now achieved a unity of its own; but it was loud, and vain, and endlessly repeated; and it had little harmony, but rather a clamorous unison as of many trumpets braying upon a few notes. And it essayed to drown the other music out by the violence of its voice, but it seemed that its most triumphant notes were taken by the other and woven into its own solemn pattern.[305]

Tolkien's first music, which is overseen by the angelic, benevolent Valar, is cosmic in the Greek sense of having order – and thus clear spatial dimensions of depth and width – and ornamentation or 'beauty'. In contrast, the second music, which is overseen by the Satanic Melkor, is unordered or chaotic in its jumbled polyphony, having 'little harmony', it is not beautiful to listen to, being loud and repetitive, and, lastly, it is destructive in its aims. This musical contrast picks up several of the characteristics evident in the Ovidian battle between the Orphic and the Maenadic modes, not least the references to the amplitude and jumbled polyphony of the Maenadic – and, importantly, its destructive aims as it 'drowned' (*obstrepuere*)[306] the ordered Orphic music. Yet Tolkien's musical cosmogony has rewritten the Ovidian passage – 'a kind of Orpheus-legend in reverse' – such that the music is not drowned out by the cacophonic form but instead interweaves the latter into its pattern to further enhance its 'cosmic' – its beautiful, ordered – effects. That the destructive, polyphonic music does not hold sway is obviously a testament to the dominant creative design which underlies this music, and so all existence, in Tolkien's legendarium, Ilúvatar.

Interestingly, the idea of a musical contest is repeated in the Old Forest sequence,[307] where the hobbits also experience two types of music: first, Old Man Willow, who is 'singing [...] cool words [...] about water and sleep';[308] and then Tom Bombadil, who 'began singing in a low voice.'[309] Formally at least, the two musics of Old Man Willow and Tom Bombadil are quite similar, a kind of gentle, low lullaby to lull the listeners into sleep, yet their songs are governed by entirely contrary intentions: Old Man Willow's singing is a means by which he can destroy the hobbits, crushing Merry and Pippin inside his bark and drowning Frodo; Tom's singing, like Orpheus', is aimed at taming or bringing order to a volatile nature – 'Eat earth! Dig deep!' – and, again like Orpheus' 'eukatabatic ability',[310] at restoring life to the hobbits from the clutches of death – an almost literally described rebirthing from the tree in the case of Merry and Pippin.[311] In this musical contest, there is only one winner: 'A shudder ran through the tree from root to tip, and complete silence fell'[312] because Tom 'know[s] the tune for him [Old Man Willow]'.[313] The music of Old Man Willow, representing the destructive impulses of nature, if not compositionally the 'Bacchic dithyrambs' of Melkorian song, is silenced by that of Tom, who possesses the mastering melody, which is concerned with maintaining order and beauty in nature and, above all, the creation of life.

There are several other passages which show how Tom's 'Orphic' song seems to engender or lead the way to order and beauty in nature and in his general spatial, material environment. It is Tom Bombadil's singing, appropriately, that leads the hobbits to his bright, well-ordered home in the middle of the dark forest.[314] This spatial symbol of lightness in Bombadil's house is likely a token of heavenly bliss, reflective of Tolkien's Edenic Valinor. Indeed, as Beal shows,[315] the description of Bombadil's house that Frodo later realizes in a half-dream state at the start of the chapter 'Fog on the Barrow-Downs' is explicitly picked up at the end of *The Lord of the Rings*, when Frodo is finally granted rest from his sufferings in Valinor.[316] Against critics, including film-makers, who have regarded the Tom Bombadil episode as superfluous to the telling of the epic, these descriptive parallels between the narrative in Bombadil's house and in Valinor – similarities in colour (green, gold, silver), in colour transitions (from greyer to lighter shades) and in singing – declare the symbolic importance of the hobbits' experience in Tom's home; it provides them with a sublime realization of a peaceful, essentially Christian view of heaven – even if, strictly speaking, Tolkien's hobbits, like men, do not attain a terrestrial paradise on Arda (or 'earth') as the elves do.[317] Importantly, Tom's Orphic musical abilities stimulate this delightful vision: it is his 'sweet singing', which reflects the beauty of the Valars' music, that triggers the imagined visual picture of paradise and penetrates through 'the grey curtain' and the 'veil', being the essential illusion of destruction, in Tolkien's anti-Nietzschean thought. The comparison of Tom's whistling 'to a tree full of birds' in this passage – Orpheus' death is mourned by birds[318] – continues the Orphic association between his ordered control over nature and the beautiful quality of his simple melodies (whistling).

Unlike the classical Orpheus, however, who is slaughtered by Maenads and who is relegated to a dreary afterlife in the Ovidian underworld,[319] Tolkien's rewritten Orphic bard is triumphant in his musical ordering of nature: Tom cannot be mastered by any entity in the natural mini-cosmos of the Old Forest, to paraphrase Goldberry,[320] least of all any Maenadic 'evil' song of nature which seeks to dissolve or dismember individuals into chaos, as in Ovid's *Metamorphoses*; moreover, far from descending into a dreary, 'classical' underworld future, Tolkien's Orphic bard reigns in a realm which is as close to heavenly paradise as any place on Middle-earth.[321] In the sylvan episodes narrated in the *Metamorphoses*, 'Ovid's scenery does not form a similar "spiritual landscape"';[322] despite Orpheus' best efforts to create controlled, beautiful nature through his divine-inspired music, the Ovidian universe is essentially one of diversity, change, violence and confusion for human beings:

'the very mysteriousness of these Ovidian landscapes befits the arbitrariness and incomprehensibility of a world in which the human individual has little or no power to protect his person',[323] whereby Ovid stresses the 'powerlessness of song and the degree to which passion and violence are impervious to it'.[324]

In short, the musical, natural arena of the Old Forest acts as a kind of symbolic microcosm for key theological principles of Tolkien's universal mechanics (spelled out in *The Silmarillion*[325]) regarding notions, on the one hand, of destruction, which is associated with ideas of chaos, disorder and darkness and, on the other hand, of cosmic creation, which is associated with notions of order and beauty (*kosmos*). The four hobbits travel deep into the Old Forest, a katabatic journey into darkness,[326] a place haunted by a nightmarish tree who threatens them with his song of devouring destruction; instead, in this sylvan sublime episode, they encounter a different kind of song by an Orphic figure, but this music, unlike its classical paradigm, is rewritten, it is triumphant against the destructive forces,[327] and it propagates cosmic order, beauty and creation in nature – much like Orpheus in manner, if not in successful execution. In Tolkien's literary masterpiece, elements of destruction, whether realized through spatial (darkness, chaos) or musical metaphor (disharmony, amplitude), are illusions which can be pierced by cosmic music and light and which, therefore, only serve to further enhance the beauty in the patterns of creation. This is the key spiritual lesson which the hobbits learn in their sublime encounter with Tom after their experience in the Old Forest.[328]

## Conclusion: Tolkien's Classical Sublime – walking among the ruins of Graeco-Roman Númenor

Instead of focusing on further subjective experiences in other natural arenas, such as mountains (Caradhras), rivers (the Anduin) and plains (Rohan), this final section considers the (pre-)romantic idea of the ancient world *itself* as a sublime object in Tolkien's Middle-earth. The sublime object in late-eighteenth and early-nineteenth-century British romantic thought was represented not only by individual encounters with the natural world, such as Wordsworth's famous experience of crossing the Alps,[329] an adventure which Tolkien too enjoyed, but also by poets and intellectuals visiting, and later reflecting on through their writings, the classical world of Greece and Rome – or, at least, its architectural vestiges, historical landscapes and material remains. For a romantic such as Lord Byron, classical Greece both serves as a sublime object through its impressive historical sites such as Thermopylae and also offers a particular form of moral transcendence, a restoration of an ideal of Hellenism.[330] The romantic notion of the classical or Greek sublime evolved from the actual experiences of European travellers throughout the seventeenth and eighteenth centuries, individuals who visited specific classical sites and perceived something extraordinary, 'an entire new way of life'.[331] This romantic classicism was realized far more through an engagement and experience with sheer materiality than through the 'Enlightenment' of texts; Sachs gives the example of Keats's poem 'Ode on a Grecian Urn' as the popular iconic example of this romantic relationship to the material objects of the classical past.[332] This is not to say that such a material-focused sublime could not give rise to 'immaterial', ideological awakenings: namely, the fascination with Hellenism, which would subsequently play its part in renovating the British educational system, in influencing political discourses on democracy and national patriotism, and even in promoting new heroic models of masculinity and sexuality.[333]

This romantic fascination with travelling towards the ruins[334] of a classical civilization in search of the sublime would continue well into the twentieth century, in the modernist period – most remarkably with the rediscovery of Minoan Crete, a pre-classical, thalassocratic, proto-Occidental paradise, at least as imagined by Sir Arthur Evans;[335] archaeological sites such as Knossos and Phaistos could awaken sublime experiences among Anglo-American travel writers, including Mary Renault,[336] Lawrence Durrell,[337] and Henry Miller. The latter spells out his 'Minoan sublime' in clear terms while at Phaistos, meshing a natural object, namely a mountainous vantage, with a pre-classical site, and suggesting notions of spiritual bliss:

> From this sublime, serene height it has all the appearance of the Garden of Eden. At the very gates of Paradise the descendants of Zeus halted here on their way to eternity to cast a look earthward and saw with the eyes of innocents that the earth is indeed what they had always dreamed it to be: a place of beauty and joy and peace.[338]

Through its own hermetic, fictional constructs, Tolkien's Middle-earth preserves this tradition of (pre-)romantic and modernist encounters with the ruins of an ancient, 'classical' civilization that lead to sublime experiences. Just like our own world, the landscape of Middle-earth is dotted with the ruins of previous aeons of lost civilization;[339] the Fellowship of nine travellers, for example, happens upon Amon Sûl (Weathertop), the Mines of Moria, the Argonath and Amon Hen. In three of the above four cases, excluding the dwarven underground kingdom of Moria, the ruins belong to the Númenórean civilization and its dynastic offshoots in Arnor and Gondor, which, as has been already discussed, have parallels with various ancient-world civilizations. Tolkien's adventurers in the Fellowship, stemming from a later, more modern age, experience the various ruins of this ancient, quasi-Graeco-Roman Númenor (or Gondor orArnor) as sublime places; one might speak of a 'Númenórean sublime' in analogy with Lord Byron's Greek sublime or Henry Miller's Minoan sublime. A close reading of certain travelling narratives in *The Fellowship of the Ring* illustrates this notion as characters, typically 'modern' hobbits, witness and interact with three ancient Númenórean ruins – Amon Sûl, the Argonath and Amon Hen.

With the help of Strider, later known to them as Aragorn, whom they met at the town of Bree after their adventures in the Old Forest and Barrow-downs, the four hobbits approach the ancient hill fort of Amon Sûl, which is covered by 'the ruins of old works of stone'.[340] Like those post-classical individuals who have wandered around the monumental ancient architectural remains of Greece, Rome and Crete, Merry experiences typical unsettling feelings of the sublime among the broken stonework.[341] The ruins, which are impressive objects in their sheer magnitude, trigger cognitive confusion in him – he 'wonders', he asks seemingly unanswerable questions, he expresses uncertainty, he stutters.[342] Such cognitive confusion is a typical emotion which has been ascribed to both romantic narratives of the natural sublime, such as that of Coleridge, as well as Tolkien's own characteristic 'fantastic sublime', where the disarrangement of preconceptions will pave the path for a fresh way of thinking.[343] The grandeur of real-world ancient ruins can also, however, stimulate – and potentially even resolve – similar feelings of confusion or disorientation. In Nikos Kazantzakis' *Zorba the Greek* (1946),[344] the nameless narrator walks towards the Minoan ruins on Crete with 'a feeling of lassitude, an emotional tension in the breast, a tingling sensation throughout [his] body',[345] in the hope that 'after three of four hours' walk fatigue would calm the unrest that spring had brought';[346] it is, in fact, the Minoan ruins themselves which further destabilize the intellectual narrator's state of mind, but which eventually help him to move towards some form of new understanding about happiness in life.[347] The logophilic Henry Miller describes a similar state of perceptual strangeness among the Minoan ruins: 'I felt that the earth was bearing me through a zone I had never been carried through before. I was a little nearer to the stars and the ether was charged with nearness.'[348]

In Tolkien's narrative at the Númenórean ruins, Merry's comparison to what the hobbits experienced at the dreadful Barrow-downs also gives Weathertop the feeling of a graveyard.[349] This sense of mortuary terror, as the negative, dreadful, 'Burkean' component of sublime awe, is not unknown among those who walk among ancient ruins – as places of the dead. It is found in expressions of the Minoan sublime, for Kazantzakis' narrator, 'in old ruined cities this [noon] is a dangerous time of day, for the air is filled with cries and the noise of spirits. [...] Every inch of ground you tread is a grave, and you hear the dead groaning';[350] for Henry Miller at Phaistos, there is a sudden change in mood towards a more dangerous milieu: 'the shimmering counters massed themselves in orchestral formation, the eagles swooped out of their eyries and hung in the sky like sultry messengers of the gods. [...] The sky had become more menacing.'[351] Later, on the trip back from the ruins through the mountains, Miller perceives in the rocks a 'weird demonic stretch', 'some forbidden pass guarded by evil spirits'.[352] In truth, the very name of Tolkien's Weathertop signifies its tempestuous nature, and it does have a dark, ominous atmosphere in the chapter 'A Knife in the Dark'. This is prefigured before the hobbits even reach the hilltop, when they 'looked anxiously at the distant hills';[353] Weathertop is the place where Gandalf battled the Black Riders, phantoms of the darkness, several days before the company of five arrived there, and it is the site where Frodo receives his near-fatal stabbing at the hands of the Witch King of Angmar, the most terrible of the wraiths.

Thus far it appears that the Númenórean sublime experienced at the 'classical' ruins of Weathertop is entirely of the Burkean variety: a place of confusion and disorientation, all terror and all horror, the grave of an extinct civilization, the place where ghosts and wraiths roam. But that is only half the story. Ancient ruins represented for romantic and modernist travellers the appropriate *topos* at which to reflect and, in sublime moments, to arrive at some kind of new perspective or transcendent realization on the material or immaterial world – whether the pastoral, almost Epicurean philosophy of a simple life, partnered with Buddhist notions of the alleviation of mental cares, which Kazantzakis' narrator finds personified in the form of the witty shepherd in the Minoan ruins,[354] or the material sublime, the resplendent world divorced from thought, which Miller finds at Phaistos.[355] So too Amon Sûl is a place where revelations can be had, which offers the visiting hobbits the chance of reflection and realization. For Frodo, such a realization is, on the one hand, not entirely pleasant, as it is in this lonely place that the gravity of his predicament, 'his homelessness and danger', dawns on him;[356] on the other hand, the Númenórean ruins also offer the distressed hobbit some vague sense of hope, personified by the figure of Gandalf, who has left his rune marks on a stone atop a cairn among the ruins.[357] Hope is one of the pervasive, Christian virtues which almost all of Tolkien's positive characters exhibit at some stage or other.

The ruins at Amon Sûl also provide a kind of retrospective, historical hope in the face of grim worldly affairs. Just as Byron, experiencing the sublime landscapes of Thermopylae and Salamis, felt how the Hellenism of ancient Greece might reawaken the spirit of an oppressed modern Greece under the Ottomans,[358] so the travellers in the Fellowship are offered hope in their present through the stimulation of the ancient elven-Númenórean historical events which occurred at the ruins.[359] The stationary ruins provide a consistent spatial connection with the distant, triumphant past. The earlier defeat of Sauron at the hands of the Last Alliance, during the Second Age of Middle-earth, offers an historical precedent and, importantly, an awakened sense of hope, which motivates the quintet of travellers in their struggles against Sauron's minions in the Third Age. It is unsurprising that the four hobbits, when camping on the hill fort later on, beg Strider to tell them more about the ancient history of the elves – not for the sake of storytelling in itself but because it brings hope, lifting their hearts from the darkness which seems to surround them.[360] More abstractly, though, apart from the patriotism of past victories and the hope it stirs, for the modern dwellers of Middle-earth ancient elven-Númenórean culture functions in rather the same way that ancient Graeco-Roman and, more particularly, Classical Athenian culture has functioned for post-classical traditions. In both cases, the ancient cultures were regarded in posterity as epistemologically superior, representing the birth of creative art forms, philosophy and 'western' knowledge or lore.[361]

In sum, the ruins at Weathertop function in the characteristic manner of the 'ancient sublime object' in the post-classical imagination: acting as a grand object from the past which disorients travellers; threatening terrible, ghostly apparitions; and affording them some form of awakening – namely, a connection with the absent Gandalf, himself a spirit, with the patriotic triumphs and cultural greatness of 'classical' history and with a restoration of hope. Much later in *The Fellowship of the Ring*, after the company of nine walkers has passed by Caradhras and through Moria, where they lose Gandalf, into Lothlórien, and down the river Anduin, they confront another great relic of Númenórean power: the Argonath.[362] Tolkien neatly classifies this experience as definitively sublime when he describes how Frodo is overcome by the characteristic sublime emotions: 'awe and fear fell upon Frodo'.[363] The terrible wonder makes Frodo 'cower down'; he is struck by the awe-inspiring grandness of the sublime object, which 'seemed to him [as] vast grey figures silent but threatening'.[364] Sam too experiences the terrible awe of the sublime statues: 'What a horrible place! Just let me get out of this boat, and I'll never wet my toes in a puddle again.'[365] In spite of the hobbits' timid reaction, the ancient statues also seem to offer some form of awakening or epiphany,[366] and Frodo, turning back from the statues to the company, sees Strider as Aragorn for the first time, the future king of Gondor, and indeed much of Middle-earth, but also the last true descendant in the line of Númenor.[367] As with Byron's renewed Hellenism, inspired by classical sites and designed to 'reawaken' Greek nationalism, the ideal which is stirred by the Argonath and reflected in Aragorn is, in part, patriotic pride and reverence; Boromir reveals as much by bowing his head and in his subsequent appeals to the party and to Frodo, specifically, to 'make Gondor great again'.[368]

The final ruin which is visited by Frodo, at the moment when the Fellowship disintegrates and the various members go on their various paths, is Amon Hen. Still wearing the One Ring, which he slipped on to escape the maddened Boromir, Frodo is gifted a kind of second sight by virtue of his position on 'the ancient chair' around the crumbling ruins of Amon Hen;[369] this is a place of visual transcendence which enables the hobbit to behold all the lands to the north, west, south and east and the preparations which are being made for war by both sides.

In summary, then, the ancient ruins of Númenor, which are scattered around Middle-earth do not function as simple theatrical backdrops in front of which the action occurs; they are imbued with ancient cultural meanings, and function as places where the various characters, especially the mundane hobbits Merry, Sam and Frodo, can experience the 'Númenórean sublime', just as various romantics experienced the sublime at Graeco-Roman ruins and moderns at the ruins at Knossos and other Minoan sites. There is a sense of cognitive dissonance at the immensity of the ruins – the great, 'Egyptian' monumental architecture of the Argonath perhaps recalling ancient superstructures such as the Colossi of Memnon[370] or even the Colossus of Rhodes, which also guards a waterway. At the ruins the travellers experience typical feelings of wonder, awe and terror, the last of which can lead to feelings of wraith-like horror, to nightmares, to the apparitions of thecemetery. Yet in Tolkien's optimistic sublime there is always the chance for transcendence above the ordinary experience, which can be expressed in varying terms: the perspective of the greater world which Frodo gains, literally at Amon Hen and psychologically at Amon Sûl; a sense of renewed national spirit and of pride being awakened; the chance to learn about the greatness of 'classical' history; and, perhaps most importantly, the pervasive sense of hope in the face of grimness and defeat which underlies much of Tolkien's Christian-inspired philosophy.

# Epilogue

## Ancient Trees in Tolkien's Forest

Northern Irish writer C.S. Lewis was Tolkien's close friend for many years, a firm ally in the Oxford English Faculty, and also a fellow member of the creative-writers circle called the Inklings. In his seven-part children's series *The Chronicles of Narnia* (1950–6), Lewis constructs a fantasy world with permeable borders that allows for the physical intrusion of his own mid-twentieth-century British society: thus, the four Pevensie children (Peter, Susan, Edmund and Lucy) and their friends may enter Narnia through a magical wardrobe, a painting and a mundane railway station. Lewis also does not try to shut out the direct intrusion of his own inherited, 'real-world' cultural histories, literatures and myths from Narnia. This means that a character such as Father Christmas can sleigh over the frozen landscapes of Narnia and delight the Pevensie children with gifts. It also means that a host of classical creatures and characters frequent Lewis' children's stories and that there are direct references to Graeco-Roman literature. For instance, one of the main characters in *The Lion, the Witch and the Wardrobe* (1950) is a Roman faun with the Latin name of Mr Tumnus, while satyrs, fauns and dryads all make an appearance in *The Silver Chair* (1953);[1] and perhaps the most noteworthy classical intrusion occurs in *Prince Caspian* (1951),[2] with a Euripidean cast that includes Bacchus, Silenus and Maenads, who prove unstoppable in supplanting the greedy Telmarines. At one point during their sea adventure in *The Voyage of the Dawn Treader* (1952),[3] the talking mouse Reepicheep suggests binding Prince Caspian to the ship's mast, to which Edmund makes the obvious Ulyssean analogy.

There is none of this overt, direct Lewisian intrusion of figures and events from classical literature into the fantasy landscape of Middle-earth, apart from one anomalous, brief reference to a 'dryad loveliness'[4] in 'classical' Ithilien.[5] Middle-earth seems hermetically sealed off from our own world. There are no open doorways, whether cultural or physical, as graphically represented in Lewis' *The Magician's Nephew* (1955).[6] While there are vague memories of mythic and historical figures and events from classical literature in Tolkien's writing – such that one might identify Aragorn with the Roman founder-restorer duo of Aeneas and Augustus, Bilbo with trickster hero Odysseus, who reclaims his home, or Tom Bombadil with a musician such as Orpheus, who enchants the natural world – the opaqueness of Middle-earth, its ou-topian wonder and newness, can never totally be shaken off by a reader. One reason for this opaque, hermetic quality is the sheer density of Tolkien's accumulated, inherited traditions. Tolkien employed two interesting metaphors to describe his creative processes: he compared his stories to a cauldron of soup which receives flavour from different bones, so revising a metaphor from folklorist Sir George Webbe Dasent,[7] and to a compost heap, a whole which is matured from individual leaves.[8] Both these comparisons bring up the same idea. There is an integration of multiple, different leaves or bones into the mixture of a story – in classical reception terms, the mixing of classical and non-classical contexts together. As a reader with a strong classical background might detect the influence of Aeneas or Augustus in the figure of Aragorn, scholars with expertise in Old English heroic epic, Celtic mythology or medieval romance have discovered different Aragorns. Tolkien's classical reception is thus always mixed with other literary, mythic traditions; it is always partial.[9]

Importantly, unlike Lewis, Tolkien's reception is also always indirect – allusive, covert or symbolic. This, to continue the soup and compost metaphors, is because the creative processes of brewing or composting ensure that the 'matter' which is ladled to the reader of the stories, or the matter which Tolkien uses to garden, is new, distinct, valuable and worth understanding in terms of its *own creation*, within the logic of Tolkien's hermetic universe. It was perhaps the fear of future scholars excavating the bones and, by extension, reducing the soup to a mere sum of its parts which led to Tolkien's rather disparaging thoughts on the virtues of source-based studies. One might appropriate another well-known proverbial metaphor and declare that the dendrophilic Tolkien was perhaps concerned that his readers would not see the forest for the trees. This study of classical reception has been largely concerned with examining 'ancient trees' for the express purpose of appreciating and understanding Tolkien's 'forest'.

This has meant not simply examining the transmission of individual classical 'trees' in Tolkien's stories in Middle-earth – parallels between characters, objects, events and places – but identifying *broader narratives* that have been received and rewritten from ancient literature and thought, 'clusters of trees' which inform our reading of Tolkien's works. Thus, lapsarian narratives which are centred on the decline, collapse and, sometimes, the restoration of ancient communities or cities, including Atlantis and Rome, inform the stories of declining communities in Middle-earth, such as Númenor and Gondor; the seminal Western hospitality narrative of Homer's *Odyssey*, which explores the proper relationship between hosts and guests in a home, provides an ethical framework for appreciating *The Hobbit*; and sublime narratives in natural arenas, such as the archetypal forest of Ovid's *Metamorphoses*, provide a basis for Tolkien's rewriting of his own sublime narratives, as in the Old Forest sequence of *The Fellowship of the Ring*.

In analyzing Tolkien's receptions of these ancient narratives, one needs to look beyond the individual trees as structural units and appreciate the meaning behind these narrative receptions, to our understanding of the 'forest', the broader architecture of Middle-earth, in which Tolkien's stories take place. Tolkien's engagement with such ancient narratives is, in the analysis of this book, governed by an overarching utopianism. On the one hand, Tolkien's utopianism entails an imaginative, defamiliarizing usage of narrative space, with Middle-earth representing a strange, other, foreign ou-topia to be discovered by the reader; on the other hand, Tolkien's narrative exploration of Middle-earth is really a kind of re-exploration, and indeed rewriting, of places past, such that one might better call it a retrotopianism. It is clear that certain places in Middle-earth – be they communities, individual homes or natural environments – seem to draw on a rich classical (and post-classical) narrative imagination of similar places. What is important to recognize in this retrotopianism is Tolkien's great interest in the potential eu-topianism of these ancient narrative spaces:[10] the ability of lapsarian narratives to provide utopian visions of perfective communities which can be restored, often in quite specific political, religious, moral or philosophical respects; of hospitality narratives to explore the ethical ideal of the home, meandering between idyllic visions and the entirely inhospitable towards a reciprocal model; of sublime narratives to act as an ambiguous, dangerous site where characters can experience the awakening of both the material (the natural world) and the immaterial (the divine).

This is not to say that the actual ideals which Tolkien discovers are necessarily always the very same as those of ancient texts, although Platonic moderation, Augustan restoration, Homeric xenophilia and the Ovidian material sublime are all reflected in his works. Tolkien's retrotopianism always entails a rewriting of ancient narratives in post-classical and modern contexts.[11] One way of appreciating this is to compare and contrast his retrotopianism with that of other twentieth-century literary and philosophical texts. Firstly, just as Tolkien explains the falls of various 'ancient-world' cities in his legendarium in a manner which conforms to the author's Catholic, religiously conservative, anti-modern, anti-imperial, politically liberal worldview, so too modern cinema has often explained *why* 'the ancient city must fall' in concrete modern terms: because of anti-Christian paganism (*Quo Vadis*), because of anti-republican, fascist government (*Gladiator*), because of dangerous, anti-rational, religious thought (*Troy*). Secondly, Tolkien's ethical explorations of the home through a Homeric lens puts him in conversation with several twentieth-century writings which used paradigms borrowed from ancient Greek contexts to explore the ideals of hospitality and xenophilia, not least Jacques Derrida; interestingly, like Derrida, Tolkien not only idealizes an ancient form of hospitality but puts this traditional, religiously sanctioned form in jeopardy in a modernizing, technocratic world governed by state hospitality (Saruman) and commercial hospitality (the Master of Lake-town). Lastly, Tolkien's representations of the sublime draw on various early modern and romantic narratives, where the transformative experience of this phenomenon was often encouraged by coming into contact not only with the natural world but also with 'ancient-world' Númenórean ruins; such sublime narratives centred on ancient ruins have been a particular feature of travel and semi-autobiographic writings – in Tolkien's lifetime the Minoan ruins at Knossos and elsewhere in Crete gave writers such as Henry Miller, Lawrence Durrell and Nikos Kazantzakis a chance to experience sublime revelations.

Ultimately, it must be conceded that many modern thinkers will find the concrete version of utopia which Tolkien's narratives tend to construct disappointingly retrogressive or conservative. From the findings of this book, one might draw up an ideal Tolkienian settlement in the Morean tradition of utopian fiction. From a political perspective, it must surely be an imperial, 'Augustan' regency backed up by a Platonic sophocratic nobility, with perhaps further medieval class hierarchies implied; the church and state are not separate entities here, since it is a religiously pious, blessed and ultimately Catholic utopia where technology is regarded as essentially the corruption of the Devil. Economically, all mass commercial trade is regarded as destructive to sound morals, especially if trade comes over the sea from the Orient, although bartering and exchange on the Homeric level of the *oikos* are not frowned upon; yet on an individual level, free movement across roads and reciprocal exchanges with individuals from other cultures is particularly welcomed as a means of ensuring that the utopia does not become stagnant and provincial in its ways. On the level of 'sound morals', traditional families are probably given state subsidies in this utopia, although bachelor heroes can also rise to prominence. On a more abstract philosophical level, a general principle of moderation and balance holds sway. Lastly, this utopian 'city' itself is necessarily dressed in green gardens, and outside its borders lies the dangerous archetypal forest, wherein can be found a universal truth which lies outside the limited utopian structures of the City of Man, although this sublime truth is ultimately that of the Gospels, the City of God.

A modern, hyper-technocratic, secular, post-humanist progressive might find Tolkien's utopian ideas to be, essentially, dystopian, and the reader is reminded here that one man's utopia is another woman's dystopia, as many female readers of Thomas More's eponymous book have discovered. Still, over and above concrete utopia, there is something to be said in favour of the long-lasting importance of Tolkien's *utopianism*, as a form of literary thought, to the modern fantasy genre: first, it simultaneously defamiliarizes and refamiliarizes physical space for the reader – so providing the blueprint for modern fantasy, which draws on but also necessarily *obscures* and rewrites antiquity and the medieval world; second, it has established a set of common places – the paradisical island, the city, the home, the forest – which are peculiar to the utopian thought of fantasy literature (as opposed to the interstellar realms of science fiction); and third, it is, above all, concerned with the narrative exploration of what these places mean on the level of ideals and ethics.

# Notes

## Introduction

1 Morson 1981: 74; Williams 2021a: xvi–xviii.
2 See Kawin 2012: 2, 13–14.
3 James and Mendlesohn 2012: 3.
4 Shippey 2014: xvii–xviii.
5 Vieira 2010: 5.
6 Cf. Suvin 2010: 17.
7 *Definition of utopianism* 2021.
8 See Vieira 2010: 3, 6–7.
9 See Marty 2003: 82; Morris and Kross 2009: xxi, xxxvi–xxxvii; Vieira 2010: 21–2; on utopianism as communism or totalitarianism, see Evans 2008: 1; Suvin 2010: 12–14; Vieira 2010: 20.
10 Morris and Kross 2009: xxi; see Ferns 1999: 5; Suvin 2010: 21–2.
11 See Morris and Kross 2009: xxxviii; Suvin 2010: 19; cf. Ferns 1999: 4–5.
12 See Morris and Kross 2009: xxiii–xxiv.
13 Bruce 1999: xi; Suvin 2010: 19–21, 24–6.
14 Bruce 1999: xi–xii; Vieira 2010: 5–6.
15 Vieira 2010: 7–18.
16 See Wolf 2012: 86.
17 See Ferns 1999: 2; Suvin 2010: 30.
18 Bruce 1999: xiv.
19 Bruce 1999: xxi; see Davis 2010: 38.
20 Bruce 1999: xiv, xix–xxv; Davis 2010: 31–2, 40; Ferns 1999: 3.
21 Bruce 1999: xxvi; for receptions of More's *Utopia*, see Bruce 1999: xxi; Davis 2010: 30.
22 See Bruce 1999: xiv.
23 See Wolf 2012: 95–6.
24 Bruce 1999: xv.
25 Suvin 2010: 17.
26 Cf. Bruce 1999: xi, xiii–xv.
27 Adams [1972] 1982.
28 Durrell [1947] 2001.

29 Cf. Bruce 1999: ix–x; Ferns 1999: 2–3; Rothstein 2003: 2, 7.
30 On such pragmatic utopianism, see Vieira 2010: 22.
31 On the distinction between constructed utopias and utopianism as a form of thought, see Evans 2008: 2; Rothstein 2003: 11.
32 See Ferns 1999: 13–27; Vieira 2010: 7ff.
33 See Bruce 1999: x–xi; Ferns 1999: 19; Morris and Kross 2009: xxvi–xxvii; Vieira 2010: 4.
34 Thus, the traveller of utopian fiction became a mere tourist; see Ferns 1999: 19–20.
35 Ferns 1999: 176; Wolf 2012: 95–6.
36 Wolf 2012: 96.
37 On 'mapping' utopian fiction, see Bruce 1999: xii.
38 Fimi and Honegger 2019: ii.
39 Wolf 2012: 130–4.
40 Wolf 2019: 2–5.
41 Wolf 2019: 2.
42 On worldbuilding as beyond the story narrative, see Wolf 2012: 7–12.
43 Bregman 2017; for utopianism as a process or a strategy, see Vieira 2010: 22–3.
44 According to Wolf (2019: 5–12), invented worlds are always dependent on or built on familiar, 'real-world' constructs; no work of literature can create an absolute otherness, an entirely 'new continent' – rather only the appearance of one.
45 See Lee (ed.) 2014: Essays 15 to 20. *Contra*, on the modernity of Tolkien's writings, see Honegger and Weinreich (eds) 2006a; 2006b; Ordway 2021; Shippey 2014: xxvii; Vaninskaya 2014.
46 Fisher 2011: 32–4; Honegger 2005: 45–6, 54–65. For linguistic contexts, see Atherton 2014; Birkett 2014; Solopova 2014. In general, the works of Thomas Honegger, Tom Shippey and Jane Chance are good starting points to understand Tolkien's medievalism.
47 For a summary of the Christian character of Tolkien's literary works, see Birzer 2007a: 88–9; 2007b: 99–101.
48 See Honegger 2005: 50–1; 2014.
49 For a summary of the role of Christian, Catholic faith in Tolkien's life, see Birzer 2007a: 85–9; 2007c: 101–3; Pinsent 2014: 448–9.
50 On classical education in England during the Victorian and (post-)Edwardian periods, see Stray 1992; 1998.
51 Carpenter [1977] 2002: 38.
52 Carpenter [1977] 2002: 42, 53.
53 Carpenter [1977] 2002: 45, 47.
54 *Letters* no. 163, p. 213.
55 Williams 2021c: 6–7: see Hutton 1952: 107.

56 Carpenter [1977] 2002: 54–5.
57 Williams 2021c: 7–8 (with a list of likely prescribed texts); cf. *Letters* no. 272, pp. 356–7.
58 Williams 2021c: 8; as indicated by examinations, cf. Williams 2021c: 11–12.
59 Carpenter [1977] 2002: 73; Scull and Hammond 2006a: 14; Williams 2021c: 9–10.
60 Carpenter [1977] 2002: 74; Garth 2003: 18; Scull and Hammond 2006b: 226; Williams 2021c: 10.
61 Scull and Hammond 2006a: 11.
62 *Letters* no. 272, p. 357.
63 For further information on these examinations, see Williams 2021c: 10–12.
64 For quotations from the original examination reports, see Williams 2021c: 12.
65 On Tolkien's scholarships, see Williams 2021c: 13.
66 On Tolkien's university syllabus, see Scull and Hammond 2006b: 173–4. On classical education at Oxford (including Tolkien's period), see Stray (ed.) 2013.
67 Carpenter [1977] 2002: 80; Garth 2014: 21.
68 See Garth 2003: 30; Garth 2014: 19; Scull and Hammond 2006a: 33, 38; Williams 2021c: 14–15.
69 Carpenter [1977] 2002: 90; cf. Garth 2003: 3–4, 30.
70 Williams 2021c: 16–19.
71 Stray 1998: 186; cf. Fletcher 1910: 106; Wells 1918: 184.
72 Garth 2014: 21; Williams 2021c: 16.
73 Carpenter [1977] 2002: 57; Garth 2003: 15; Librán-Moreno 2007b: 344–5; Williams 2021c: 6.
74 Williams 2021c: 17; cf. Carpenter [1977] 2002: 82.
75 Carpenter [1977] 2002: 80; Garth 2014: 21.
76 *Letters* no. 131, p. 144.
77 Livingston 2013: 78–9.
78 *Letters* no. 156, p. 201; Livingston 2013: 79.
79 On Petrarch's characterization of medieval culture with regard to Classics, see Kallendorf 2007: 1–3.
80 See Stray 2007: 6.
81 See Hardwick and Stray 2008: 4–5.
82 See Hardwick 2007: 4.
83 Simpson and Weiner (eds) 1989: 281.
84 Hardwick 2007: 1–4.
85 Rogers and Stevens 2017: 9.
86 On Tolkien's broader, Indo-European understanding of the classical world, see Burton 2021.
87 *Letters* no. 131, p. 150, 154.
88 *WR* 229–30; *SD* 281.

89 *Letters* no. 294, p. 377; Renault [1958] 1961, [1960] 2015.
90 Scull and Hammond 2006a: 51.
91 Scull and Hammond 2006a: 341.
92 Williams 2021c: 25–9: *Letters* no. 52, pp. 63–4; no. 77, p. 89.
93 Carpenter [1977] 2002: 162.
94 Birzer 2007a: 86.
95 Scull and Hammond 2006a: 153.
96 *Letters* no. 294, p. 376.
97 See Stray 1998: 178–83.
98 Morse 1986; Reckford 1974.
99 E.g. Bruce 2012; Fenwick 1996; Greenman 1992; Reckford 2003.
100 See Fisher 2011: 30, 40–1; Risden 2011: 20.
101 Freeman 2021.
102 Stevens 2017; 2021.
103 Pezzini 2021.
104 Williams (ed.) 2021b.
105 For Wolf (2019: 5–9), the strangeness of a constructed world, the 'new continent' in Shippey's terms, has to always be constrained and familiarized by certain elements.
106 On interactions between classical and non-classical contexts in classical reception studies, see Hardwick and Stray 2008: 1.
107 On the ideal of direct influences in Tolkien's works, see Risden 2011: 17–18.

# 1 Lapsarian Narratives: The Decline and Fall of Utopian Communities in Middle-earth

1 Potts 2016: 149; Rateliff 2006: 67, 80; Sanford 1995; Stoddard 2010.
2 'Lapsarian' is used here as an adjectival synonym for 'of the fall' – a sense including both decline (a process of falling) and collapse (an apparently terminal point) – without any implications about the order of divine decrees in theology (see Allen 2009: 299–315)
3 *Letters* no. 131, p. 147.
4 *Letters* no. 131.
5 *Letters* no. 96, p. 109–10.
6 *Letters* no. 43, p. 48.
7 See Tolkien's warnings to his middle son Michael: *Letters* no. 43, p. 48, 51.
8 On biblical narratives in *The Silmarillion*, see Garbowski 1998: 49–62; Huttar 2008: 8; Sanford 1995: 15; Shippey 1992: 209, 213ff. On Milton's *Paradise Lost* and

Tolkien's use of the fall, see Huttar 1975: 138; Shippey 1992: 209–10, 213. For the Garden of Eden in Tolkien's *Leaf by Niggle*, see Kaufmann 1975.
9  Kowalik 2020: 46.
10 For the importance of biblical temptation in narratives of decline in Tolkien's work, see Sanford 1995: 16–19; for allusions to Christian ideas on materialism and idolatry in the Silmarils, see Shippey 1992: 214.
11 *Letters* no. 43, p. 48, 51; see Pinsent 2014: 453–4.
12 On Christian readings of Boromir's story (temptation, betrayal, redemption, confession), see Neubauer 2020; Wood 2003: 63–4, 154–5.
13 Watts 2021: 109–10.
14 *Letters* no. 195, p. 255.
15 See Devine 2016: 10–11.
16 See Devine 2016: 10.
17 See Huttar 2008: 4. For three ages in Christian thought, see Fasching 1993: 22.
18 Potts 2016: 150.
19 See Sanford 1995: 19; cf. Huttar 2008: 12–13.
20 See Huttar 2008: 4; Wicher 2020: 116–17.
21 See Birzer 2002: 55–6.
22 Huttar 2008: 4–5.
23 Huttar 2008: 4–5.
24 *Letters* no. 131, p. 150.
25 Szyjewski 2020.
26 Eilmann 2021.
27 *Letters* no. 131, p. 150.
28 On his schoolboy interactions with Greek drama, see Carpenter [1977] 2002: 74; Scull and Hammond 2006b: 315. For Tolkien's views on Shakespeare, see *Letters* no. 76, p. 88; no. 156, p. 201; cf. Shippey 1992: 163.
29 Librán-Moreno 2005: 17–21.
30 Drout 2004: 139–41, 144–9; Freeman 2021: 146–50 (an anti-Priam).
31 Shippey 1992: 165.
32 Harrisson 2021: 342; Stevens 2021: 111.
33 See *OFS* 75.
34 Stevens 2021: 123; see Harrisson 2021: 342.
35 See Potts 2016; Rateliff 2006; Stevens 2021; Stoddard 2010.
36 Huttar 2008: 8; Stoddard 2010: 153; Stevens 2021: 115.
37 Rateliff 2006: 67.
38 Huttar 2008: 12; Stoddard 2010: 151–2; Stevens 2021: 107.
39 *TT* 88.
40 *RK* 289.

41 See Potts 2016: 149–50; Stoddard 2010: 154–9.
42 Rateliff 2006: 68–9, *passim*.
43 See Huttar 1975: 131.
44 *BLT2* 196–7.
45 *BLT2* 203.
46 Shepard and Powell (eds) 2004; for Tolkien's reception of these medieval Trojan myths, see Livingston 2013.
47 Naquet 2007; for Tolkien's knowledge of post-Platonic Atlantis traditions, see Kleu 2021: 206–9; Leśniewski 2020: 9–11.
48 Watts 2021: 102ff.
49 Ford 2005: 53–8.
50 Watts 2021: 226–33.
51 Potts 2016: 151–3; Watts 2021: 222–6; for the influence of Spenglerian tropes on Tolkien, see Potts 2016.
52 Hesiod, *Works and Days* 106–26; Ovid, *Metamorphoses* 1.89–112; Most 1997: 104. For similar golden-age constructs in Cratinus, Pausanias, Tibullus, Virgil and Seneca, see Heinberg 1989: 48–9; Most 1997: 105. For other anthropological contexts of the golden-age motif, see Heinberg 1989: 39–56.
53 Evans 2008: 17.
54 Hesiod, *Works and Days* 170–3; Ovid *Metamorphoses* 1.94–6.
55 On characteristics of the 'Hesiodic' golden-age paradise, see Dougherty 2001: 88; Fontenrose 1974: 5.
56 Diodorus Siculus, *Library of History* 5.19; Strabo, *The Geography* 1.1.5; Plutarch, *Life of Sertorius* 8.
57 On Alcinous' perennial garden, see Homer, *Odyssey* 7.115–26; De Jong [2001] 2004: 176; Edwards 1993: 47–8.
58 Segal 1962: 27–8.
59 See Homer, *Odyssey* 7.203; Dougherty 2001: 88–9.
60 On other spatially (though not necessarily temporally) remote paradisical islands in classical literature, see Evans 2008: 14–17.
61 Most 1997: 104.
62 The myth of the 'four (/three) ages' can be found in Aratus, Horace, Antipater of Thessalonica, Seneca, Juvenal and Proclus (Most 1997: 105–6).
63 Hesiod, *Works and Days* 106–81; Ovid, *Metamorphoses* 1.89–150, 177–98. This is a generalization. Hesiod's fourth 'race of heroes' briefly restores the golden race; see Hesiod, *Works and Days* 167–173; Most 1997: 104; Querbach 1985: 8.
64 Plato, *Timaeus* 25c–25d.
65 Homer, *Odyssey* 13.96–187.
66 *UT* 216–17.

67 Hamfast ('Gaffer') Gamgee best exemplifies this sense of hobbitish otium; see *FR* 28–31, 34.
68 *S* 56–63.
69 Kowalik 2020: 58.
70 Bruce 1999: xii.
71 See Evans 2008: 1–2, 6; Marty 2003: 58; Morson 1981: 76; Suvin 2010: 37, 39.
72 Huttar 2008: 3.
73 Cf. Morson 1981: 74.
74 For this sub-genre of utopian literature, see Ferns 1999: 105–38; Morson 1981: 73; Rothstein 2003: 3–4; Wolf 2012: 95.
75 For the fluctuation between utopian and dystopian imaginings in post–Second World War science fiction, see Moylan 2000: 9.
76 On the paradisical countryside versus the utopian city, see Evans 2008: 12.
77 Evans 2008: 3, 12, 17; Suvin 2010: 22–3, 39. On this religious/secular division, see Heinberg 1989: 146; Marty 2003: 64–5; cf. Bruce 1999: xii. *Contra* secular idealism of utopian literature in the early modern period, see Morris and Kross 2009: xxv–xxvii.
78 Boym 2007: 13.
79 For the intersection of ideas of progress with constructions of utopias, see Marty 2003: 82; Rothstein 2003: 3.
80 Suvin 2010: 30; cf. Bruce 1999: xii–xiii.
81 See Evans 2008: 1–2, 32.
82 Most 1997: 108.
83 Most 1997: 115–16.
84 Most 1997: 108; see Evans 2008: 34.
85 Most 1997: 116.
86 See Most 1997: 108.
87 Evans 2008: 36–48.
88 Evans 2008: 3. For golden-age myths as forward-looking, see Heinberg 1989: xxx.
89 Evans 2008: 38–9.
90 On the city as an important *topos* of utopia/dystopia, and the Graeco-Roman roots behind this *topos*, see Evans 2008: 3–4.
91 Watts 2021: 3; particularly strong are the moral aspects of decline; see Evans 2008: 5–6.
92 Watts 2021: 7–15.
93 Watts 2021: 16–23.
94 Watts 2021: 23–8; 40–52.
95 Watts 2021: 102–17; see Ando 2008: 31.
96 See Watts 2021: 1–3ff.

97 Evans 2008: 31.
98 See Huttar 2008: 6.
99 *UT* 216–17; *S* 311–13. While such longevity is a biblical motif, Hesiod's golden race of men do enjoy long-lasting youth (Hesiod, *Works and Days* 113–16).
100 *Letters* no. 131, p. 150–7.
101 Plato, *Critias* 108e–121c; *Timaeus* 20c–26c.
102 Delattre 2007: 305–8; Kleu 2021: 201–6; Leśniewski 2020: 13–18; Ponsen 1985: 23–6.
103 See *Letters* no. 131, p. 150–1; no. 144, p. 175; no. 151, p. 186; no. 154, p. 197–8; no. 156, p. 206; no. 163, p. 213; no. 227, p. 303; no. 252, p. 342; no. 257, p. 347; no. 276, p. 361; no. 294, p. 378.
104 *S* 337.
105 *SD* 281.
106 Kleu 2021: 206.
107 For a further overview of similarities, see Kleu 2021: 201–3; Ponsen 1985: 23–6.
108 *Letters* no. 131, p. 154.
109 *Letters* no. 131, p. 155.
110 *Letters* no. 131, p. 154.
111 Plato, *Timaeus* 23b–c, 25c–d.
112 Williams 2020a: 146–50.
113 See *Letters* no. 154, p. 197–8; no. 227, p. 303; no. 276, p. 361; no. 294, p. 378.
114 Tolkien's assumption does not necessarily imply that there *was* an actual mythic tradition of such seafaring communities in the ancient Greek imagination.
115 *Letters* no. 227, p. 303.
116 *Letters* no. 163, p. 213; no. 180, p. 232; no. 257, p. 347.
117 *Letters* no. 227, p. 303.
118 See Fraser 1929: 157; Shewan 1919: 8–10.
119 Plato, *Timaeus* 25b = *S* 332–4.
120 *S* 334 = Herodotus 7.170; cf. Diodorus Siculus 4.79.5–7.
121 *S* 334.
122 Homer *Odyssey* 13.96–187.
123 *S* 334–5 = Plato, *Timaeus* 25d. On modern theories of Minoan natural catastrophe, some of which predate Tolkien's creative output, see Middleton 2017: 114–18; Ponsen 1985: 38.
124 Plato, *Timaeus* 20d–23a.
125 *Timaeus* 26a.
126 *UT* 213.
127 *UT* 213.
128 See Vidal-Naquet 2007: 17.

129 *UT* 213.
130 Harrisson 2021: 334–5.
131 *UT* 213.
132 The term 'thalassocracy' refers to a political entity, such as an empire or a kingdom, which has attained prominence through the domination of the seas, for example through establishing a powerful navy or strong trade networks.
133 On Tolkien's familiarity with Thucydides, see Williams 2021c: 7–8; there is probably an allusion to Herodotus' Xerxes at *Letters* no. 52.
134 Clare 2021: 43–56.
135 To be clear, this book uses the terms 'Orient', 'Oriental', 'Orientalized' (etc.) to designate an Occidental-centric discourse, a 'Western' school of representing the culturally imagined 'East', in line with the work of Edward Said ([1978] 1979). This 'Orient' is, in no way, regarded as the 'real East', as experienced by its inhabitants (if indeed such an overarching term is in itself helpful). Similarly, 'Occident' and 'Occidental' refer to a 'Western' imaginary, discourse and representation of itself. Uncapitalized forms of 'east' and 'west' in this book refer, without ideology, to the mere cartographic directions.
136 See Taylor (transl.) [1929] 2013: 104–5; Vidal-Naquet 2007: 24–5.
137 See Plato, *Timaeus* 20d–23c, 24b; Ponsen 1985: 27; Taylor (transl.) [1929] 2013: 21. On Egypt as Oriental and Graeco-Roman ethnic stereotyping, see Sidebottom 2004: 16–21.
138 Herodotus 1.98–9 = Plato, *Critias* 115c–116d.
139 Herodotus 1.185–6 = Plato, *Critias* 118c–e; Gill 1977: 292; cf. Taylor (transl.) [1929] 2013: 103–4.
140 Rowe 2007: 102; see Welliver 1977: 41, 43.
141 Plato, *Timaeus* 24e–25b.
142 *Timaeus* 25a–b.
143 *Timaeus* 24e; Lee (transl.) 2008: 15.
144 It is problematic to draw textual links between the narratives of (supposed) divine punishment, the defeat to Athens and the (global) natural catastrophe. For further literature on such problems, see Kleu 2021: 196n9–10; Williams 2020a: 158–9.
145 Cairns 1996: 14.
146 Plato, *Critias* 121b.
147 See Cairns 1996: 13, 17–22; Robertson 1955: 81–3; on problems defining *hybris* (e.g. as dispositional or behavioural; traditional or new/'Platonic'), see Cairns 1996.
148 This god remains nameless; Taylor ((transl.) [1929] 2013: 127) suspects Zeus.
149 Plato, *Critias* 120d–e.

150 Cf. Welliver 1977: 35–6, 40.
151 On Herodotean Xerxes as *hybristēs*, see Cairns 1996: 13.
152 Cf. Gill 1977: 298; Welliver 1977: 43.
153 *S* 313.
154 *S* 313.
155 *S* 313.
156 *S* 311.
157 *S* 319.
158 *S* 319. For Oriental, Persian elements in the imperialism of these late Númenóreans in Middle-earth, see Williams 2020b: 414–16; see also Ar-Pharazôn's Egyptian name (Walsh 2007b: 145).
159 *S* 333–4.
160 Plato, *Critias* 121a. On the tension in ancient representations of golden ages between wealth (profusive nature, etc.) as a marker of, for instance, divine benediction and wealth as a sign of material (Orientalized) decay, see Evans 2008: 14–21.
161 Plato, *Critias* 119c–d.
162 *Critias* 119d–120b.
163 *Critias* 115b.
164 *Critias* 121a; Lee (transl.) 2008: 15.
165 *Critias* 120e.
166 Homer, *Odyssey* 7.159–66.
167 *Odyssey* 6.10.
168 *Odyssey* 8.570–1.
169 *Odyssey* 13.181–4.
170 *UT* 214.
171 Plato, *Critias* 113d.
172 *UT* 214–15; see Rosario Monteiro 1993: 635.
173 *Knossos* 1.
174 See *Letters* no. 156, p. 206.
175 *S* 318.
176 *S* 319.
177 *S* 327.
178 *S* 313.
179 Cf. *S* 315.
180 On this Oriental-materialist association, see Dougherty 2001: 116–17; Rhodes 2007: 36–7.
181 Plato, *Critias* 116d.
182 *Critias* 117b; Welliver 1977: 43.

183 Plato, *Critias* 117b.
184 Gill 1977: 294; see Taylor (transl.) [1929] 2013: 105.
185 See Plato, *Critias* 120e–121a. On the combination of a love of wealth and a drop in divine essence as causing Atlantean fall, see Gill 1977: 297.
186 See Plato, *Laws* 695–6; Gill 1977: 294n32.
187 Gill 1977: 297; cf. Welliver 1977: 42.
188 Plato, *Critias* 110c–112d; Gill 1977: 295.
189 Gill 1977: 297; see Plato, *Gorgias* 515Cff.; 517Bff. For the trope of Occidental asceticism in the *Odyssey*, see Homer, *Odyssey* 9.27; Austin 1975: 97.
190 For Atlantis as a reflection of Persianized Athens in the fifth century; see Vidal-Naquet 2007: 23; Welliver 1977: 41–3.
191 *S* 312.
192 *UT* 219; see Rosario Monteiro 1993: 636.
193 *Letters* no. 131, p. 155; cf. *S* 318. On the Oriental, Egyptian connotations of the great tombs and mortuary culture, see *Letters* no. 131, p. 155; Ponsen 1985: 26; Scull and Hammond 2006b: 370.
194 *UT* 219.
195 *S* 319.
196 *S* 319.
197 Plato, *Laws* 704C–705B.
198 *Laws* 706C–707D.
199 *Laws* 704D; Bury (transl.) 1956: 257.
200 *Laws* 704D–E; Bury (transl.) 1956: 257.
201 *Laws* 705A; Bury (transl.) 1956: 257.
202 *Laws* 706A–C.
203 *Laws* 706B–C.
204 For other ideas on geography, climate and people in Plato, cf. Romm 2010: 224–5.
205 *UT* 220.
206 *UT* 220–1.
207 *UT* 213–19.
208 *UT* 219.
209 *Letters* no. 131, p. 155.
210 See Delattre 2007: 306–7.
211 *UT* 246.
212 Hoiem 2005: 78.
213 *UT* 223–73.
214 Plato, *Republic* 488a–489a. For an excellent reading of this Platonic passage, I am indebted (as an admiring editor) to an upcoming essay by Prof. Gabriele Cornelli (forthcoming).

215 *Letters* p. 440.
216 *Letters* no. 94, p. 107.
217 *Letters* no. 94, p. 107.
218 *S* 312–13.
219 *S* 318.
220 *S* 320.
221 *RK* 91.
222 *RK* 90–3, 95–6.
223 *TT* 352; on Faramir's (Virgilian) piety, see Freeman 2021: 143–6.
224 *TT* 350.
225 *RK* 295, 297–8.
226 *TT* 344–5.
227 *TT* 346.
228 To come
229 Straubhaar 2007: 249; on 'ancient' Gondor, see Ford 2005; Freeman 2021: 143–53; Harrisson 2021: 333–40; Librán-Moreno 2011.
230 *Letters* no. 211, p. 281; Harrisson 2021: 333–5; Walsh 2007b: 145.
231 See *Letters* no. 294, p. 376; Harrisson 2021: 335–6; Livingston 2013: 80–81, 87–9.
232 Harrisson 2021: 335–6; Librán-Moreno 2011: 87–8.
233 Straubhaar 2007: 249; see Harrisson 2021: 339.
234 *Letters* no. 294, p. 376; see Straubhaar 2007: 249.
235 Ford 2005: 60–2, 67–8; Harrisson 2021: 339.
236 Ford 2005: 62.
237 See *RK* 396; for 'Roman' acculturation in the First Age, see Gallant 2021; for Tolkien's reception of Roman (Tacitus') ethnographies of barbarian peoples, see Ford 2005: 64–5; Straubhaar 2004: 101–9.
238 *RK* 398.
239 Straubhaar 2007: 249.
240 *RK* 396.
241 *RK* 395.
242 *RK* 401.
243 On this long decay, see Ford 2005: 59.
244 Ford 2005: 59.
245 Ford 2005: 70–1.
246 *FR* 522–5.
247 Ford 2005: 62.
248 Ford 2005: 60–1; cf. Librán-Moreno 2011: 87.
249 *RK* 36–7.
250 Librán-Moreno 2011: 88.

251 See Ford 2005: 54.
252 Ford 2005: 62; cf. Harrisson 2021: 338–9.
253 See *RK* 454–69.
254 Librán-Moreno 2011: 87.
255 Harrisson 2021: 337–8; Librán-Moreno 2011.
256 *Letters* no. 131, p. 157.
257 On Gondor's typical 'Roman' (or 'Byzantine') enemies, see Ford 2005: 63–6; Librán-Moreno 2011: 87–108.
258 Ford 2005: 64.
259 *RK* 135–6; cf. Harrisson 2021: 342; Librán-Moreno 2011: 100.
260 Comparing the two battles, see Librán-Moreno 2011: 100–1.
261 See Straubhaar 2007: 249.
262 On the Wainriders as (medieval-focalized) Huns, see Ford 2005: 65–6.
263 Harrisson 2021: 340–5.
264 Ford 2005; cf. Harrisson 2021: 342–435. Or a fairy tale of a restored Troy; see Livingston 2013: 89.
265 *Letters* no. 294, p. 376; see Librán-Moreno 2011: 85.
266 Ford 2005: 69–70; Librán-Moreno 2011: 111–12.
267 Ford 2005: 71.
268 For such post-classical reimaginings, see Ford 2005: 55–8; Watts 2021: 118ff.
269 Straubhaar 2004: 110; *contra*, cf. Librán-Moreno 2011: 85.
270 Stevens 2021: 110.
271 Ford 2005: 59; Aragorn's elvish name literally means 'the Restorer'.
272 Ford 2005: 66.
273 Ford 2005: 66–9.
274 Anzinger 2010: 376–83; Freeman 2021: 132–3.
275 Anzinger 2010: 391–2.
276 Anzinger 2010: 376–80.
277 There are two brothers in each myth; see Straubhaar 2007: 249.
278 Straubhaar 2007: 249.
279 Suetonius *Life of Augustus* 7; see Anzinger 2010: 394–5; Galinksy 2013: 67, 77–8.
280 Ford 2005: 59.
281 For a similar classification of different forms of restoration, see Watts 2021: 27.
282 Watts 2021: 24. Some 'Augustan' Roman writers were critical of the *princeps*: Ovid, Livy and perhaps even Virgil; see Evans 2008: 57; Watts 2021: 24. For a summary of posthumous assessments (ancient and modern) of Augustus, see Galinksy 2013: 179–86. The stylization of an 'Augustan Golden Age' is also, to an extent, a post-classical myth (as this analysis attests); see Galinksy 2013: 84.
283 Ford 2005: 54.

284 See Evans 2008: 4; Watts 2021: 23. For the Juvenalian theme of a dystopian Rome, infrastructure falling apart, see Evans 2008: 4.
285 Suetonius, *Life of Augustus* 28.3; Graves (transl.) [1957] 1979: 61.
286 *Life of Augustus* 29; see Evans 2008: 4.
287 Evans 2008: 4.
288 *RK* 12.
289 *RK* 13.
290 *RK* 14–15.
291 *RK* 170.
292 *RK* 28.
293 *RK* 107.
294 *RK* 297.
295 Jordan 2021: 356; see Horace, *Satires* 1.8.
296 *RK* 169; see *RK* 170. For 'Justinian' architectural renewal in Gondor, see Librán-Moreno 2011: 89.
297 Ovid, *Metamorphoses* 15.833–4; Evans 2008: 69; Watts 2021: 27.
298 *RK* 297–8; for Augustus' advocation of clemency, see Galinsky 2013: 70.
299 Suetonius, *Life of Augustus* 29.1–3; Galinsky 2013: 67–8, 99–107.
300 *RK* 299–302.
301 For the connection with Valinor, see Reckford 1974: 63.
302 For Aragorn's piety in his duties as modelled on Aeneas, see Anzinger 2010: 382–3.
303 Galinsky 2013: 61–3 (citing Augustus' *Res Gestae*); Watts 2021: 24; although this may be regarded as pure propaganda; see Galinsky 2013: 182.
304 *RK* 294.
305 Evans 2008: 6.
306 Ford 2005: 63.
307 Ford 2005: 63; see Galinsky 2013: 96–9; Watts 2021: 25–6.
308 *RK* 12; cf. *RK* 406.
309 *RK* 12; Ford 2005: 53.
310 *RK* 28–9.
311 *RK* 297.
312 *RK* 297.
313 Evans 2008: 21.
314 Evans 2008: 21.
315 Evans 2008: 22.
316 Evans 2008: 22–3.
317 Suetonius, *Life of Augustus* 9–17.
318 *Life of Augustus* 20–1.

319 *Life of Augustus* 21.1-2; Graves (transl.) [1957] 1979: 55-6; for a full discussion of *pax Augusta*, see Galinsky 2013: 85-99.
320 Suetonius, *Life of Augustus* 21.3; see also Horace, *Odes* 4.15.1-6.
321 *RK* 408.
322 *RK* 297.
323 *RK* 314.
324 Suetonius, *Life of Augustus* 21.3.
325 E.g. Watts 2021: 25.
326 Cf. Evans 2008: 2-1, 67-9; Galinsky 2013: 93-5.
327 Virgil, *Aeneid* 6.791-796; Knight (transl.) [1956] 1968: 171.
328 Virgil, *Eclogues* 1.40-5.
329 Virgil, *Georgics* 1.489-7; Galinksy 2013: 92; Watts 2021: 24.
330 *RK* 469-70.
331 See Jordan 2021.
332 Watts 2021: 28.
333 Galinsky 2013: 84.
334 Watts 2021: 228-33.
335 Watts 2021: 223-6.
336 Watts 2021: 234-42; cf. Wyke 1997: 43.
337 See Evans 2008: 31-2.
338 See Wyke 1997: 61-8.
339 Elliot 2014.
340 Winkler 2001: 51.
341 Wyke 1997: 40.
342 Winkler 2001: 51.
343 See Elliot 2014: 10; Richards 2014: 20.
344 Wyke 1997: 74.
345 Wyke 1997: 94-7.
346 Wyke 1997: 114-19.
347 Wyke 1997: 119-20.
348 Elliot 2014: 11.
349 Wyke 1997: 121-35.
350 Wyke 1997: 110.
351 Richards 2014: 22-5.
352 See Wyke 1997: 40-1.
353 See Elliot 2014: 11.
354 The recent Netflix miniseries *Troy: Fall of a City* (2018-present) represents a postcolonial, more critical-leftist interpretation of the narrative.

355 On anti-fundamentalist representations in recent ancient-epic films, see Elliot 2014: 11.
356 For a similar comparison using ancient sources, see Clare 2021: 59–62.
357 See Wyke 1997: 67, 198–9.
358 Wyke 1997: 63; see 252.
359 Wyke 1997: 199. Sienkiewicz' *Quo Vadis* (1895–6) draws heavily on Christian eschatological literature rather than on ancient biography; see Wyke 1997: 199–211.
360 See Wyke 1997: 199–200.
361 On a Christian Spartacus, see Wyke 1997: 103–4, 122–3.
362 *S* 325–6.
363 *S* 326.
364 *S* 328.
365 *S* 325.
366 On the early 'underground' Christian church, see Clare 2021: 60.
367 *S* 327.
368 *S* 327.
369 *S* 328.
370 *S* 328.
371 *S* 329.
372 *S* 288.
373 *S* 328.
374 Cf. *S* 319.
375 *S* 330–1, 33–6.
376 *RK* 107.
377 See Clare 2021: 62.
378 Carpenter [1977] 2002: 40–1, 50–1.
379 *Letters* no. 306, p. 394–5.
380 *Letters* no. 83, p. 94–6.
381 Kazantzakis [1981] 1988; Renault [1958] 1961; Caldecott [1979] 2005.
382 Anderson [1971] 1972.
383 For important scholarship, see Gere 2010; Momigliano 2020; Momigliano and Farnoux (eds) 2017.
384 Evans 1921,
385 For Evans's Minoan ethnography, see *Knossos* 1–31.
386 Cf. *Knossos* 26–7.
387 *Knossos* 2.
388 *Knossos* 22–3.
389 *Knossos* 27.
390 *Knossos* 27–8.

391 Middleton 2017: 114.
392 See *Knossos* 15.
393 *UT* 213–21.
394 For Númenor as a critique of British imperialism, see Hoiem 2005.
395 See *PK* 1.
396 *PK* 4, 86, 193–4.
397 *PK* 153.
398 *PK* 132.
399 Cf. *PK* 20.
400 See *PK* 21, 30; on Aryan Athenians, cf. *PK* 128, 130, 182–3, 187.
401 See *PK* 95.
402 Cf. *PK* 18, 150, 163; see Momigliano 2020: 100–1.
403 See *PK* 27.
404 On the wing-freedom motif, see *PK* 81, 143–4.
405 *PK* 141, 172.
406 *PK* 117.
407 *Letters* no. 294, p. 377.
408 *KMD* 253.
409 *KMD* 47–9; cf. 219, 225.
410 *KMD* 187, 222–6.
411 See Evans 2008: 6–7.
412 *UT* 256–8.
413 See Evans 2008: 6–7.
414 *UT* 258–9.

## 2 Hospitality Narratives: The Ideal of the Home in an Odyssean *Hobbit*

1 On the 'homely houses' in the first chapters of *The Fellowship of the Ring*, see Shippey 2014: 63–5.
2 *Hobbit* Contents.
3 *FR* 297.
4 *Hobbit* 55, 60.
5 *Hobbit* 74.
6 *Hobbit* 228.
7 *Hobbit* 241.
8 De Jong 2012: 1–2. On the neglect of space in literary studies, see Bal 2009: 134; Zoran 1984: 310; on literature as a temporal art, cf. Genette 1980: 215.

9 De Jong 2012: 1–13.
10 De Jong 2012: 13–16.
11 Ruud 2011: 111.
12 Green 1995; 2008.
13 Weinberg 1986.
14 On symbolic rebirths from cave-wombs in the *Odyssey*, see Schein 1995: 19; Segal 1962: 48–9; Weinberg 1986: 30; *contra*, see Ustinova 2009: 3–4.
15 Green 1995: 63.
16 For a similar division of different functions of space in Tolkien's work, also with a focus on the moral aspects of space, see Honegger 2004: 62, 77, *passim*.
17 Michelet 2015: 24.
18 Heffernan 2014. For definitions of hospitality, see Michelet 2015: 23.
19 *Hobbit* Contents.
20 On a didactic *Hobbit*, see Stevens and Stevens 2008: 20.
21 Shippey 2011: 10.
22 See Pinsent 2014: 449–50.
23 *Letters* no. 142, p. 172.
24 *Letters* no. 142, p. 172.
25 Cilli 2019: 126.
26 Cilli 2019: 126.
27 Carpenter [1977] 2002: 58; *contra*, this might be an allusion to John Keats's sonnet 'On First Looking into Chapman's Homer'; thanks to Thomas Honegger for this remark (and many others!)
28 Scull and Hammond 2006b: 173–4.
29 Scull and Hammond 2006a: 34.
30 Scull and Hammond 2006a: 37.
31 *Letters* no. 156, p. 201.
32 *Letters* no. 131, p. 154.
33 *Letters* no. 131, p. 154.
34 *WR* 229.
35 See Scull and Hammond 2006b: 174.
36 Fenwick 1996; Greenman 1992: 7–9; Larini 2019; Librán-Moreno 2005; Pezzini 2021; Reckford 2003; Spirito 2009: 195–6; Williams 2019c: 117–22.
37 Greenman 1992.
38 See Larini 2019.
39 Pezzini 2021.
40 See Belmont 1962; Donlan 1982; Edwards 1975; Katz 1994; Reece 1993; Van Wees 1992. For hospitality in archaic Greek society more broadly, see Most 1989a; Nagy 1981.

41 Gross 1976; Most 1989b; Rose 1969.
42 Newton 2008; Podlecki 1961.
43 Levy 1963.
44 Edwards 1975; Reece 1993.
45 Lord [1960] 1971: 68.
46 Armstrong 1958.
47 Fenik 1968.
48 Edwards 1992: 287, 290; see Belmont 1962: 114–16; Lord [1960] 1971: 68–98; Minchin 2001: 32–72.
49 Reece 1993: 6.
50 On repetition in Homeric poetry, see Fenik 1974: 135.
51 Reece 1993: 6–7.
52 Reece 1993: 5.
53 Homer, *Odyssey* 6.119–21; Shewring (transl.) [1980] 2008: 69–70; see *Odyssey* 8.576, 9.176, 13.202.
54 *Odyssey* 8.544, 546–7; Shewring (transl.) [1980] 2008: 97–8.
55 *Odyssey* 9.259–80.
56 Louden 2011: 37; Most 1989b: 24–5; Rose 1969: 389, 394; Webber 1989: 3; *contra*, cf. Reece 1993: 10; Schmiel 1972: 470–1.
57 Alden 2000: 4–5; Levy 1963.
58 On the suitors as bad guests, see Bakker 2013: 43–8; cf. McInerney 2010: 86.
59 Homer, *Odyssey* 1.248–51; 2.48–9; 4.318–20; Bakker 2013: 44–5; Howe 2008: 40.
60 Homer, *Odyssey* 4.660–72.
61 Katz 1994.
62 Silk 2004: 38.
63 De Jong [2001] 2004: 4.
64 Silk 2004: 37.
65 See Most 1989b; Murnaghan 2011: 74–8 (the Phaeacian narrative); Murnaghan 2011: 79–86 (Books 13–24).
66 Homer, *Odyssey* 9.229.
67 See *Odyssey* 9.266–71.
68 Gould 1973: 76; Pedrick 1982: 126–7.
69 Homer, *Odyssey* 9.268.
70 Fuqua 1991: 53–4; Muellner 1996: 35–7.
71 Homer, *Odyssey* 9.271.
72 *Odyssey* 9.270.
73 Cf. Homer, *Iliad* 13.624; Tsagarakis 1977: 24–7.
74 Tsagarakis 1977: 25.
75 Levy 1963: 148; Van Wees 1992: 72–3, 104, 106, 233.

76 Homer, *Iliad* 6.232–6.
77 *Hobbit* 3.
78 *Hobbit* 3.
79 *Hobbit* 3.
80 *Hobbit* 3.
81 *Hobbit* 6.
82 *Hobbit* 6.
83 *Hobbit* 6–7.
84 *Hobbit* 7.
85 *Hobbit* 7–9.
86 *Hobbit* 7.
87 *Hobbit* 7.
88 Rateliff 2007: 45.
89 Green 2001: 57.
90 Green 2001: 57–8.
91 On a Victorian *Hobbit*, see Green 2001: 53–64.
92 Homer, *Odyssey* 1.11–15.
93 *Odyssey* 5.57–9.
94 *Odyssey* 5.59–61.
95 *Odyssey* 5.61.
96 *Odyssey* 5.62.
97 *Odyssey* 5.63–73.
98 *Odyssey* 5.73–4; Shewring (transl.) [1980] 2008: 56.
99 *Odyssey* 5.75–6.
100 De Jong [2001] 2004: 123.
101 Homer, *Odyssey* 5.86.
102 *Odyssey* 5.88–91.
103 *Odyssey* 5.86, 92–5.
104 See De Jong [2001] 2004: 130.
105 De Jong [2001] 2004: 128–9.
106 Homer, *Odyssey* 5.135–6.
107 De Jong [2001] 2004: 136–7.
108 De Jong [2001] 2004: 129; see 130.
109 Homer, *Odyssey* 5.160–4.
110 *Odyssey* 1.14–15; 4.557–8; see 7.315–16; De Jong [2001] 2004: 130.
111 Homer, *Odyssey* 5.219–20.
112 *Odyssey* 9.27–36.
113 *Hobbit* 6–7.
114 Homer, *Odyssey* 9.35.

115 *Odyssey* 5.1–58.
116 *Hobbit* 8.
117 *UT* 502–20.
118 Bakker 2013: 43–8.
119 *Hobbit* 16.
120 Homer, *Odyssey* 2.138–43; cf. *Odyssey* 11.116; Bakker 2013: 45.
121 Homer, *Odyssey* 2.144–5.
122 *Hobbit* 27.
123 Homer, *Odyssey* 2.85–128.
124 *Odyssey* 4.660–72.
125 Ruud 2011: 111, 115; Scott 1918: 421–3.
126 On Telemachus' education and development, see Scott 1918: 426–7; Schmiel 1972: 465.
127 Scott 1918: 422–3.
128 *Hobbit* 23–4.
129 Rateliff 2007: 103; Ruud 2011: 112–13.
130 Williams 2019c: 114–16.
131 Larini 2019; Reckford 2003: 8–9; Ruud 2011: 113.
132 Homer, *Odyssey* 9.113–15; *Hobbit* 37.
133 *Odyssey* 9.177–82; *Hobbit* 38–9.
134 *Odyssey* 9.182–86; *Hobbit* 39.
135 *Odyssey* 9.167; *Hobbit* 40.
136 *Odyssey* 9.187–92; *Hobbit* 40.
137 *Odyssey* 9.224–9; *Hobbit* 42.
138 *Odyssey* 9.371–4; *Hobbit* 42, 44.
139 *Odyssey* 9.223; *Hobbit* 43–4, 48.
140 *Hobbit* 44.
141 Homer, *Odyssey* 9.347–52.
142 *Odyssey* 9.375–97; *Hobbit* 46.
143 *Odyssey* 9.287–93; *Hobbit* 48.
144 *Odyssey* 9.364–7; *Hobbit* 48–9.
145 *Odyssey* 9.182; *Hobbit* 50.
146 *Odyssey* 9.240–3; *Hobbit* 51.
147 *Odyssey* 9.219–22, 374; *Hobbit* 51.
148 *Odyssey* 9.319–20; *Hobbit* 51.
149 *Odyssey* 9.464–6; *Hobbit* 52.
150 Reece 1993: 124–5.
151 Homer, *Odyssey* 9.273–8; Reece 1993: 133–4.
152 Homer, *Odyssey* 9.288–93; Reece 1993: 134–6.

153 Homer, *Odyssey* 9.370; Reece 1993: 138–9.
154 Homer, *Odyssey* 9.231–3.
155 *Odyssey* 9.224–7; Pucci 1998: 116–17.
156 *Hobbit* 40.
157 *Hobbit* 40.
158 *Hobbit* 40.
159 Williams 2019a.
160 *Hobbit* 42.
161 Austin 1983: 20; Glenn 1971: 169–71, 180–1; Newton 1983: 137–42.
162 *Hobbit* 41.
163 Homer, *Odyssey* 9.289.
164 *Hobbit* 44.
165 Stevens and Stevens 2008: 23.
166 E.g. Homer, *Odyssey* 9.287–98.
167 *Hobbit* 43–4, 48–9.
168 Homer, *Odyssey* 9.375–97.
169 *Hobbit* 46.
170 Homer, *Odyssey* 9.366.
171 *Odyssey* 9.408.
172 *Hobbit* 48–50.
173 Homer, *Odyssey* 9.565–6.
174 *Hobbit* 54.
175 *Hobbit* 54–6.
176 Homer, *Odyssey* 10.3.
177 *Odyssey* 10.21–2.
178 *FR* 293–4.
179 Dougherty 2001: 97; Homer, *Odyssey* 21–2.
180 *Odyssey* 10.14; Cook 1995: 72–3; Pucci 1998: 114; Reinhardt 1996: 88–9.
181 Homer, *Odyssey* 10.8–10; Shewring (transl.) [1980] 2008: 113.
182 *Hobbit* 61.
183 *Hobbit* 60.
184 Homer, *Odyssey* 10.19–27.
185 *Hobbit* 61.
186 *Hobbit* 61.
187 Homer, *Odyssey* 10.13–27.
188 *Hobbit* 60–4.
189 *Hobbit* 60.
190 *Hobbit* 60.
191 Homer, *Odyssey* 10.72–5; Shewring (transl.) [1980] 2008: 114.

192 E.g. Homer, *Odyssey* 1.1–5, 2.343, 8.166–85, 9.12–15; see Bassi 1999: 414–18, 421–2; Cook 1999; De Jong [2001] 2004: 6; Nagler 1990: 337.
193 *FR* 302.
194 *S* 36.
195 As in Bilbo's song 'The Road Goes Ever On and On' (e.g. *FR* 47).
196 *Letters* no. 96, p. 110.
197 E.g. *Letters* no. 250, pp. 336–41; for a Catholic reading of hospitality in *The Hobbit*, see Pinsent 2014: 449–53.
198 See e.g. Genesis 18, 19.1-18; Leviticus 19.33-4; Matthew 25; Luke 14.12-14; for scholarship, see Michelet 2015: 24–5; Wood 2003: 89–90.
199 Carpenter [1977] 2002: 50.
200 *Letters* no. 250, p. 340; no. 267, p. 354.
201 Walsh 2007a: 56.
202 Anderson 2002: 168.
203 See Pollington 2011: 19–20, 22–5.
204 *Hobbit* 148.
205 *Hobbit* 137.
206 Burton 2021: 282–5.
207 *TT* 351–2.
208 Walsh 2007a: 56. On hospitality in *Beowulf*, see Michelet 2015. For Beorn as Beowulf, see Shippey 1992: 73–4; Walsh 2007a: 56. For shapeshifters in Norse mythology, see Ruud 2011: 116–17.
209 *Hobbit* 134–5.
210 His name is a pun on the Old Norse words for 'warrior' and 'bear' (Ruud 2001: 117).
211 Reece 1993: 10.
212 Most 1989b; Reece 1993; Rose 1969.
213 Homer, *Odyssey* 6.273–84, 7.32–3; Rose 1969: 388, 390–1.
214 Homer, *Odyssey* 6.303–15, 7.53–77.
215 Fenik 1974: 5–6; Rose 1969: 404; Whittaker 1999: 147.
216 Rose 1969: 393–97.
217 Homer, *Odyssey* 8.131–64; Louden 2011: 157; Rose 1969: 402–3.
218 Most 1989b: 28.
219 Homer, *Odyssey* 7.311–14; Most 1989b: 27–8; see Pucci 1998: 145–6; Reinhardt 1996: 122–3.
220 Austin 1975: 157–9; De Vries 1977: 121; Fenik 1974: 8–9; Garvie 1994: 24–5; Segal 1962: 22.
221 E.g. Homer, *Odyssey* 8.31–3; Austin 1975: 162; Reinhardt 1996: 128–9; Segal 1962: 21–2.

222 Homer, *Odyssey* 13.70–125; Segal 1962: 22, 38.
223 Fenik 1974: 165.
224 Katz 1994: 58; Louden 2011: 137; Reece 1993: 109–13.
225 E.g. Most 1989b; Rose 1969.
226 Rose 1969: 398, 400–2.
227 Fenik 1974: 105–6.
228 Most 1989b: 19.
229 Most 1989b: 20–4.
230 Homer, *Odyssey* 11.334.
231 *Hobbit* 138.
232 *Hobbit* 141.
233 *Hobbit* 143.
234 *Hobbit* 145.
235 *Hobbit* 142.
236 Reece 1993: 28.
237 Segal 1968: 420–5.
238 Homer, *Odyssey* 10.220–43.
239 *Odyssey* 10.323–45.
240 *Odyssey* 10.449–68; Segal 1968: 421–2.
241 *Hobbit* 149–50.
242 Homer, *Odyssey* 10.237–40.
243 *Hobbit* 151.
244 Homer, *Odyssey* 10.212–19.
245 Segal 1968: 428.
246 Homer, *Odyssey* 12.320–3.
247 *Hobbit* 159.
248 Homer, *Odyssey* 12.271–6.
249 *Odyssey* 10.150, 210; *Hobbit* 163–98.
250 *Odyssey* 10.168; *Hobbit* 168–9.
251 *Hobbit* 172–3.
252 Homer, *Odyssey* 10.144–50.
253 *Hobbit* 175–9.
254 Homer, *Odyssey* 10.220–8.
255 Most 1989b: 23–4; see Redfield 1983: 237–8.
256 Bakker 2013: 42.
257 Bakker 2013: 88; Segal 1968: 420.
258 Also apparent in the episodes of the lotus-eaters and sirens; see Schein 1995: 20–1.
259 *Hobbit* 201.

260 Ruud 2011: 119.
261 My thanks to Thomas Honegger for pointing out a related example of an entirely negative hospitality scene in *The Lord of the Rings*: Gandalf is kept as prisoner-'guest' in Saruman's tower of Orthanc because he does not provide Saruman with the desired intelligence or news, namely, the whereabouts of the One Ring (*FR* 288–9, 336–41). Subsequently, in *The Two Towers*, when Gandalf responds to the honeyed rhetoric of a beleaguered Saruman, who has invited him inside Orthanc once more, he reflects proverbially on the earlier inhospitality: 'the guest who has escaped from the roof, will think twice before he comes back in by the door' (*TT* 227).
262 *Hobbit* 201; Ruud 2011: 119.
263 Homer, *Odyssey* 3.69–74 (news for the host); *Odyssey* 3.102–200 (news for the guest).
264 Reece 1993: 28.
265 Ruud 2011: 119.
266 Homer, *Odyssey* 10.286–92.
267 Not yet the One Ring of Sauron in Tolkien's legendarium, but here functioning as a 'simple ring of invisibility' (Rateliff 2014: 129); on changing the nature of the Ring, see *Letters* no. 109, p. 122.
268 Ruud 2011: 119.
269 Homer, *Odyssey* 22; *Hobbit* 289–90.
270 *Odyssey* 24.412ff.
271 *Hobbit* 302–8.
272 Homer, *Odyssey* 24.502–48.
273 *Hobbit* 323.
274 *Hobbit* 323.
275 Odysseus is characterized in the Homeric poems as 'polymetic': a man of many crafts or wiles (Homer, *Iliad* 1.311; *Odyssey* 21.274).
276 *Hobbit* 255.
277 *Hobbit* 300.
278 *Hobbit* 300–2.
279 Green 2008: 34.
280 *Hobbit* 307.
281 *Hobbit* 308.
282 Homer, *Odyssey* 17.462–5.
283 *Hobbit* 336.
284 *Hobbit* 348.
285 *Hobbit* 348.
286 See *UT* 415–22.

287  Ruud 2011: 96.
288  Homer, *Odyssey* 9.266–71.
289  *Odyssey* 5.1–58.
290  E.g. *Odyssey* 2.399–405.
291  *Odyssey* 10.8–14.
292  *Odyssey* 10.286–305.
293  E.g. *Odyssey* 6.1–42, 7.139–45; Rose 1969: 400–1.
294  Homer, *Odyssey* 24.502ff.
295  Louden 2011: 30–7.
296  Louden 2011: 32; cf. Kearns 1982. Such theoxenies occur in the Bible, e.g. in the case of Lot: *Genesis* 18, 19.1-18.
297  Homer, *Odyssey* 9.366.
298  Most 1989b.
299  See Pucci 1987.
300  Homer, *Odyssey* 13.291–3.
301  *Odyssey* 13.298–9; Pucci 1987: 16, 22.
302  *LfgrE* 464–9.
303  Reece 1993: 108.
304  Van Wees 1992: 44–5, 169–71, 228–37.
305  Homer, *Odyssey* 16.241–57.
306  *FR* 31; see also *FR* 58–60.
307  *FR* 60.
308  *FR* 92.
309  *FR* 475–6.
310  *RK* 334–64.
311  *RK* 324.
312  *RK* 334; see 328.
313  *RK* 344.
314  *RK* 370.
315  *RK* 469–71.
316  See *Letters* no. 53, p. 65.
317  *MC* 191.
318  Miller [1941] 2016; Durrell [1978] 2002.
319  Derrida [1998] 2000.
320  *OH* 5–45.
321  *OH* 3ff.
322  *OH* 15, 17.
323  *OH* 25.
324  *OH* 61.

325 Plato, *Apology of Socrates* 17d.
326 *OH* 15, 17.
327 *OH* 15.
328 *OH* 15, 17.
329 *Hobbit* 6.
330 *Hobbit* 348.
331 *OH* 25.
332 *OH* 17–27.
333 *OH* 27.
334 *OH* 25.
335 *Hobbit* 338.
336 *Hobbit* 338.
337 *FR* 48.
338 *FR* 48.
339 Heffernan 2014.
340 See Garbowski 2014.
341 *OH* 61.
342 *RK* 336–40.
343 *RK* 340.
344 *RK* 353–4, 360, 363.
345 Cf. *Letters* no. 52, p. 63.
346 *Hobbit* 338, 349–50.
347 *RK* 297–8, 314.
348 *RK* 329.

## 3 Sublime Narratives: Classical Transcendence in Nature and Beyond in *The Fellowship of the Ring*

1 See Dickerson and Evans 2006: xvi; Simpson 2017: 75, 76.
2 For philological interpretations, see Dickerson and Evans 2006: xxi–xxii, 128–9; cf. Curry [1997] 1998: 60; *Letters* no. 148, p. 183–4.
3 For a definition, see Wilson 2007: 189.
4 Dickerson and Evans 2006: xviii; Flieger 2012: 262–3. For a succinct definition of the field's goals, see Siewers 2007: 166.
5 Campbell 2014: 431–3.
6 Carpenter [1977] 2002: 35–43.
7 Carpenter [1977] 2002: 36.
8 Carpenter [1977] 2002: 36–7.

9   Carpenter [1977] 2002: 35; see Campbell 2014: 432.
10  Carpenter [1977] 2002: 43.
11  Carpenter [1977] 2002: 43.
12  Dickerson and Evans 2006: 79.
13  Curry [1997] 1998: 83.
14  Curry [1997] 1998: 65–6, 83–5.
15  *Letters* no. 339, p. 420.
16  Dickerson and Evans 2006: 78; see Curry [1997] 1998: 65.
17  *Letters* no. 339, p. 419; see also *Letters* no. 165, p. 220; no. 210, p. 275; no. 213, p. 288–9.
18  On fauna in Tolkien, see Simpson 2017.
19  See Curry 2007b: 454.
20  Campbell 2014: 433.
21  Dickerson and Evans 2006: xvi–xvii.
22  Curry [1997] 1998: 64–5.
23  *TT* 78.
24  *TT* 83.
25  *TT* 85.
26  *TT* 83–5; Simpson 2017: 77–8.
27  Campbell 2014: 442.
28  Campbell 2014: 433.
29  Curry 2007a: 165.
30  *RK* 235; see Campbell 2014: 438–9.
31  *RK* 360–1.
32  Flieger 2012: 265.
33  *RK* 367–9.
34  Flieger 2012: 265.
35  Dickerson and Evans 2006: 12–13, 72–3, 85–7, 90.
36  See Brisbois 2005: 197–8; Campbell 2014: 436–7; Curry 2007b: 453; Light 2003: 152–3. For such ethno-topographic thought in Tolkien, see Williams 2019b.
37  See Birzer 2002: 128; Light 2003: 151; Siewers 2007: 166–7.
38  Dickerson and Evans 2006: xvii.
39  Birzer 2002: 128; see Dickerson and Evans 2006: xxii.
40  See Birzer 2002: 127–8; Curry 2007a: 165; Light 2003: 150–1; Potts 2016: 163–4; Siewers 2007: 166.
41  Flieger 2012: 263; see Birzer 2002: 128.
42  See Siewers 2007: 166; Wilson 2007: 190–5.
43  Conrad-O'Briain and Hynes 2013: 14.
44  Flieger 2012: 263; see Conrad-O'Briain and Hynes 2013: 13.

45 Flieger 2012: 264.
46 Flieger 2012: 263–5; Hjulstad 2020: 10–14.
47 Flieger 2012: 264.
48 Brisbois 2005: 206–7.
49 Burton 2021: 277.
50 Burton 2021: 277–82.
51 Reckford 1974: 57–8.
52 Reckford 1974: 58.
53 See Reckford 1974: 58–63.
54 Burton 2021: 280.
55 Burton 2021: 280. On the symbolism of Tolkien's fictional trees, see Cohen 2009: 99–102.
56 On nature and Tolkien's creative imagination, see Campbell 2014: 431–2, 441–2.
57 See Carpenter [1977] 2002: 171, 237–8; Letters no. 324, p. 409.
58 See Curry 2007b: 453.
59 Williams 2019b: 300–8.
60 *FR* 376–86.
61 *FR* 379.
62 *Hobbit* 67.
63 Homer, *Odyssey* 9.536–42; 10.118–24; 11.308–20.
64 See Segal 1992: 497.
65 Campbell 2014: 435; Dickerson and Evans 2006: xix–xx; Siewers 2007: 167.
66 Birzer 2002: 128.
67 *PME* 413; for a recent reading on 'The New Shadow', see Danielson 2021: 179–94.
68 On Christian stewardship in Tolkien's environmental vision, see Dickerson and Evans 2006: 37–67.
69 Campbell 2014: 442.
70 Cohen 2009: 102; 104–5.
71 *S* 31–2.
72 Campbell 2014: 435–6.
73 See Campbell 2014: 440.
74 Campbell 2014: 431; Curry 2007b: 453. For a good recent example of such a study on real nature, see Judd and Judd 2017.
75 Brisbois 2005: 198–200.
76 Campbell 2014: 433.
77 Cohen 2009: 96.
78 Campbell 2014: 431.
79 Hynes 2012: 21–30.
80 See Curry [1997] 1998: 60.

81  Campbell 2014: 436–7. On post-humanist readings of nature in Middle-earth, see Curry 2007a: 165; 2007b: 453–4; Light 2003: 155–63; Simpson 2017: 71–89.
82  Cohen 2009: 111–16; see Light 2003: 153–4.
83  Simpson 2017: 78.
84  For detailed explanations of these terms, see Genette 1980: 228–31.
85  For a brief etymological history of the word *sublime*, see Costelloe 2012: 3.
86  Heath 2012.
87  Porter 2016: 18–23.
88  Brady 2012: 172; Costelloe 2012: 7.
89  See Potkay 2012.
90  See Costelloe 2012: 1.
91  Porter 2016: 1–5.
92  Costelloe 2012: 2.
93  Costelloe 2012: 2.
94  See Brady 2012: 176; Porter 2016: 5; Potkay 2012: 208.
95  On the moral sublime in romantic thought, see Potkay 2012: 207.
96  Brady 2012: 174–6; Porter 2016: 43.
97  For example, the romantic transcendence allows for ideas of 'magnanimity, generosity, patriotism, and universal benevolence' (Potkay 2012: 205).
98  See Porter 2016: 5; Potkay 2012: 203.
99  See Potkay 2012: 208–9.
100 On the romantic sublime as drawing on the classical sublime, see Potkay 2012: 204.
101 See Brady 2012: 173; Potkay 2012: 204, 216.
102 Sander 1997: 4–6; for Tolkien as romantic, see Eilmann 2017.
103 See Costelloe 2012: 4–5, 7; Porter 2016: 49–50.
104 Porter 2016: 9–13, 15, 27.
105 Porter 2016: *passim*.
106 Heath 2012: 12, 23; Potkay 2012: 208–9; see Longinus, *On the Sublime*, 35.
107 Porter 2016: 6, 13, *passim*.
108 Porter 2016: 15–16.
109 Porter 2016: 7, 24–5, 32, 38, *passim*.
110 See Heath 2012: 13.
111 Potkay 2012: 208–9.
112 *FR* 107.
113 *FR* 107.
114 See Brady 2012: 172; Costelloe 2012: 2; Sander 1997: 4.
115 Burke ([1757] 2015).
116 *PESB* 59.

117 *PESB* 48–9.
118 *PESB* 49.
119 See *FR* 107.
120 *FR* 376.
121 *FR* 377.
122 See Sander 1997: 4.
123 *FR* 107. For these typical emotions of the sublime across linguistic and cultural contexts, see *PESB* 48.
124 Merkelbach 2013: 57.
125 For a sociocultural history on the spiritual (and religious) value of forests, see Konijnendijk 2018: 19–35.
126 *FR* 109.
127 *FR* 109.
128 *FR* 109.
129 *FR* 109.
130 *S* 3–5.
131 See Beal 2018: 8–9, *passim*; Kowalik 2020: 44–5.
132 *FR* 106.
133 See Porter 2016: 27, 42–3; *contra*, on the secularism of the romantic sublime, see Brady 2012: 185; Potkay 2012: 203–4.
134 See Sander 1997: 6.
135 *Letters* no. 89, p. 100. For Christian 'joy' in Tolkien's letters, see *Letters* no. 43, p. 53–4; no. 54, p. 66; no. 89, p. 99.
136 See *Letters* no. 89, p. 101.
137 *PESB* 47.
138 *PESB* 49.
139 *PESB* 70.
140 Virgil, *Aeneid* 7.81–4; as transl. by Guyer in *PESB* 148.
141 *PESB* 54.
142 Nietzsche [1872] 2003.
143 Guyer (ed.) in *PESB* xxix.
144 *BT* 20.
145 *BT* 20, 22–3.
146 *BT* 22–3.
147 Cf. Cilli 2019: 36, 223.
148 *Letters* no. 163, p. 214.
149 Mantovani 2019: 14.
150 Cilli 2019: 229.
151 SL 194; *Metamorphoses* 2.235–6.

152 Stevens 2004.
153 Sundt 2021.
154 Hinds 2006: 122; Segal 1969: 14–15. For the importance of the natural world as providing unity to Ovid's constructed spatial-moral world, see Segal 1969: 4–19, *passim*.
155 For this ancient sylvan motif in Virgil and Statius, see Segal 1969: 4; Newlands 2004, respectively.
156 Segal 1969: 4.
157 Ovid, *Metamorphoses* 2.836–4.603.
158 Newlands 2004: 133–4; see Hinds 2006: 127–8.
159 Newlands 2004: 137; see Parry 1964: 268.
160 Newlands 2004: 136–7; see Segal 1969: 8. Merkelbach (2013: 58–66) compares transformative sylvan experiences in Tolkien to those in fairy stories and folk tales.
161 Segal 1969: 15.
162 Ovid, *Metamorphoses* 3.28–32; Melville (transl.) 2008: 52.
163 *Metamorphoses* 3.24–27.
164 *Metamorphoses* 3.40.
165 *Metamorphoses* 3.39–40; Melville (transl.) 2008: 52.
166 *Metamorphoses* 3.48–9.
167 *Metamorphoses* 3.146; Melville (transl.) 2008: 55.
168 *Metamorphoses* 3.155–252.
169 *Metamorphoses* 3.388.
170 *Metamorphoses* 3.407–510.
171 *Metamorphoses* 3.393–401.
172 *Metamorphoses* 3.708–9; Melville (transl.) 2008: 72.
173 *Metamorphoses* 3.710–33.
174 *Metamorphoses* 10.687.
175 *Metamorphoses* 10.686–704.
176 On influences of sylvan narratives from fairy tales and folklore (Germanic, Norwegian or Finnish), see Hjulstad 2020: 7–8; Szyjewski 2020: 108–9.
177 See Segal 1969: 5.
178 Ovid, *Metamorphoses* 3.28.
179 *Metamorphoses* 10.691–4; Melville (transl.) 2008: 247.
180 FR 147; see Hjulstad 2020: 6.
181 Ovid, *Metamorphoses* 3.28; Melville (transl.) 2008: 52.
182 *Metamorphoses* 3.29–31.
183 *Metamorphoses* 3.155–62.
184 FR 146–7.
185 FR 146.

186 *FR* 146–7.
187 See Konijnendijk 2018: 21.
188 Hinds 2006: 124–5; see Segal 1969: 5.
189 *FR* 141–2.
190 Ovid, *Metamorphoses* 10.86–105.
191 *FR* 145–6.
192 See Segal 1969: 17–18.
193 Ovid, *Metamorphoses* 3.141–2.
194 *Metamorphoses* 3.174–6; Melville (transl.) 2008: 56.
195 Hjulstad 2020: 8.
196 *FR* 146.
197 *FR* 147.
198 *FR* 151.
199 Ovid, *Metamorphoses* 3.176; Melville (transl.) 2008: 56.
200 *FR* 151.
201 Ovid, *Metamorphoses* 3.201.
202 *Metamorphoses* 3.357–69.
203 *FR* 147.
204 *FR* 149.
205 Ovid, *Metamorphoses* 3.155, 157–8; Melville (transl.) 2008: 55.
206 Parry 1964: 278–80; Segal 1969: 23–33.
207 Ovid, *Metamorphoses* 3.27, 30–1; Melville (transl.) 2008: 52.
208 *Metamorphoses* 3.161.
209 *Metamorphoses* 3.407.
210 *FR* 150.
211 *FR* 150.
212 *Contra*, cf. Merkelbach 2013: 65.
213 Segal 1969: 15.
214 Hinds 2006: 126–7.
215 Ovid, *Metamorphoses* 160–4; Melville (transl.) 2008: 56.
216 *Metamorphoses* 3.164.
217 See Parry 1964: 279. On the sexual, erotic nature of these sylvan encounters, see Hinds 2006: 130–6; Segal 1969: 8–9.
218 Segal 1969: 10.
219 Ovid, *Metamorphoses* 3.411–12; Melville (transl.) 2008: 63.
220 Segal 1969: 43.
221 Hinds 2006: 123.
222 Ovid, *Metamorphoses* 10.86–105.
223 *Metamorphoses* 3.206–27.

224 See Hjulstad 2020: 8–9.
225 *FR* 152.
226 *FR* 152.
227 *FR* 154.
228 Newman 2005: 140.
229 Segal 1969: 15.
230 Hjulstad 2020: 9.
231 Hjulstad 2020: 10; Newlands 2004: 140–5.
232 Newlands 2004: 140.
233 *FR* 152–4.
234 Parry 1964: 277; see Segal 1969: 4.
235 See Hjulstad 2020: 9–10.
236 Newlands 2004: 136–7; see Hinds 2006: 130–6.
237 Segal 1969: 15. On variations of this motif in Germanic, Celtic or Christian traditions, see Konijnendijk 2018: 21.
238 Parry 1964: 278.
239 *FR* 154–6.
240 See Newlands 2004: 137–8.
241 *FR* 171.
242 Ovid, *Metamorphoses* 3.413–15.
243 *Metamorphoses* 5.594; Melville (transl.) 2008: 117.
244 *Metamorphoses* 5.585–641.
245 *Metamorphoses* 10.495–8; Melville (transl.) 2008: 240.
246 *Metamorphoses* 8.738–884.
247 Lucan, 3.399–452; Newlands 2004: 139.
248 *FR* 156.
249 *FR* 156.
250 Newlands 2004: 137.
251 Newlands 2004: 137–8.
252 *FR* 157ff.
253 *Letters* no. 144, p. 174; Dickerson and Evans 2006: 18.
254 Hargrove 1986: 20; Jenike 2010: 67.
255 See Pezzini 2021: 99.
256 Beal 2018: 15–17; Campbell 2010: 43; Hargrove 1986: 21–3; Jenike 2010: 69–70. On Bombadil outside *The Lord of the Rings*, see Beal 2018: 12–14.
257 Campbell 2010: 43.
258 Sundt 2021: 184–6.
259 Sundt 2021: 166–7.
260 See Honegger 2010: 117 n. 2; Hostetter 2007.

261 Sundt 2021: 177–8.
262 *Letters* no. 153, p. 193.
263 Beal 2014; Librán-Moreno 2007a; Sundt 2021: 170–6.
264 Sundt 2021: 184–6.
265 Sundt 2021: 167.
266 Ovid, *Metamorphoses* 9. 8–10.
267 *FR* 162.
268 *FR* 162; Sundt 2021: 186.
269 Sundt 2021: 186. This resurrection may be viewed in light of Christian stories; see Beal 2018: 22–7.
270 *FR* 187–9.
271 Ovid, *Metamorphoses* 10.88–105; Melville (transl.) 2008: 227.
272 *FR* 158.
273 *FR* 158.
274 Sundt 2021: 186; cf. *FR* 190.
275 For Ovidian natural descriptions in post-classical visual arts, see Hinds 2006: 142–7.
276 See Porter 2016: 5.
277 *FR* 160.
278 *FR* 154–5.
279 *FR* 167–8.
280 See Campbell 2010: 45.
281 *FR* 171.
282 See Hinds 2006: 127.
283 Campbell 2010: 45.
284 See Hjulstad 2020.
285 See Brady 2012: 172, 177–80.
286 *FR* 164.
287 Hinds 2006: 127.
288 *FR* 171; see Campbell 2010: 44–5.
289 *FR* 158.
290 *FR* 158.
291 *FR* 158.
292 Or perhaps Pan; see Campbell 2010: 43.
293 For such a modern depiction of Bacchus, with which Tolkien was probably familiar, see C.S. Lewis's *Prince Caspian* ([1951] 2010: 166–9).
294 Ovid, *Metamorphoses* 11.1–19; Melville (transl.) 2008: 249.
295 *Metamorphoses* 11.17.
296 *Metamorphoses* 11.1.
297 *Metamorphoses* 11.14.

298 *Metamorphoses* 11.20–21; Melville (transl.) 2008: 249.
299 See Segal 1969: 76–7.
300 *BT* 14–18.
301 *BT* 18.
302 *BT* 20–1.
303 *BT* 24.
304 *BT* 25.
305 *S* 4–5.
306 Ovid, *Metamorphoses* 11.18; Melville (transl.) 2008: 249.
307 For the analogy between the Music of the Ainur and that of Tom, see Beal 2018: 17 n. 45.
308 *FR* 154.
309 *FR* 158–9.
310 For the coinage, see Stevens 2021: 111–12.
311 *FR* 159.
312 *FR* 159.
313 *FR* 158.
314 *FR* 161.
315 Beal 2018: 10–12.
316 *FR* 178 = *RK* 377–8.
317 Beal 2018: 9–10.
318 Ovid, *Metamorphoses* 11.44.
319 *Metamorphoses* 11.61–6.
320 *FR* 164.
321 On the story of Beren and Lúthien as rewriting Orpheus' classical, underworld fate through Christian resurrection, see Stevens 2021: 114.
322 Segal 1969: 9.
323 Segal 1969: 15.
324 Segal 1969: 76.
325 Cf. Campbell 2010: 46.
326 See Huttar 1975: 120.
327 On Tom's spiritual triumph, see Beal 2018: 22.
328 For other lessons learned by the hobbits in their sylvan sublime, see Merkelbach 2013: 59, 62–3.
329 Potkay 2012: 203.
330 Potkay 2012: 212.
331 Sachs 2009: 316.
332 Sachs 2009: 314.
333 Sachs 2009: 317–22.

334 Sander 1997: 4.
335 E.g. *Knossos* 22–3.
336 Sweetman 1993: 167–70.
337 *GI* 57, 62, 71.
338 *CM* 133.
339 See Stevens 2021: 115 n. 31.
340 *FR* 243.
341 *FR* 244.
342 *FR* 244.
343 Sander 1997: 4–5. On the element of mystery in sublime narratives, see Brady 2012: 174–5, 180; Potkay 2012: 207.
344 Kazantzakis [1946] 2008.
345 *ZG* 180.
346 *ZG* 180.
347 *ZG* 181–3.
348 *CM* 125.
349 *FR* 244.
350 *ZG* 181.
351 *CM* 135.
352 *CM* 136.
353 *FR* 242.
354 *ZG* 182–3.
355 *CM* 134–5.
356 *FR* 248.
357 *FR* 247.
358 Potkay 2012: 212.
359 *FR* 244.
360 *FR* 252.
361 Clare 2021: 55–6.
362 *FR* 516.
363 *FR* 516.
364 *FR* 516.
365 *FR* 516.
366 See Newman 2005: 243.
367 *FR* 516.
368 For an alternate reading of this moment as a divine epiphany drawing on Apollonius Argonautica, see Newman 2005: 242–3.
369 *FR* 525–6.
370 Harrisson 2021: 333–4.

## Epilogue: Ancient Trees in Tolkien's Forest

1. Lewis [1950] 2010; Lewis [1953] 2010.
2. Lewis [1951] 2010.
3. Lewis[1952] 2010.
4. *TT* 318.
5. Burton 2021: 281–2.
6. Lewis [1955] 2010.
7. *OFS* 39–40.
8. Carpenter [1977] 2002: 171. For further discussions on leaves, see Carpenter [1977] 2002: 237–8; *Letters* no. 324, p. 409.
9. See Livingston 2013: 78.
10. While it is anachronistic to talk about a 'utopian genre' in ancient writings, utopianism as a more general form of thought seems to have existed in pre-modern, ancient thought; see Vieira 2010: 5–6.
11. Livingston 2013: 89.

# References

Adams, R. ([1972] 1982), *Watership Down*, London: Allen Lane/Kestrel Books.
Alden, M. (2000), *Homer Beside Himself: Para-Narratives in the* Iliad, Oxford: Oxford University Press.
Allen, M. (2009), 'Jonathan Edwards and the Lapsarian Debate', *Scottish Journal of Theology*, 62 (3): 299–315.
Anderson, D.A. (2002), *The Annotated Hobbit*, revised and expanded edition, Boston, New York: Houghton Mifflin Company.
Anderson, P. ([1971] 1972), *The Dancer from Atlantis*, New York: The New American Library.
Ando, C. (2008), 'Decline, Fall, and Transformation', *Journal of Late Antiquity*, 1 (1): 31–60.
Anzinger, S. (2010), 'Von Troja nach Gondor. Tolkiens "The Lord of the Rings" als Epos in vergilischer Tradition', in T. Burkard, M. Schauer, and C. Wiener (eds), *Vestigia Vergiliana: Vergil-Rezeption in Der Neuzeit*, 363–401, Berlin: De Gruyter.
Armstrong, J. (1958), 'The Arming Motif in the *Iliad*', *American Journal of Philology*, 79 (4): 337–54.
Atherton, M. (2014), 'Old English', in S.D. Lee (ed.), *A Companion to J.R.R. Tolkien*, 217–29, Chichester: Wiley Blackwell.
Austin, N. (1975), *Archery at the Dark of the Moon: Poetic Problems in Homer's Odyssey*, Berkeley: University of California Press.
Austin, N. (1983), 'Odysseus and the Cyclops: Who is Who?', in C.A. Rubino and C.W. Shelmerdine (eds), *Approaches to Homer*, 3–37, Austin: University of Texas Press.
Bakker, E.J. (2013), *The Meaning of Meat and the Structure of the* Odyssey, Cambridge: Cambridge University Press.
Bal, M. (2009), *Narratology: Introduction to the Theory of Narrative*, third edition, Toronto: University of Toronto Press.
Bassi, K. (1999), 'Nostos, Domos, and the Architecture of the Ancient Stage', *The South Atlantic Quarterly*, 98 (3): 415–49.
Beal, J. (2014), 'Orphic Powers in J.R.R. Tolkien's Legend of Beren and Lúthien', *Journal of Tolkien Research*, 1 (1): 1–25.
Beal, J. (2018), 'Who is Tom Bombadil?: Interpreting the Light in Frodo Baggins and Tom Bombadil's Role in the Healing of Traumatic Memory in J.R.R. Tolkien's *The Lord of the Rings*', *Journal of Tolkien Research*, 6 (1): Article 1, 1–34.

Belmont, D.E. (1962), 'Early Greek Guest-Friendship and Its Role in Homer's *Odyssey*', PhD Thesis, Princeton: Princeton University Press.

Birkett, T. (2014), 'Old Norse', in S.D. Lee (ed.), *A Companion to J.R.R. Tolkien*, 244–58, Chichester: Wiley Blackwell.

Birzer, B.J. (2002), *J.R.R. Tolkien's Sanctifying Myth: Understanding Middle-earth*, Wilmington, Delaware: ISI Books.

Birzer, B.J. (2007a), 'Catholicism, Roman', in M.D.C. Drout (ed.), *J.R.R. Tolkien Encyclopedia: Scholarship and Critical Assessment*, 85–9, London: Routledge.

Birzer, B.J. (2007b), 'Christian Readings of Tolkien', in M.D.C. Drout (ed.), *J.R.R. Tolkien Encyclopedia: Scholarship and Critical Assessment*, 99–101, London: Routledge.

Birzer, B.J. (2007c), 'Christianity', in M.D.C. Drout (ed.), *J.R.R. Tolkien Encyclopedia: Scholarship and Critical Assessment*, 101–3, London: Routledge.

Boym, S. (2007), 'Nostalgia and Its Discontents', *The Hedgehog Review*, 9 (2): 7–19.

Brady, E. (2012), 'The Environmental Sublime', in T.M. Costelloe (ed.), *The Sublime from Antiquity to the Present*, 171–82, Cambridge: Cambridge University Press.

Bregman, R. (2017), *Utopias for Realists: And How We Can Get There*, London: Bloomsbury Publishing.

Brisbois, M.J. (2005), 'Tolkien's Imaginary Nature: An Analysis of the Structure of Middle-earth', *Tolkien Studies* 2: 197–216.

Bruce, A.M. (2012), 'The Fall of Gondolin and the Fall of Troy: Tolkien and Book II of *The Aeneid*', *Mythlore* 30 (3): 103–15.

Bruce, S. (1999), 'Introduction', in S. Bruce (ed.), *Three Early Modern Utopias: Utopia, New Atlantis, The Isles of the Pines*, ix–xlii, Oxford: Oxford University Press.

Burke, E. ([1757] 2015), *A Philosophical Enquiry into the Sublime and Beautiful*, P. Guyer (ed.), Oxford: Oxford University Press.

Burton, P. (2021), '"Eastwards and Southwards": Philological and Historical Perspectives on Tolkien and Classicism', in H. Williams (ed.), *Tolkien and the Classical World*, 273–304, Zurich, Jena: Walking Tree Publishers.

Bury, R.G. (transl.) (1956), *Plato: Laws*, Cambridge, Massachusetts: Harvard University Press.

Cairns, D.L. (1996), 'Hybris, Dishonour, and Thinking Big', *The Journal of Hellenic Studies*, 116: 1–32.

Caldecott, M. ([1979] 2005), *The Lily and the Bull*, Bath: Bladud Books.

Campbell, L. (2010), 'The Enigmatic Mr. Bombadil: Tom Bombadil's Role as a Representation of Nature in *The Lord of the Rings*', in K. Dubbs and J. Kaščáková, *Middle-earth and Beyond: Essays on the World of J.R.R. Tolkien*, 41–65, Newcastle upon Tyne: Cambridge Scholars Publishing.

Campbell, L. (2014), 'Nature', in S. Lee (ed.), *A Companion to J.R.R. Tolkien*, 431–45, Chichester: Wiley Blackwell.

Carpenter, H. ([1977] 2002), *J.R.R. Tolkien: A Biography*, London: HarperCollinsPublishers.

Cilli, O. (2019), *Tolkien's Library: An Annotated Checklist*. Edinburgh: Luna Press Publishing.

Clare, R. (2021), 'Greek and Roman Historiographies in Tolkien's Númenor', in H. Williams (ed.), *Tolkien and the Classical World*, 37–68, Zurich, Jena: Walking Tree Publishers.

Cohen, C.M. (2009), 'The Unique Representation of Trees in *The Lord of the Rings*', *Tolkien Studies*, 6: 91–125.

Conrad-O'Briain, H. and G. Hynes (2013), 'Introduction', in H. Conrad-O'Briain and G. Hynes (eds), *J.R.R. Tolkien: The Forest and the City*, 13–18, Dublin: Four Courts Press.

Cook, E.F. (1995), *The* Odyssey *in Athens: Myths of Cultural Origins*, Ithaca: Cornell University Press.

Cook, E.F. (1999), '"Active" and "Passive" Heroics in the "Odyssey"', *Classical World*, 93 (2): 149–67.

Cornelli, G. (forthcoming), 'Plato Sailing Against the Current: The Image of the Ship in the *Republic*', in H. Williams and R. Clare (eds), *The Ancient Sea: The Utopian and Catastrophic in Classical Narratives and Their Reception*, Liverpool: Liverpool University Press.

Costelloe, T. (2012), 'The Sublime', in T. Costelloe (ed.), *The Sublime: From Antiquity to the Present*, 1–8, Cambridge: Cambridge University Press.

Curry, P. ([1997] 1998), *Defending Middle-earth. Tolkien: Myth and Modernity*, London: HarperCollinsPublishers.

Curry, P. (2007a), 'Environmentalism and Eco-Criticism', in M.D.C. Drout (ed.), *J.R.R. Tolkien Encyclopedia: Scholarship and Critical Assessment*, 165, New York, London: Routledge.

Curry, P. (2007b), 'Nature', in M.D.C. Drout (ed.), *J.R.R. Tolkien Encyclopedia: Scholarship and Critical Assessment*, 453–4, New York, London: Routledge.

Danielson, S. (2021), '"To Trees All Men Are Orcs": The Environmental Ethics of J.R.R. Tolkien's "The New Shadow"', *Tolkien Studies*, 18: 179–94.

Davis, J. (2010), 'Thomas More's Utopia: Sources, legacy, and interpretation', in G. Claeys (ed.), *The Cambridge Companion to Utopian Literature*, 28–50, Cambridge: Cambridge University Press.

(2021). *Definition of utopianism* [online], Oxford University Press. Available at: https://www.lexico.com/definition/utopianism (accessed 11 August 2022).

De Jong, I.J.F. ([2001] 2004), *A Narratological Commentary on the Odyssey*, Cambridge: Cambridge University Press.

De Jong, I.J.F. (2012), 'Introduction: Narratological Theory on Space', in I.J.F. de Jong (ed.), *Space in Ancient Greek Literature*, 1–20, Leiden: Brill.

Delattre, C. (2007), 'Númenor et l'Atlantide: Une Écriture en Héritage', *Revue de Littérature Comparée*, 323 (3): 303–22.

Derrida, J. ([1998] 2000), *Of Hospitality: Anne Dufourmantelle Invites Jacques Derrida to Respond*, transl. Rachel Bowlby, Stanford, California: Stanford University Press.

Devine, C. (2016), 'Fertility and Grace in *The Lord of the Rings*', *Mallorn*, 57: 10–11.

De Vries, G.J. (1977), 'Phaeacian Manners', *Mnemosyne*, 30 (2): 113–21.

Dickerson, M. and J. Evans (2006), *Ents, Elves, and Eriador*, Lexington: The University Press of Kentucky.

Donlan, W. (1982), 'Reciprocities in Homer', *Classical World*, 75 (3): 137–75.

Dougherty, C. (2001), *The Raft of Odysseus: The Ethnographic Imagination of Homer's Odyssey*, Oxford: Oxford University Press.

*Downsizing* (2017), [Film] Dir. A. Payne, US: Paramount Pictures.

Drout, M.D.C. (2004), 'Tolkien's Prose Style and Its Literary and Rhetorical Effects', *Tolkien Studies*, 1: 137–62.

Durrell, L. ([1947] 2001), *The Dark Labyrinth*, London: Faber and Faber.

Durrell, L. ([1978] 2002), *The Greek Islands*, London: Faber and Faber.

Edwards, A.T. (1993), 'Homer's Ethical Geography: Country and City in the *Odyssey*', *Transactions of the American Philological Association*, 123: 27–78.

Edwards, M.W. (1975), 'Type-Scenes and Homeric Hospitality', *Transactions of the American Philological Association*, 105: 51–72.

Edwards, M.W. (1992), 'Homer and Oral Tradition: The Type Scene', *Oral Tradition*, 7 (2): 284–330.

Eilmann, J. (2017), *J.R.R. Tolkien: Romanticist and Poet*, Zurich, Jena: Walking Tree Publishers.

Eilmann, J. (2021), 'Horror and Fury: J.R.R. Tolkien's *The Children of Húrin* and the Aristotelian Theory of Tragedy', in H. Williams (ed.), *Tolkien and the Classical World*, 247–68, Zurich, Jena: Walking Tree Publishers.

Elliot, A.B.R. (2014), 'Introduction: The Return of the Epic', in A.B.R. Elliot (ed.), *The Return of the Epic Film: Genre, Aesthetics, and History in the 21st Century*, 1–16, Edinburgh: Edinburgh University Press.

Evans, A. (1921), *The Palace of Minos at Knossos*, Volume I, London: Macmillan.

Evans, R. (2008), *Utopia Antiqua: Readings of the Golden Age and Decline at Rome*, London, New York: Routledge.

Fasching, D.J. (1993), *The Ethical Challenge of Auschwitz and Hiroshima: Apocalypse or Utopia*, New York: State University of New York Press.

Fenik, B. (1968), *Typical Battle Scenes in the* Iliad, Wiesbaden: Franz Steiner Verlag GMBH.

Fenik, B. (1974), *Studies in the Odyssey*, Wiesbaden: Franz Steiner Verlag GMBH.

Fenwick, A. (1996), 'Breastplates of Silk: Homeric Women in *The Lord of the Rings*', *Mythlore*, 21 (3): 17–23.

Ferns, C. (1999), *Narrating Utopia: Ideology, Gender, Form in Utopian Literature*, Liverpool: Liverpool University Press.

Fimi, D. and T. Honegger (2019), 'Introduction', in D. Fimi and T. Honegger (eds), *Subcreating Arda: World-Building in J.R.R. Tolkien's Work, Its Precursors and Its Legacies*, i–vi, Zurich, Jena: Walking Tree Publishers.

Fisher, J. (2011), 'Tolkien and Source Criticism: Remarking and Remaking', in J. Fisher (ed.), *Tolkien and the Study of His Sources*, 29–44, Jefferson, London: McFarland & Company.

Fletcher, F. (1910), 'Comparison of English and German Classical Schools', in J.W. Headlam, F. Fletcher and J.L.A Paton (eds), *The Teaching of Classics in Secondary Schools in Germany. Board of Education: Special Reports on Educational Subjects*, volume 20, 106–17, London: Wyman & Sons.

Flieger, V. (2012), *Green Suns and Faërie: Essays on J.R.R. Tolkien*, Kent, Ohio: The Kent State University Press.

Fontenrose, J. (1974), 'Work, Justice, and Hesiod's Five Ages', *Classical Philology*, 69 (1): 1–16.

Ford, J.A. (2005), 'The White City: *The Lord of the Rings* as an Early Medieval Myth of the Restoration of the Roman Empire', *Tolkien Studies*, 2: 53–73.

Fraser, A.D. (1929), 'Scheria and the Phaeacians', *Transactions and Proceedings of the American Philological Association*, 60: 155–78.

Freeman, A.M. (2021), '*Pietas* and the Fall of the City: A Neglected Virgilian Influence on Middle-earth's Chief Virtue', in H. Williams (ed.), *Tolkien and the Classical World*, 131–63, Zurich, Jena: Walking Tree Publishers.

Fuqua, C. (1991), 'Proper Behavior in the *Odyssey*', *Illinois Classical Studies*, 16 (1/2): 49–58.

Galinsky, K. (2013), *Augustus: Introduction to the Life of an Emperor*, Cambridge: Cambridge University Press.

Gallant, R. (2021), 'The Noldorization of the Edain: The Roman-Germani Paradigm for the Noldor and Edain in Tolkien's Migration Era', in H. Williams (ed.), *Tolkien and the Classical World*, 305–27, Zurich, Jena: Walking Tree Publishers.

Garbowski, C. (1998), 'The *Silmarillion* and *Genesis*: The Contemporary Artist and the Present Revelation', *Annales Universitatis Mariae Curie-Skłodowska*, 16: 49–62.

Garbowski, C. (2014), 'Evil', in S.D. Lee, *A Companion to J.R.R. Tolkien*, 418–30, Malden, Oxford, Chichester: Wiley Blackwell.

Garth, J. (2003), *Tolkien and the Great War: The Threshold of Middle-earth*, London: HarperCollinsPublishers.

Garth, J. (2014), *Tolkien at Exeter College: How an Oxford Undergraduate Created Middle-Earth*, Oxford: Exeter College.

Garvie, A.F. (1994), *Homer: Odyssey. Books VI–VIII*, Cambridge: Cambridge University Press.

Genette, G. (1980), *Narrative Discourse: An Essay in Method*, transl. J.E. Lewin, Ithaca: Cornell University Press.

Gere, C. (2010), *Knossos and the Prophets of Modernism*, Chicago: University of Chicago Press.

Gill, C. (1977), 'The Genre of the Atlantis Story', *Classical Philology*, 72 (4): 287–304.

*Gladiator* (2000), [Film] Dir. R. Scott, US: DreamWorks Pictures and Universal Pictures.

Glenn, J. (1971), 'The Polyphemus Folktale and Homer's Kyklôpeia', *Transactions and Proceedings of the American Philological Association*, 102: 133–81.

Gould, J. (1973), 'Hiketeia', *Journal of Hellenic Studies*, 93: 74–103.

Graves, R. (transl.) ([1957] 1979), *Gaius Suetonius Tranquillus: The Twelve Caesars*, London: Penguin Books.

Green, W.H. (1995), *The Hobbit: A Journey into Maturity*, New York: Simon and Schuster Macmillan.

Green, W.H. (2001), 'King Thorin's Mines: *The Hobbit* as Victorian Adventure Novel', *Extrapolation*, 42 (1): 53–64.

Green, W.H. (2008), 'Bilbo's Adventures in Wilderland', in H. Bloom (ed.), *Bloom's Modern Critical Views: J.R.R. Tolkien*, 27–42, New York: Infobase Publishing.

Greenman, D. (1992), 'Aeneidic and Odyssean Patterns of Escape and Return in Tolkien's "Fall of Gondolin" and *The Return of the King*', *Mythlore*, 18 (2): 4–11.

Gross, N.P. (1976), 'Nausicaa: A Feminine Threat', *Classical World*, 69 (5): 311–17.

*Hail Caesar* (2004), [Film] Dir. J. Coen and E. Coen, US: Universal Pictures.

Hardwick, L. (2007), 'Introduction', in L. Hardwick and C. Gillespie (eds), *Classics in Postcolonial Worlds*, 1–11, Oxford: Oxford University Press.

Hardwick, L. and C. Stray (2008), 'Introduction: Making Connections', in L. Hardwick and C. Stray (eds), *A Companion to Classical Receptions*, 1–9, Malden, Oxford, Carlton: Blackwell Publishing.

Hargrove, G. (1986), 'Who is Tom Bombadil?', *Mythlore* 13 (1): 20–4.

Harrisson, J. (2021), '"Escape and Consolation": Gondor as the Ancient Mediterranean and Rohan as the Germanic World in *The Lord of the Rings*', in H. Williams (ed.), *Tolkien and the Classical World*, 329–48, Zurich, Jena: Walking Tree Publishers.

Heath, M. (2012), 'Longinus and the Ancient Sublime', in T. Costelloe (ed.), *The Sublime: From Antiquity to the Present*, 11–23, Cambridge: Cambridge University Press.

Heffernan, J. (2014), *Hospitality and Treachery in Western Literature*, Yale: Yale University Press.

Heinberg, R. (1989), *Memories and Visions of Paradise: Exploring the Universal Myth of a Lost Golden Age*, New York: St. Martin's Press.

*Helen of Troy* (1956), [Film] Dir. R. Wise, US, Italy, France: Warner Bros.

Hinds, S. (2006), 'Landscape with Figures: Aesthetics of Place in the *Metamorphoses* and ts Tradition', in P. Hardie (ed.), *The Cambridge Companion to Ovid*, 122–49, Cambridge: Cambridge University Press.

Hjulstad, K.L.A. (2020), 'The Tale of the Old Forest: The Damaging Effects of Forestry in J.R.R. Tolkien's Written Works', *Journal of Tolkien Research*, 10 (2): Article 7, 1–16.

Hoiem, E.M. (2005), 'World Creation as Colonization: British Imperialism in Aldarion and Erendis', *Tolkien Studies* 2: 75–92.

Honegger, T. (2004), 'From Bag End to Lórien: The Creation of a Literary World', in P. Buchs and T. Honegger, *News from the Shire and Beyond: Studies on Tolkien*, 59–81, Zurich, Jena: Walking Tree Publishers.

Honegger, T. (2005), 'Tolkien through the Eyes of a Medievalist', in T. Honegger (ed.), *Reconsidering Tolkien*, 45–66, Zurich, Jena: Walking Tree Publishers.

Honegger, T. (2010), 'Fantasy, Escape, Recovery, and Consolation in *Sir Orfeo*: The Medieval Foundation of Tolkienian Fantasy', *Tolkien Studies*, 7: 117–36.

Honegger, T. (2011), 'The Rohirrim: "Anglo-Saxons on Horseback"? An Inquiry into Tolkien's Use of Sources', in J. Fisher (ed.), *Tolkien and the Study of His Sources*, 116–32, Jefferson, North Carolina and London: McFarland & Company.

Honegger, T. (2014), 'Academic Writings', in S.D. Lee (ed.), *A Companion to J.R.R. Tolkien*, 27–40, Chichester: Wiley Blackwell.

Honegger, T. and F. Weinreich (eds) (2006a), *Tolkien and Modernity 1*, Zurich, Jena: Walking Tree Publishers.

Honegger, T. and F. Weinreich (eds) (2006b), *Tolkien and Modernity 2*, Zurich, Jena: Walking Tree Publishers.

Hostetter, C.F. (2007), 'Orfeo, Sir', in M.D.C. Drout (ed.), *J.R.R. Tolkien Encyclopedia: Scholarship and Critical Assessment*, 487–8, New York, London: Routledge.

Howe, T. (2008), *Pastoral Politics: Animals, Agriculture and Society in Ancient Greece*, Claremont: Gorgias Press.

Huttar, C.A. (1975), 'Hell and the City: Tolkien and the Traditions of Western Literature', in J. Lobdell (ed.), *A Tolkien Compass*, 143–52, La Salle, Illinois: Open Court Publishing Company.

Huttar, C.A. (2008), 'Tolkien, Epic Traditions, and Golden Age Myths', in H. Bloom (ed.), *Bloom's Modern Critical Views: J.R.R. Tolkien*, 3–16, New York: Infobase Publishing.

Hutton, T.W. (1952), *King Edward's School Birmingham 1552–1952*, Oxford: Basil Blackwell.

Hynes, G. (2012), 'Beneath the Earth's Dark Keel', *Tolkien Studies*, 9: 21–36.

James, E. and F. Mendlesohn (2012), 'Introduction', in E. James and F. Mendlesohn (eds), *The Cambridge Companion to Fantasy Literature*, 1–4, Cambridge: Cambridge University Press.

Jenike, K. (2010), 'Tom Bombadil: Man of Mystery', in K. Dubbs and J. Kaščáková (eds), *Middle-earth and Beyond: Essays on the World of J.R.R. Tolkien*, 67–74, Newcastle upon Tyne: Cambridge Scholars Publishing.

Jordan, A.M. (2021), 'Shepherds and the Shire', in H. Williams (ed.), *Tolkien and the Classical World*, 353–63, Zurich, Jena: Walking Tree Publishers.

Judd, W.S. and G.A. Judd (2017), *Flora of Middle-earth: Plants of J.R.R. Tolkien's Legendarium*, Oxford: Oxford University Press.

Kallendorf, C.W. (2007), 'Introduction', in C.W. Kallendorf (ed.), *A Companion to the Classical Tradition*, 1–4, Malden, Oxford, Victoria: Blackwell Publishing.

Katz, M.A. (1994), 'Homecoming and Hospitality: Recognition and the Construction of Identity in the *Odyssey*', in S.M. Oberhelman, V. Kelly and R.J. Gols (eds), *Epic and Epoch*, 49–75, Lubbock: Texas Tech University Press.

Kaufmann, U.M. (1975), 'Aspects of the Paradisical in Tolkien's Works', in J. Lobdell (ed.), *A Tolkien Compass*, 143–52, La Salle, Illinois: Open Court Publishing Company.

Kawin, B.F. (2012), *Horror and the Horror Film*, London: Anthem Press.

Kazantzakis, N. ([1981] 1988), *At the Palaces of Knossos*, transl. T. Vasils and T. Vasils, Athens, Ohio: Ohio University Press.

Kazantzakis, N. ([1946] 2008), *Zorba the Greek*, transl. C. Wildman, London: Faber and Faber.

Kearns, E. (1982), 'The Return of Odysseus: A Homeric Theoxeny', *Classical Quarterly*, 32 (1): 2–8.

Kleu, M. (2021), 'Plato's Atlantis and the Post-Platonic Tradition in Tolkien's Downfall of Númenor', in H. Williams (ed.), *Tolkien and the Classical World*, 193–215, Zurich, Jena: Walking Tree Publishers.

Knight, F.W.J. (transl.) ([1956] 1968), *Virgil: The Aeneid*, Baltimore: Penguin.

Konijnendijk, C.C. (2018), *The Forest and the City: The Cultural Landscape of Urban Woodland*, Cham, Switzerland: Springer.

Kowalik, B. (2020), 'Tolkien's Use of the Motif of Goldsmith-Craft and the Middle English *Pearl*: Ring or Hand?', in Ł. Neubauer (ed.), *Middle-earth, or There and Back Again*, 39–70, Zurich, Jena: Walking Tree Publishers.

Larini, G. (2019), 'The Trolls in *The Hobbit* and Polyphemus in the *Odyssey*', in R. Arduini, G. Canzonieri and C.A. Testi (eds), *Tolkien and the Classics*, 3–12, Zurich, Jena: Walking Tree Publishers.

Lee, D. (transl.) (2008), *Plato: Timaeus and Critias*, London: Penguin.

Lee, S., ed. (2014), *A Companion to J.R.R. Tolkien*, Chichester: Wiley Blackwell.

Leśniewski, M. (2020), 'Tolkien and the Myth of Atlantis, or the Usefulness of Dreams and the Methodology of Mythmaking', in Ł. Neubauer (ed.), *Middle-earth, or There and Back Again*, 1–24, Zurich, Jena: Walking Tree Publishers.

Levy, H.L. (1963), 'The Odyssean Suitors and the Host-Guest Relationship', *Transactions and Proceedings of the American Philological Association*, 94: 145–53.

Lewis, C.S. ([1951] 2010), *Prince Caspian*, New York: Harper Collins.

Lewis, C.S. ([1950] 2010), *The Lion, the Witch and the Wardrobe*, New York: Harper Collins.

Lewis, C.S. ([1955] 2010), *The Magician's Nephew*, New York: Harper Collins.

Lewis, C.S. ([1953] 2010), *The Silver Chair*, New York: Harper Collins.

Lewis, C.S. ([1952] 2010), *The Voyage of the Dawn Treader*, New York: Harper Collins.

*Lexikon des frühgriechischen Epos* (2004), Göttingen: Vandenhoeck & Ruprecht.

Librán-Moreno, M. (2005), 'Parallel Lives: The Sons of Denethor and the Sons of Telamon', *Tolkien Studies*, 2: 15–52.

Librán-Moreno, M. (2007a), '"A Kind of Orpheus-Legend in Reverse": Two Classical Myths in the Story of Beren and Lúthien', in E. Segura and T. Honegger, *Myth and Magic: Art According to the Inklings*, 143–85, Zurich, Berne: Walking Tree Publishers.

Librán-Moreno, M. (2007b), 'Latin Language', in M.D.C. Drout (ed.), *J.R.R. Tolkien Encyclopedia: Scholarship and Critical Assessment*, 244–345, New York: Routledge.

Librán-Moreno, M. (2011), '"Byzantium, New Rome!" Goths, Langobards, and Byzantium in *The Lord of the Rings*', in J. Fisher (ed.), *Tolkien and the Study of His Sources*, 85–115, Jefferson, North Carolina, London: McFarland & Company.

Light, A. (2003), 'Tolkien's Green Time: Environmental Themes in *The Lord of the Rings*', in G. Bassham and E. Bronson (eds), *The Lord of the Rings and Philosophy: One Book to Rule Them All*, 150–63, Chicago and La Salle, Illinois: Open Court.

Livingston, M. (2013), 'Troy and the Rings: Tolkien and the Medieval Myth of England', *Mythlore*, 32 (1): 75–93.

Lord, A.B. ([1960] 1971), *The Singer of Tales*, New York: Athenaeum.

Louden, B. (2011), *Homer's* Odyssey *and the Near East*, Cambridge: Cambridge University Press.

McInerney, J. (2010), *The Cattle of the Sun: Cows and Culture in the World of the Ancient Greeks*, Princeton: Princeton University Press.

Mantovani, L. (2019), 'Renewing the Epic: Tolkien and Apollonius Rhodius', in R. Arduini, G. Canzonieri, and C.A. Testi (eds), *Tolkien and the Classics*, 13–24, Zurich, Jena: Walking Tree Publishers.

Marty, M. (2003), '"But Even So: Look at That": An Ironic Perspective on Utopias', in E. Rothstein, H. Muschamp, and M.E. Marty (eds), *Visions of Utopia*, 49–88, Oxford: Oxford University Press.

Melville, A.D. (transl.) (2008), *Ovid: Metamorphoses*, E.J. Kenney (ed.), Oxford: Oxford University Press.

Merkelbach, R. (2013), 'Deeper and Deeper into the Wood: Forests as Places of Transformation in *The Lord of the Rings*', in H. Conrad-O'Briain and G. Hynes, *J.R.R. Tolkien: The Forest and the City*, 57–66, Dublin: Four Courts Press.

Michelet, F.L. (2015), 'Hospitality, Hostility, and Peacemaking in *Beowulf*', *Philological Quarterly*, 94 (1–2): 23–50.

Middleton, G.D. (2017), *Understanding Collapse*, Cambridge: Cambridge University Press.

Miller, H. ([1941] 2016), *The Colossus of Maroussi*, London: Penguin Books.

Minchin, E. (2001), *Homer and the Resources of Memory: Some Applications of Cognitive Theory to the* Iliad *and the* Odyssey, Oxford: Oxford University Press.

Momigliano, N. (2020), *In Search of the Labyrinth*, London: Bloomsbury.

Momigliano, N. and A. Farnoux, eds (2017), *Cretomania: Modern Desires for the Minoan Past*, London: Routledge.

Morris, J.M. and A.L. Kross (2009), *The A to Z of Utopianism*, The A to Z Guide Series, No. 36, Lanham, Toronto, Plymouth: The Scarecrow Press.

Morse, R.E. (1986), *Evocation of Virgil in Tolkien's Art: Geritol for the Classics*, Wauconda, Illinois: Bolchazy-Carducci Publishers.

Morson, G.S. (1981), *The Boundaries of Genre: Dostoevsky's Diary of a Writer and the Traditions of Literary Utopia*, Evanston: Northwestern University Press.

Most, G.W. (1989a), 'The Stranger's Stratagem: Self-Disclosure and Self-Sufficiency in Greek Culture', *Journal of Hellenic Studies*, 109: 114–33.

Most, G.W. (1989b), 'The Structure and Function of Odysseus' *Apologoi*', *Transactions of the American Philological Association*, 119: 15–30.

Most, G.W. (1997), 'Hesiod's Myth of the Five (or Three or Four) Races', *Proceedings of the Cambridge Philological Society*, 43: 104–27.

Moylan, T. (2000), *Scraps of the Untainted Sky: Science Fiction, Utopia, Dystopia*, Boulder: Westview Press.

Muellner, L. (1996), *The Anger of Achilles*, Ithaca: Cornell University Press.

Murnaghan, S. (2011), *Disguise and Recognition in the* Odyssey, Lanham: Lexington Books.

Nagler, M.N. (1990), 'The Proem and the Problem', *Classical Antiquity*, 9 (2): 335–56.

Nagy, J.F. (1981), 'The Deceptive Gift in Greek Mythology', *Arethusa*, 14 (2): 191–204.

Naquet, V. (2007), *The Atlantis Story: A Short History of Plato's Myth*, Exeter: University of Exeter Press.

Neubauer, Ł. (2020), '"What News from the North?": The Compositional Fabric, Intricate Imagery and Heroic Christian Character of the "Lament for Boromir"', in J. Eilmann and F. Schneidewind (eds), *Music in Tolkien's Work and Beyond*, 83–116. Zurich, Jena: Walking Tree Publishers.

Newlands, C. (2004), 'Statius and Ovid: Transforming the Landscape', *Transactions of the American Philological Association*, 134: 133–55.

Newman, J.K. (2005), 'J.R.R. Tolkien's *The Lord of the Rings*: A Classical Perspective', *Illinois Classical Studies*, 30: 229–47.

Newton, R.M. (1983), 'Poor Polyphemus: Emotional Ambivalence in "Odyssey" 9 and 17', *Classical World*, 76 (3): 137–42.

Newton, R.M. (2008), 'Assembly and Hospitality in the *Cyclopeia*', *College Literature*, 35 (4): 1–44.

Nietzsche, F. ([1872] 2003), *The Birth of Tragedy Out of the Spirit of Music*, transl. S. Whiteside, ed. M. Tanner, London: Penguin Books.

Ordway, H. (2021), *Tolkien's Modern Reading: Middle-earth Beyond the Middle Ages*, Des Plaines, Illinois: Word on Fire Academic.

Parry, H. (1964), 'Ovid's *Metamorphoses*: Violence in a Pastoral Landscape', *Transactions and Proceedings of the American Philological Association*, 95: 268–82.

Pedrick, V. (1982), 'Supplication in the *Iliad* and the *Odyssey*', *Transactions of the American Philological Association*, 112: 125–40.

Pezzini, G. (2021), 'The Gods in (Tolkien's) Epic: Classical Patterns of Divine Interaction', in H. Williams (ed.), *Tolkien and the Classical World*, 73–103, Zurich, Jena: Walking Tree Publishers.

Pinsent, P. (2014), 'Religion: An Implicit Catholicism', in S.D. Lee (ed.), *A Companion to J.R.R. Tolkien*, 446–60, Chichester: Wiley Blackwell.

Podlecki, A.J. (1961), 'Guest-Gifts and Nobodies in "Odyssey 9"', *Phoenix*, 15 (3): 125–33.

Pollington, S. (2011), 'The Mead-Hall Community', *Journal of Medieval History*, 37 (1): 19–33.

Ponsen, A. (1985), 'Het Atlantis Complex: Een "Niet-Relevante" Studie van de Overeenkomsten Tussen Plato's Atlantis en het Númenor van Tolkien', in R. Vink and A. Ponsen (eds), *Lembas Extra 1985*, 17–42, Beverwijk: Tolkien Genootschap Unquendor.

Porter, J.I. (2016), *The Sublime in Antiquity*, Cambridge: Cambridge University Press.

Potkay, A. (2012), 'The British Romantic Sublime', in T.M. Costelloe (ed.), *The Sublime: From Antiquity to the Present*, 203–16, Cambridge: Cambridge University Press.

Potts, M. (2016), '"Evening-Lands": Spenglerian Tropes in *The Lord of the Rings*', *Tolkien Studies* 13: 149–68.

Pucci, P. (1987), *Odysseus Polutropos: Intertextual Readings in the* Odyssey *and the* Iliad, Ithaca: Cornell University Press.

Pucci, P. (1998), *The Song of the Sirens: Essays on Homer*, Lanham: Rowman & Littlefield Publishers.

Querbach, C.W. (1985), 'Hesiod's Myth of the Four Races', *The Classical Journal*, 81 (1): 1–12.

*Quo Vadis* (1951), [Film] Dir. M. LeRoy, US: Metro-Goldwyn-Mayer.

Rateliff, J.D. (2006), '"And All the Days of Her Life Are Forgotten": The Lord of the Rings as Mythic Prehistory', in W. Hammond and C. Scull (eds), *The Lord of the Rings 1954–2004: Scholarship in Honour of Richard E. Blackwelder*, 67–100, Milwaukee, WI: Marquette University Press.

Rateliff, J.D. (2007), *The History of the Hobbit, Part One: Mr Baggins*. London: HarperCollinsPublishers.

Rateliff, J.D. (2014), '*The Hobbit*: A Turning Point', in S.D. Lee (ed.), *A Companion to J.R.R. Tolkien*, 119–32, Malden, Oxford: Wiley Blackwell.

Reckford, K.J. (1974), 'Some Trees in Virgil and Tolkien', in G.K. Galinsky (ed.), *Perspectives of Roman Poetry*, 57–92, Austin: The University of Texas Press.

Reckford, K.J. (2003), '"There and Back Again" – Odysseus and Bilbo Baggins', *Amphora*, 2 (1): 8–9, 15.

Redfield, J.M. (1983), 'The Economic Man', in C.A. Rubino and C.W. Shelmerdine (eds), *Approaches to Homer*, 218–47, Austin: University of Texas Press.

Reece, S. (1993), *The Stranger's Welcome: Oral Theory and the Aesthetics of the Homeric Hospitality Scene*, Ann Arbor: The University of Michigan Press.

Reinhardt, K. (1996), 'The Adventures in the *Odyssey*', in S.L. Schein (ed.), transl. H.I. Flower, *Reading the* Odyssey: *Selected Interpretative Essays*, 63–132, Princeton: Princeton University Press.

Renault, M, ([1958] 1961), *The King Must Die*, Sevenoaks, Kent: New English Library.

Renault, M ([1962] 2015), *The Bull from the Sea*, London: Virago.

Rhodes, P.J. (2007), 'The Impact of the Persian Wars on Classical Greece', in E. Bridges, E. Hall, and P.J. Rhodes (eds), *Cultural Responses to the Persian Wars: Antiquity to the Third Millennium*, 31–45, Oxford: Oxford University Press.

Richards, J. (2014), 'Sir Ridley Scott and the Rebirth of Historical Epic', in A.B.R. Elliot (ed.), *The Return of the Epic Film: Genre, Aesthetics, and History in the 21st Century*, 19–35, Edinburgh: Edinburgh University Press.

Risden, E.L. (2011), 'Source Criticism: Background and Applications', in J. Fisher (ed.), *Tolkien and the Study of His Sources*, 17–28, Jefferson, London: McFarland & Company.

Robertson, H.G. (1955), 'The Hybristes in Homer', *The Classical Journal*, 51 (2): 81–3.
Rogers, B.M. and B.E. Stevens (2017), 'Introduction: Fantasies of Antiquity', in B.M. Rogers and B.E. Stevens (eds), *Classical Traditions in Modern Fantasy*, 1–22, Oxford: Oxford University Press.
Romm, J. (2010), 'Continents, Climates, and Cultures: Greek Theories of Global Structure', in R.J.A. Talbert and K.A. Raaflaub (eds), *Geography and Ethnography: Perceptions of the World in Pre-Modern Societies*, 215–35, Chichester: Blackwell Publishing.
Rosario Monteiro, M. (1993), 'Númenor: Tolkien's Literary Utopia', *History of European Ideas*, 16 (4–6): 633–8.
Rose, G.P. (1969), 'The Unfriendly Phaeacians', *Transactions and Proceedings of the American Philological Association*, 100: 387–406.
Rothstein, E. (2003), 'Utopia and Its Discontents', in E. Rothstein, H. Muschamp, and M.E. Marty (eds), *Visions of Utopia*, 1–28, Oxford: Oxford University Press.
Rowe, C. (2007), 'Plato and the Persian Wars', in E. Bridges, E. Hall, and P.J. Rhodes (eds), *Cultural Responses to the Persian Wars: Antiquity to the Third Millennium*, 85–104, Oxford: Oxford University Press.
Ruud, J. (2011), *Critical Companion to J.R.R. Tolkien: A Literary Reference to His Life and Work*, New York: Infobase Learning.
Sachs, J. (2009), 'Greece or Rome?: The Uses of Antiquity in Late Eighteenth- and Early Nineteenth-Century British Literature', *Literature Compass*, 6 (2): 314–31.
Said, E.W. ([1978] 1979), *Orientalism*, New York: Vintage Books.
Sander, D. (1997), 'The Fantastic Sublime: Tolkien's "On Fairy Stories" and the Romantic Sublime', *Mythlore*, 22 (1): 4–7.
Sanford, L. (1995), 'The Fall from Grace – Decline and Fall in Middle-earth: Metaphors for Nordic and Christian Theology in *The Lord of the Rings* and *The Silmarillion*', *Mallorn*, 32: 15–20.
Schein, S. (1995), 'Female Representations and Interpreting the *Odyssey*', in B. Cohen (ed.), *The Distaff Side: Representing the Female in Homer's* Odyssey, 17–27, New York: Oxford University Press.
Schmiel, R. (1972), 'Telemachus in Sparta', *Transactions and Proceedings of the American Philological Association*, 103: 463–72.
Scott, J.A. (1918), 'The Journey Made by Telemachus and Its Influence on the Action of the "Odyssey"', *The Classical Journal*, 13 (6): 420–8.
Scull, C. and W.G. Hammond (2006a), *The J.R.R. Tolkien Companion and Guide: Chronology*, London: HarperCollinsPublishers.
Scull, C. and W.G. Hammond (2006b), *The J.R.R. Tolkien Companion and Guide: Reader's Guide*. London: HarperCollinsPublishers.

Segal, C. (1962), 'The Phaeacians and the Symbolism of Odysseus' Return', *Arion*, 1 (4): 17–64.
Segal, C. (1968), 'Circean Temptations: Homer, Vergil, Ovid', *Transactions and Proceedings of the American Philological Association*, 99: 419–42.
Segal, C. (1969), *Landscape in Ovid's Metamorphoses: A Study in the Transformations of a Literary Symbol*, Wiesbaden: Franz Steiner Verlag GMBH.
Segal, C. (1992), 'Divine Justice in the *Odyssey*: Poseidon, Cyclops, and Helios', *American Journal of Philology*. 113 (4): 489–518.
Shepard, A., and S.D. Powell (eds) (2004), *Fantasies of Troy: Classical Tales and the Social Imaginary in Medieval and Early-Modern Europe*, Toronto: Centre for Reformation and Renaissance Studies.
Shewan, A. (1919), 'The Scheria of the *Odyssey*', *The Classical Quarterly*, 13 (1): 4–11.
Shewring, W. (transl.) ([1980] 2008), *Homer: The Odyssey*, Oxford: Oxford University Press.
Shippey, T. (1992), *The Road to Middle-earth: How J.R.R. Tolkien Created a New Mythology*, London: HarperCollinsPublishers.
Shippey, T. (2011), 'Introduction: Why Source Criticism', in J. Fisher (ed.), *Tolkien and the Study of His Sources*, 7–16, Jefferson and London, McFarland & Company.
Shippey, T. (2014), *J.R.R. Tolkien: Author of the Century*, London: HarperCollinsPublishers.
Sidebottom, H. (2004). *Ancient Warfare: A Very Short Introduction*. New York, Oxford: Oxford University Press.
Siewers, A.K. (2007), 'Environmentalist Readings of Tolkien', in M.D.C. Drout (ed.), *J.R.R. Tolkien Encyclopedia: Scholarship and Critical Assessment*, 166–7, New York, London: Routledge.
Silk, M. (2004), 'The *Odyssey* and Its Explorations', in R. Fowler (ed.), *The Cambridge Companion to Homer*, 31–44, Cambridge: Cambridge University Press.
Simpson, E.R. (2017), 'The Evolution of J.R.R. Tolkien's Portrayal of Nature', *Tolkien Studies*, 14: 71–89.
Simpson, J.A. and E.S.C. Weiner, eds (1989), *The Oxford English Dictionary*, second edition, third volume, Oxford: Clarendon Press.
Solopova, E. (2014), 'Middle English', in S.D. Lee (ed.), *A Companion to J.R.R. Tolkien*, 230–43, Chichester: Wiley Blackwell.
*Spartacus* (1960), [Film] Dir. S. Kubrick, US: Universal International.
Spirito, G. (2009), 'The Legends of the Trojan War in J.R.R. Tolkien', *Hither Shore*, 6: 182–200.
Stevens, B.E. (2017), 'Ancient Underworlds in J.R.R. Tolkien's *The Hobbit*', in B.M. Rogers and B.E. Stevens (eds), *Classical Traditions in Modern Fantasy*, 121–44, Oxford: Oxford University Press.

Stevens, B.E. (2021), 'Middle-earth as Underworld: From *Katabasis* to *Eucatastrophe*', in H. Williams (ed.), *Tolkien and the Classical World*, 105–30, Zurich, Jena: Walking Tree Publishers.

Stevens, D. and C.D. Stevens (2008), 'The Hobbit', in H. Bloom (ed.), *Bloom's Modern Critical Views: J.R.R. Tolkien*, 17–26, New York: Infobase Publishing.

Stevens, J. (2004), 'From Catastrophe to Eucatastrophe. J.R.R. Tolkien's Transformation of Ovid's Pyramus and Thisbe into Beren and Lúthien', in J. Chance (ed.), *Tolkien and the Invention of Myth: A Reader*, 119–32, Lexington, KY: University of Kentucky Press.

Stoddard, W.H. (2010), '"Simbelmynë": Mortality and Memory in Middle-earth', *Mythlore*, 29 (1/2): 151–60.

Straubhaar, S.B. (2004), 'Myth, Late Roman History, and Multiculturalism in Middle-earth', in J. Chance (ed.), *Tolkien and the Invention of Myth: A Reader*, 101–17, Lexington, Kentucky: The University Press of Kentucky.

Straubhaar, S.B. (2007), 'Gondor', in M.D.C. Drout (ed.), *J.R.R. Tolkien Encyclopedia: Scholarship and Critical Assessment*, 248–9, New York, London: Routledge.

Stray, C. (1992), *The Living Word: W.H.D. Rouse and the Crisis of Classics in Edwardian England*, London: Bristol Classical Press.

Stray, C. (1998), *Classics Transformed: Schools, University, and Society in England, 1830–1960*, Oxford: Oxford University Press.

Stray, C. (2007), 'Education', in C.W. Kallendorf (ed.), *A Companion to the Classical Tradition*, 5–14, Malden, Oxford, Victoria: Blackwell Publishing.

Stray, C., ed. (2013), *Oxford Classics: Teaching and Learning 1800–2000*, London: Bloomsbury.

Sundt, P. (2021), 'The Love Story of Orpheus and Eurydice in Tolkien's Orphic Middle-earth', in H. Williams (ed.), *Tolkien and the Classical World*, 165–89, Zurich, Jena: Walking Tree Publishers.

Suvin, D. (2010), *Defined by a Hollow: Essays on Utopia, Science Fiction and Political Epistemology*, Oxford: Peter Lang.

Sweetman, D. (1993), *Mary Renault: A Biography*, San Diego, New York, London: Harcourt Brace & Company.

Szyjewski, A. (2020), 'The Mythical Model of the World in *The Story of Kullervo*', in Ł. Neubauer (ed.), *Middle-earth, or There and Back Again*, 83–112, Zurich, Jena: Walking Tree Publishers.

Taylor, A.E. (transl.) ([1929] 2013), *Plato: Timaeus and Critias: Translated into English with Introductions and Notes on the Text*, London: Routledge.

*The Happening* (2008), [Film] Dir. M. Night Shyamalan, US: 20th Century Fox Productions.

*The Lord of the Rings: The Fellowship of the Ring* (2001), [Film] Dir. P. Jackson, US: New Line Cinema.

*The Man Who Would Be King* (1975), [Film] Dir. J. Huston, US: Columbia Pictures.
'The Time Monster' (1972), [TV series], *Doctor Who*, Season 9, Serial 5, Episodes 1–6, Dir. P. Bernard, UK: BBC One (aired on 20 May 1972).
*The Trojan War* (or: *The Trojan Horse*) (1961), [Film] Dir. G. Ferroni, Italy: Variety Distribution.
Tolkien, J.R.R. (1932), 'Sigelwara Land', *Medium Aevum*, 1 (3): 183–96.
Tolkien, J.R.R. (1984), *The Book of Lost Tales Part II*, ed. C. Tolkien, New York: Ballantine Books.
Tolkien, J.R.R. ([1996] 1997), *The Peoples of Middle-earth*, The History of Middle-earth Volume 12, ed. C. Tolkien, London: HarperCollinsPublishers.
Tolkien, J.R.R. ([1990] 2000), *The War of the Ring*, Part 3 of the History of the Lord of the Rings, ed. C. Tolkien, Boston: Houghton Mifflin Company.
Tolkien, J.R.R. ([1954] 2001a), *The Lord of the Rings: The Fellowship of the Ring*, London: HarperCollinsPublishers.
Tolkien, J.R.R. ([1954] 2001b), *The Lord of the Rings: The Two Towers*, London: HarperCollinsPublishers.
Tolkien, J.R.R. ([1955] 2001c), *The Lord of the Rings: The Return of the King*, London: HarperCollinsPublishers.
Tolkien, J.R.R. ([1992] 2002a), *Sauron Defeated: The History of The Lord of the Rings Part 4*, ed. C. Tolkien, London: HarperCollinsPublishers.
Tolkien, J.R.R. ([1977] 2002b), *The Silmarillion*, New York: Del Rey Books.
Tolkien, J.R.R. ([1937] 2006a), *The Hobbit*, London: HarperCollinsPublishers.
Tolkien, J.R.R. ([1981] 2006b), *The Letters of J.R.R. Tolkien*, ed. C. Tolkien, London: HarperCollinsPublishers.
Tolkien, J.R.R. ([1983] 2006c), *The Monsters and the Critics and Other Essays*, ed. C. Tolkien, London: HarperCollinsPublishers.
Tolkien, J.R.R. ([1947] 2014a), *Tolkien On Fairy Stories: Expanded Edition, With Commentary and Notes*, eds V. Flieger and D.A. Anderson, London: HarperCollinsPublishers.
Tolkien, J.R.R. ([1980] 2014b), *Unfinished Tales of Númenor and Middle-earth*, ed. C. Tolkien, London: HarperCollinsPublishers.
*Troy* (2004), [Film] Dir. W. Peterson, US: Warner Bros. Pictures.
Tsagarakis, O. (1977), *Nature and Background of Major Concepts of Divine Power in Homer*, Amsterdam: B.R. Grüner Publishing.
Ustinova, Y. (2009), *Caves and the Ancient Greek Mind: Descending Underground in the Search for Ultimate Truth*, Oxford: Oxford University Press.
Vaninskaya, A. (2014), 'Modernity: Tolkien and His Contemporaries', in S.D. Lee (ed.), *A Companion to J.R.R. Tolkien*, 350–66, Chichester: Wiley Blackwell.

Van Wees, H. (1992), *Status Warriors: War, Violence, and Society in Homer and History*, Amsterdam: J.C. Gieben.

Vidal-Naquet, P. (2007), *The Atlantis Story: A Short History of Plato's Myth*, Exeter: University of Exeter Press.

Vieira, F. (2010), 'The Concept of Utopia', in G. Claeys (ed.), *The Cambridge Companion to Utopian Literature*, 3–27, Cambridge: Cambridge University Press.

Walsh, J. (2007a), 'Beorn', in M.D.C. Drout (ed.), *J.R.R. Tolkien Encyclopedia: Scholarship and Critical Assessment*, 56, New York, London: Routledge.

Walsh, J. (2007b), 'Egypt: Relationship to Númenóreans', in M.D.C. Drout (ed.), *J.R.R. Tolkien Encyclopedia: Scholarship and Critical Assessment*, 145, New York, London: Routledge.

Watts, E.J. (2021), *The Eternal Decline and Fall of Rome: The History of a Dangerous Idea*, Oxford: Oxford University Press.

Webber, A. (1989), 'The Hero Tells His Name: Formula and Variation in the Phaeacian Episode of the *Odyssey*', *Transactions of the American Philological Association*, 119: 1–13.

Weinberg, F.M. (1986), *The Cave: The Evolution of a Metaphoric Field from Homer to Ariosto*, New York: Peter Lang.

Welliver, W. (1977), *Character, Plot and Thought in Plato's Timaeus and Critias*, Leiden: Brill.

Wells, H.G. (1918), 'The Case against the Classical Languages', in R. Lankester (ed.), *Natural Science and the Classical System in Education*, 183–95, London: William Heinemann.

Whittaker, H. (1999), 'The Status of Arete in the Phaeacian Episode of the *Odyssey*', *Symbolae Osloenses*, 74 (1): 140–50.

Wicher, A. (2020), 'The Wisdom of Galadriel: A Study in the Theology of J.R.R. Tolkien's *The Lord of the Rings*', in Ł. Neubauer (ed.), *Middle-earth, or There and Back Again*, 113–30, Zurich, Jena: Walking Tree Publishers.

Williams, H. (2019a), 'Acts of Eating in the *Apologue*: Destruction and Delay', *Hermes*, 147 (1): 3–20.

Williams, H. (2019b), 'Mountain People in Middle-earth: Ecology and the Primitive', in T. Honegger and D. Fimi (eds), *Sub-Creating Arda: World-Building in J.R.R. Tolkien's Work, Its Precursors, and Its Legacies*, 285–311, Zurich, Jena: Walking Tree Publishers.

Williams, H. (2019c), 'Tolkien's Trolls: Intertextuality in "Roast Mutton" and Monstrous Incarnations after *The Hobbit*', in R. Vink (ed.), *Lembas Extra 2019: The World Tolkien Built*, 111–27, IJmond, Netherlands: Tolkien Genootschap Unquendor.

Williams, H. (2020a), 'Tolkien's Thalassocracy and Ancient Greek Seafaring People: Minoans, Phaeacians, Atlantans, and Númenóreans', *Tolkien Studies*, 17: 137–62.

Williams, H. (2020b), 'Westwards, Utopia; Eastwards, Decline: The Reception of Classical Occidentalism and Orientalism in Tolkien's Atlantic Paradise', *Journal of the Fantastic in the Arts*, 31 (3): 404–23.

Williams, H. (2021a), 'Classical Tradition, Modern Fantasy, and the Generic Contracts of Readers', in H. Williams (ed.), *Tolkien and the Classical World*, xi–xxvi, Zurich, Jena: Walking Tree Publishers.

Willams, H., ed. (2021b), *Tolkien and the Classical World*, Zurich, Jena: Walking Tree Publishers.

Williams, H. (2021c), 'Tolkien the Classicist: Scholar and Thinker', in H. Williams (ed.), *Tolkien and the Classical World*, 3–36, Zurich, Jena: Walking Tree Publishers.

Wilson, T.M. (2007), 'Blockbuster Pastoral: An Ecocritical Reading of Peter Jackson's *The Lord of the Rings* Films', in A. Lam and N. Oryshchuk (eds), *How We Became Middle-earth*, 185–96, Zurich, Jena: Walking Tree Publishers.

Winkler, M.M. (2001), 'The Roman Empire in American Cinema after 1945', in S.R. Joshel, M. Malamud, and D.T. McGuire Jr. (eds), *Imperial Projections: Ancient Rome in Modern Popular Culture*, 50–76, Baltimore: The Johns Hopkins University Press.

Wolf, M.J.P. (2012), *Building Imaginary Worlds: The Theory and History of Subcreation*, London: Routledge.

Wolf, M.J.P. (2019), 'Concerning the "Sub" in "Subcreation": The Act of Creating Under', in D. Fimi and T. Honegger (eds), *Sub-creating Arda: World-building in J.R.R. Tolkien's Work, Its Precursors and Its Legacies*, 1–15, Zurich, Jena: Walking Tree Publishers.

Wood, R.C. (2003), *The Gospel According to Tolkien: Visions of the Kingdom in Middle-earth*, Louisville, London: Westminster John Knox Press.

Wyke, M. (1997), *Projecting the Past: Ancient Rome, Cinema, and History*, New York and London: Routledge.

Zoran, G. (1984), 'Towards a Theory of Space in Narrative', *Poetics Today*, 5 (2): 309–35.

# Index

Aragorn
  Aeneas and 42
  Augustan restoration 42–9
  guest 89–90
  infrastructural renewal 43–5
  institutional renewal 45
  moral renewal 45–6
  national hero 134
  Númenórean values 27, 38
  pastoral renewal 46, 48
  *pax Gondorea* 47–8
  religious figure 54
  restorer figure 41–2, 48–9
  sources 138
Athens 25, 27–35, 37–8, 57, 133–4
Atlantis
  Athens and 30, 33–4
  decline and fall 23, 27–30, 34, 54, 139
  golden age 23
  historical analogies 31, 33–4
  (im)moderation 30–1, 33
  (im)piety 32–3
  materialism 33–4
  Minoans (Cretans) and 28–9, 55
  Númenor and 27–34, 54
  Orientalised 30–1, 33–4
  Phaeacians and 28–9
  post-classical receptions 22
  Tolkien and 12, 27
  Tolkien's Atlantis tradition 28–30, 34
Augustus
  Aragorn and 42–9, 138
  golden age 43, 46, 48
  infrastructural renewal 43–5
  institutional renewal 45
  moral renewal 45–6
  pastoral renewal 46, 48
  *pax Augusta* 47–8
  Roman restorer figure 42–3, 48–9
  in Virgil 42–3, 138

Bag End 59–62, 67–72, 77, 92–5
Baggins, Bilbo
  at Bag End 67–72
  at Beorn's home 78–82
  Calypso and 69–71
  conditional versus absolute hospitality 92–4
  eucatastrophe 20, 109
  integration versus multiculturalism 91–2
  moral progression as guest-host 70, 77, 85–9
  Odysseus and 64, 75, 83–4, 138
  at Rivendell 21, 75–7
  at Smaug's 'home' 85
  Telemachus and 70–2
  trolls and 72–5
Beorn 59–60, 78–83, 86, 88, 93
*Beowulf* 8, 10–11, 78–9
Bombadil, Tom
  Bacchus 123
  confusing sublime 122
  enigma 119
  environmental assimilation 99
  material sublime 122–3
  natural world and music 121, 123, 127–8
  Old Man Willow and 121, 127
  Orpheus and 111, 119–29, 138
  spiritual sublime 124–9
Boromir 11, 18, 20–1, 40, 134
Brandybuck, Merry 90, 109, 114–15, 118, 121, 127, 131–2, 135
Burke, Edmund 103, 106–7, 109–10, 115, 132–3

catastrophe 18–19, 20, 23, 27–8, 32, 41, 52–4, 56, 103, 108
caves 59, 60–1, 66, 69, 73, 81, 82–4, 88, 111
Christianity

# Index

absolute values 19, 94
  the church 62, 77–8
  in cinema 50–3, 140
  decline and fall 17–21, 140
  divine intervention 14
  eucatastrophe and joy 14, 18–20, 108–9
  history 4, 18–19
  hope 133, 135
  hospitality 77–8, 86–7, 90
  in Minas Tirith 54
  modernization 13, 52, 54–5
  morality 18, 50–1
  the natural world 100–3
  in Númenor 33, 53–4
  Orpheus and 120
  paganism 19, 33, 52–5, 140
  Roman decline 22
  sublime 97, 103–5, 106–9, 118, 124, 126–9
  Tolkien and 9, 17, 54–5, 77–8
  utopianism 4, 15, 141
classical reception
  and related methodologies 8, 13
  Tolkien's mixing of sources 15, 62, 105, 138
  Tolkien's retrotopianism 8, 12, 14–15, 21–2, 62, 104, 139–41
  Tolkien's rewriting 8, 14–15, 20, 41–42, 44, 49, 139–140
  Tolkien's scepticism 138–9
  types of meaning derived 14, 21–2, 67, 139
classical tradition 11–12, 21–2, 51, 61, 108, 109–11, 133–4
Classics (discipline)
  Tolkien's departure from 10–11
  in Tolkien's life 12–13
  Tolkien's school education 9–10, 62–3
  Tolkien's university education 10–11, 63

decline and fall
  Athens 30–2, 35–6
  Atlantis 22, 28–34, 37
  Atlantis tradition 28–30
  Beleriand 18–19
  Byzantine Empire 40–1
  Catholic church 13, 54–5
  Christian renewal 18–19
  elegiac genre 20
  extrasaecular 19
  the Garden of Eden 17–18
  golden ages 19, 22–6, 46–8
  Gondolin 13–14, 21
  history 18–19
  intrasaecular 19
  Knossos ('Minoan' Crete) 28–9, 32, 55–8
  legendarium 18–21
  Minas Tirith (Gondor) 38–49, 54
  narratives 26, 49
  Númenor 23, 27–39, 52–6, 58
  Persia 31–3
  Phaeacian Scheria 28–9, 32
  renewal and 21, 26, 37–9, 42–9
  Rome 22, 25–6, 39–48
  Rome in cinema 50–4
  tragic genre 19–20
  transsaecular 19
  Tolkien's self-conscious application of classical decline 21
  Troy 22
  Troy in cinema 51–2
  utopianism 20–6, 30–9, 42–58
Denethor 18, 20, 38, 44, 47, 54
Derrida, Jacques 91–5, 140
diversity 58, 89–90, 104, 116–17, 122–3, 128–9
dwarves
  at Beorn's home 78–82
  at Bilbo Baggins's home 70–2
  at the elven king's home 81–4
  hosts of the Lonely Mountain 84–6
  mountain people 99
  at Rivendell 75–7
  suitors and 70–2
  trolls and 72–5

education 9–13, 62–3
Egypt 29–30, 39, 135
elves
  alliances 84–5, 88
  Aragorn and 133
  decline and fall 18–20
  forest people 100
  Galadriel 90, 102
  Gondolin 21
  language 27, 36–7

Mirkwood 59, 82–4
Númenóreans and 27, 32–3, 53, 133
orcs and 102
Rivendell 59–60, 75–8
in Valinor 18, 23, 102
in Woody End 106–9, 118, 124
English
   Catholics 54–5
   countryside 5, 98–9
   Edwardian character 9, 16, 56, 105
   discipline 8–10
   language and classical languages 9, 13, 90–1
   literature and poetry 10–11, 40, 62–3, 103, 111, 130
   politics 36
   society 3, 13
   Victorian character 9, 13, 56, 68–9
Evans, Sir Arthur 32–3, 55–6, 130
evil 18–19, 23, 31, 58, 60, 81, 93–4, 99–101, 110, 122–3, 128, 132, 141

fairy tales and stories 20–1, 41, 53, 62, 70, 72, 75, 100, 108, 120–1
fall, *see* decline and fall
familiarization 1–3, 6–8, 13–14, 139, 141
fantasy 1–2, 6–7, 11–12, 23–4, 137–8, 141
Faramir 27, 38–9, 42, 46, 54, 78, 101
films 5, 7, 11, 49–55, 100, 128
focalization 40, 44, 59, 73–4, 107, 118, 122
freedom 5, 57–8
Frodo 18, 77–8, 89, 93, 109, 114, 116–19, 127–8, 132–5

Gandalf
   Athena and 72, 84
   at Bag End 67–72, 89–90, 92
   at Beorn's home 79–83, 93
   'divine', magical guide 70, 72, 74–5, 78, 84, 87–8
   moderating inhospitality 84, 87–8, 93
   Odysseus and 69–70, 75, 80–2, 88
   trolls and 72, 74–5
   at Weathertop 132–4
   wise 39
Garden of Eden, the 17–18, 77–8, 102, 128, 130
genres
   classical genres 10

codified 1
comedy 20, 54
dystopian fiction 4–5, 24–5, 58, 141
elegy 14, 17, 20–1
environmentalist literature 5, 100
fairy tales and stories 20–1, 41, 53, 62, 70, 72, 75, 100, 108, 120–1
fantasy codes 1–2, 11–12
fantasy and utopianism 141
historical fiction 24, 55–7
retrospective literature 23–4
speculative 'utopian' fiction 6–7
tragedy 17, 19–20, 29, 36, 42, 110–11, 114, 118, 120–3, 125–6
utopian fiction 3, 6, 23–4, 61, 141
goblins 59–60, 70, 78, 81, 84, 88
God 18, 77–8, 95, 101, 108, 119, 141
gods
   Aeolus 75–7, 82, 87
   Apolline (Nietzsche) 110, 124–6
   Artemis (Diana) 112, 114, 116–17
   Athena 70, 72, 84, 87–8
   in Atlantis 31
   Calypso 68–71, 83, 87
   Circe 66, 81–4, 87
   Dionysiac (Nietzsche) 110, 124–6
   Dionysus (Bacchus) 57, 112, 117–18, 123, 125, 137
   in forests 109–12, 114, 119–20
   Hermes (Mercury) 69–70, 83, 87
   Mars 43, 47, 112–13, 115–17
   Old Man Willow 114
   pagan gods 33, 53
   Poseidon (Neptune) 28–9, 32
   theoxenies 70, 87
   Tom Bombadil 119–21
   Zeus (Jupiter) 66, 70–1, 73, 75, 84, 87, 112, 130
golden age 12, 19, 22–6, 32, 36–7, 43, 46, 48–9, 55–6, 58
Gondor, *see* Minas Tirith
guests, *see* hospitality

heaven 18, 77, 79, 121, 128
Hesiod 19, 22–5, 27, 56
hobbits
   environmental assimilation 99
   gardeners 46
   gift-giving 93

golden age 23
pastoral ideals 48
post-classical 41, 131
xenophilic and xenophobic 58, 89–90
Homer
  Aeolus 75–7, 82, 87
  Calypso 68–71, 83, 87
  Circe 66, 81–4, 87
  eschatology 120
  hospitality motif 64–6
  Laestrygonians 101
  Menelaus 65
  Nestor 65
  Odysseus 13–14, 28–9, 64–6, 68–71, 73–7, 79–88, 138
  Phaeacians 22–3, 28–30, 32–3, 79–81, 86–8
  Polyphemus 64–6, 73–5, 81, 83–4, 87–8, 101
  Telemachus 70–2
  Tolkien and 10–12, 62–3, 110
  Virgil and 42–3
hospitality
  Aeolus 75–7, 82, 87
  Beorn 59–60, 78–83, 86, 88, 93
  biblical 62
  Bilbo Baggins 67–72, 77–82, 85–9, 91–4
  Calypso 68–71, 83, 87
  Christian 62, 77–8
  conditional versus absolute 67, 77, 92–4
  Derrida, Jacques 91–5, 140
  dwarves 70–86
  economic 66, 140
  Elrond 75–7
  elven king 81–4
  ethical quest 62, 64–7, 72, 86–7
  Gandalf 67–72, 74–5, 78–84, 87–90, 92–3
  Germanic 62, 78–9
  Homeric motif 64–6
  horror genre 1
  integration 91–2
  Lake-town 84
  Menelaus 65
  modernization 94–5
  Nestor 65
  Phaeacians 79–82
  political 64, 66, 88–9
  Polyphemus 64–6, 73–5, 81, 83–4, 87–8, 101
  reciprocity 69–70, 72, 81–3, 85, 87, 92–4, 139–40
  religious 64, 66–7, 70–2, 74–5, 78, 84, 87–8
  solipsistic 85
  suitors 65, 70–2
  theoxenia 87
  utopianism 61
  Western tradition 61, 91
hosts, *see* hospitality
*hybris* 31–2, 38

Kazantzakis, Nikos 55–7, 131–3, 140
Knossos 49, 55–8, 130, 135, 140

Lake-town 59–60, 79, 84–6, 140
languages 7–10, 13, 27, 37–8, 63, 90–2, 102, 110
lapsarianism, *see* decline and fall
Lewis, C.S. 7, 137–8
*locus amoenus* 69, 111–12, 116–17
Lonely Mountain, the 59–60, 62, 71–2, 83–5

medieval
  class hierarchies 141
  fairy tale 41–2
  fantasy codes 11–12
  receptions of classical literature 22
  Orpheus 120
  Tolkien as medievalist 8
  Tolkien's sources 9–10, 13, 54, 60–2, 90, 105, 138, 141
Melkor (Morgoth) 18–19, 53, 102, 126–7
memory 14, 20–1, 29–30, 36, 38–9, 91
Middle-earth
  defamiliarization 6–8
  Eurasia and 8, 27, 31
  hermetic 7, 103, 131, 138
  postlapsarian 18, 21, 77
  refamiliarization 8, 14–15
  ruins 20, 40, 97, 104, 129–35, 140
  utopian continent 1–2, 6–9, 13–14
Miller, Henry 91, 130–2, 140
Minas Tirith (Gondor)
  ancient Egypt and 39

Augustan restorations 42–9
Byzantine 39
cartography analogous 13
decline and fall 21, 39–41
Faramir 38–9
golden age 19
Homeric catalogue 63
infrastructural decline and restoration 43–5
institutional decline and restoration 45
moral decline and restoration 45–6
national spirit 134
and Númenor 27, 38–9, 54 131
pastoral restoration 46, 48
*pax Gondorea* 47–8
place of memory 29
protector of the Shire 90, 95
religious decline and restoration 54
Rome and 39–43
soldier's utopia 21
Troy and 39
Mines of Moria, the 4, 15, 21, 101, 131, 134
Minoan Crete 5, 28–9, 32–3, 35, 55–8, 89, 130–5, 140
Mirkwood 47, 59, 61, 79–83, 100
moderation
  Faramir 38
  the natural world 101
  Númenor 31, 33, 37
  Platonic 30–4, 37–8, 140–1
More, Thomas 3–7, 61, 141
music
  contests 124–9
  elven 108
  Nietzsche's aesthetics 110, 125–6
  Orpheus 121, 124–5, 128
  Tolkien's cosmogony 126–9
  Tom Bombadil 120–1, 127–8

natural world
  Christian 101–2, 106–9
  destructive 109–19, 125–7, 129
  ecocritical 97–100
  ecotopias 5, 100, 104
  fertility 22–3, 27, 46–6, 108, 125
  gardens 44, 46, 67, 99, 101–2, 108, 117, 141
  hospitality 81–2

industrialization 60, 78, 90, 98–9, 103
material sublime 104, 107–23, 133, 140
mountains 32, 59–60, 71, 73, 78, 81, 99, 101–3, 129, 132
Ovidian 97, 104, 109–19, 121–9, 140
pastoral 24, 48, 78, 89–90, 97, 98–9, 106–7, 133
post-humanist 5, 102–3, 123, 141
realism 102
spiritual sublime 104, 107–8, 124, 128–9
symbolic 60, 97, 100–1, 129
Tolkien and 98
in traditions of the sublime 97, 103–6
waves 28
Nero 50–4
Nietzsche, Friedrich 110, 124–6, 128
Númenor
  Aldarion 35–6, 58
  Atlantis and 27–34, 54
  classical palimpsest 29–30, 53–4
  decline and fall 18–19, 27–39, 139
  Faramir 27, 38–9, 42
  golden age 19, 23, 27, 56
  (im)moderation 30–2, 33–4
  (im)piety 32–3, 53–4
  materialism 33–4
  memory of 20, 29, 38–40
  'Minoan' Crete and 28–9, 32, 35, 55–8
  Neronian Rome and 52–4
  Phaeacian Scheria and 28–9, 32–3
  sophocracy 36–7
  sublime ruins 105, 129–35, 140
  Tolkien's Atlantis tradition 28–30, 34
  Troy 39, 41, 42
  typical coastal settlement 33–6

Oakenshield, Thorin 59–60, 71, 74, 78, 82, 84–6
Odysseus
  at Aeolus' home 76–7
  Bilbo Baggins and 13–14, 64, 75, 83–4, 138
  at Calypso's home 68–70
  at Circe's home 81–4
  Gandalf and 69–70, 75, 80–2, 88
  hospitality quest 65–6, 86–8
  at Ithaca 84–6
  among the Phaeacians 28–9, 79–81

at Polyphemus' home 66, 73–6
suffering hero 77
suitors and 65, 70–1
Thorin Oakenshield and 74
trickster hero 88
Old Forest, the 97, 100, 106–7, 109–29, 131, 139
Old Man Willow 100, 113, 118–19, 121–2, 127
Orpheus
  *katabasis* 121
  Lúthien and 111, 120
  maenads and 120, 124–5, 128
  material sublime 116, 120–3
  music 121, 124–5, 128
  ordering nature 127–9
  in Renaissance art 121
  Tolkien's rewriting of the myth 111, 120–1, 127
  Tom Bombadil and 111, 119–29, 138
  tree animation 114, 122
Ovid
  Augustus and 45
  forest motif 111–19
  golden age 19, 22–3, 25
  immaterial sublime 117, 128
  malevolent gods 113–14, 117–19
  material sublime 104–5, 113–15, 117–18, 123, 128–9
  musical contest 124–5
  Orpheus, 120–3
  Tolkien and 110–11
Oxford, University of 10, 12–13, 63, 137

paradise
  Atlantis 23, 27–9
  ecological 5, 104
  the Garden of Eden 17–18, 77–8, 102, 128, 130
  golden age 12, 19, 22–6, 32, 36–7, 43, 46, 48–9, 55–6, 58
  Hesiodic 23, 27
  Lothlórien 101–2
  Minas Tirith (Gondor) 43, 48
  'Minoan' Crete 29, 32–3, 55–6, 130
  nostalgic function 24
  Númenor 19, 23, 27–8, 56
  Ogygia 69
  Sarehole 98
  Saturnian 48
  Scheria 22–3, 29
  Rivendell 77–8
  Tom Bombadil's home 128
  utopianism 22–4, 26
  Valinor 18–19, 128
pastoral 24, 48, 89, 90, 97–9, 106–7, 133
Phaeacians
  Athena and 87
  Beorn and 86
  golden-age paradise 22–3
  (im)piety 28–9, 32
  (in)hospitality 79–81
  Númenóreans and 28–9, 32–3
  storytelling 88
  in Tolkien's Atlantis tradition 28–30
piety 29, 30, 32–4, 38, 45, 52–4, 61, 66, 87, 95, 112, 139–41
Plato
  asceticism 33–4
  coastal settlements 35–6
  Derrida's reception 91
  historical analogies 31, 33–4
  moderation 30–1, 33, 140
  More, Thomas 4
  piety 32–3
  sophocracy 36–7, 141
  sublime art 105
  utopianism 15, 26, 30
  utopias 24
  virtues 38–9
politics
  anarchism 45
  classical analogues in modern politics 13
  communism 5, 51–2
  conservatism 9, 23–4, 51–2, 54, 58, 140–1
  democracy 36, 50–1, 130
  globalization 90
  liberalism 2–3, 50–1, 57–8, 95, 140
  monarchism 31, 42, 45, 47–8
  nationalism 10–11, 39, 49–50, 52, 130, 134–5
  political realism 52
  political studies and utopias 2–4
  politicization of hospitality 89–90, 94–5
  republicanism 45, 50–1, 53, 140
  sophocracy 36–7, 141

Renault, Mary 12, 57, 130
renewal
  in Augustan Rome and Minas Tirith (Gondor) 43–9, 140
  Christian 18, 52, 54
  decline and 21, 26, 37–9, 42–9, 139
  Hellenism 130
  imperial 47–8
  infrastructural 43–5
  institutional 45
  intersaecular 19
  Minoans 55
  moral 45–6
  Roman 22, 26–6, 42, 48–9, 51
  Troy 22
retrotopianism 8, 12, 14–15, 21–2, 62, 104, 139–41
rewriting 8, 14–15, 20, 41–2, 44, 49, 139–40
Rohan 39, 41, 63, 90, 95, 129
ruins
  Graeco-Roman 40, 129–30
  in Middle-earth 20, 40
  sublime 103–4
  sublime ruins in Middle-earth 97, 131–5
  sublime ruins in Minoan Crete 130–5

Sam 18, 21, 78–9, 89–90, 99, 101–2, 107–9, 118–19, 122, 135
Saruman 20, 89–90, 93–5, 99, 140
Sauron 19, 33, 42, 53, 58, 101–2, 133
Shire, the
  garden 46, 101–2
  industrialization 99
  pastoral 48
  protectorate 47–8, 95
  scouring 94–5
  utopia 21
  Woody End 106–9
  xenophilic and xenophobic 58, 89–90, 92
Smaug 59–61, 70–1, 84–6, 88
sources
  cauldron metaphor 62, 138
  leaf metaphor 101, 105
  methodologies 8, 13
  Tolkien's mixing 15, 62, 105, 138
  Tolkien's northern sources 10–11, 15
  Tolkien's retrotopianism 8, 12, 14–15, 21–2, 62, 104, 139–41
  Tolkien's rewriting 8, 14–15, 20, 41–2, 44, 49, 139–40
  Tolkien's scepticism 138–9
  types of meaning derived 14, 21–2, 67, 139
sublime
  Burke, Edmund 103, 106–7, 109–10, 115, 132–3
  Christian 97, 103–5, 106–9, 118, 124, 126–9
  confusing 122
  destructive 109–19, 125–7, 129
  material 104, 107–23, 133, 140
  mountains 106–7
  and nature 97, 103–6
  Nietzsche, Friedrich 110, 124–6, 128
  ruins 103–4
  ruins in Middle-earth 97, 131–5
  ruins in Minoan Crete 130–5
  spiritual 104, 107–8, 124, 128–9, 133
  traditions 97, 103–6

Thebes 39, 111–14
Took, Peregrin 18, 39–40, 44–7, 63, 90, 107–9, 115, 118, 121, 127
trade 34–5, 56, 141
trees 44–5, 53, 97, 99–102, 111, 118, 121, 127–9
trolls 41, 59, 67, 71–5, 79, 83, 86–7
Troy 13–14, 21–2, 39, 42, 49, 52, 55, 140

underworld 14, 42, 120–1, 128
utopia
  absolute 4, 77–8
  Atlantis 23, 27–9
  communities 21–2, 27–58
  decline and restoration 22, 26, 30, 38–9, 43, 49–50
  dystopia 4–5, 24–5, 58, 141
  ecotopia 5, 100, 104
  in fantasy 141
  the Garden of Eden 17–18, 77–8, 102, 128, 130
  golden age 12, 19, 22–6, 32, 36–7, 43, 46, 48–9, 55–6, 58
  heaven 18, 77, 79, 121, 128
  home 61–2, 64–7, 72, 77, 86–7, 91–5

horizonal 7
hypercivilizational 28–30, 55–6
individual 5
island 15, 27–39, 53–5, 57–8, 68–9, 75–6, 82, 141
isolated 4–5
liberal 57–8
Lothlórien 101–2
Middle-earth 1–2, 6–9, 13–14
Minas Tirith (Gondor) 42–9
'Minoan' Crete 29, 32–3, 55–6, 130
mundane 5
Númenor 27–39
Ogygia 69
the Old Forest 128
paradise and 23–6
reproductive 34, 45–6
Rivendell 77–8
Scheria 22–3, 29
the Shire 21
the sublime and 104
Thomas More 3–7
Tolkien's '*Utopia*' summarised 140–1
Valinor 18–19, 128
utopian fiction (genre) 3, 6, 23–4, 61, 141
utopianism
    Christianity 4, 15, 141
    definitions 2–3
    eutopianism 3–4, 15, 23, 25, 61, 89, 139
    exploration 7–8
    familiarization 1–3, 6–8, 13–14, 139, 141
    fantasy 141
    hospitality 61
    lapsarianism 20–6, 30–9, 42–58
    in literary texts 3
    outopianism 3, 6–7, 13–14, 61, 75, 104, 138–9
    paradise 22–4, 26
    Platonic 15, 26, 30
    retrotopianism 8, 12, 14–15, 21–2, 62, 104, 139–41
    *topos* 4–5
    utopian fiction and 3, 6

Valar 18, 23, 27, 31, 33, 53, 119, 126, 128
Valinor 23, 28, 33, 70, 75, 77, 102, 119, 128
Virgil 10–11, 42–3, 48, 54, 62, 100, 109–10, 120

worldbuilding 7–8, 14, 26, 94, 100–1, 126

xenophilia and xenophobia 58, 66, 79–80, 85–7, 89–92, 94–5, 140

www.ingramcontent.com/pod-product-compliance
Lightning Source LLC
Chambersburg PA
CBHW062226300426
44115CB00012BA/2234